John Burgess Calkin

The History of the Dominion of Canada

John Burgess Calkin

The History of the Dominion of Canada

ISBN/EAN: 9783337225568

Printed in Europe, USA, Canada, Australia, Japan

Cover: Foto ©ninafisch / pixelio.de

More available books at **www.hansebooks.com**

A HISTORY

OF THE

DOMINION OF CANADA.

BY

JOHN B. CALKIN, M.A.

PRINCIPAL OF THE NORMAL SCHOOL, TRURO. N.S.

"Let all the ends thou aim'st at be thy country's,
Thy God's, and truth's.'

A. & W. MACKINLAY,
HALIFAX, N.S.
1898.

CHAPTER I.

INTRODUCTION.

	PAGE		PAGE
Extent of the Dominion	1	Present Inhabitants	3
Condition Four Hundred Years ago	2	Mother Country	4
		British Empire	4
Early Inhabitants	3	France	5

CHAPTER II.

THE DISCOVERY OF AMERICA.

The Northmen	7	Size of the Earth underestimated	11
The Route of Trade with India	8	Queen Isabella aids Columbus	12
Strange Notions	8		
Portuguese Navigators	9	Provision for the Voyage	12
Columbus	10	The Voyage	13
Form of the Earth	11	Discoveries of Columbus	14

CHAPTER III.

EARLY EXPLORERS.

The Cabots	16	Cartier's Second Voyage	23
Americus Vespucius	18	Cartier's Third Voyage	24
Discovery of the Pacific Ocean	19	Troubles in France	25
		Fisheries	25
Magellan	19	Fur Trade	26
Francis I.	20	De la Roche	26
De Léry	21	Chauvin and Pontgravé	27
Verrazano	21	Aymar de Chastes	27
Jacques Cartier	21	Champlain	28

CHAPTER IV.

FIRST CHAPTER IN THE HISTORY OF ACADIE.

	PAGE		PAGE
De Monts sails for Acadie	30	Port Royal abandoned	35
Port Royal	31	Return to Port Royal	35
St. Croix	32	Troubles	36
Port Royal founded	32	Jamestown	36
Poutrincourt	33	Port Royal destroyed	37
Lescarbot	33	Nova Scotia and Sir William Alexander	37
Order of the "Good" Time	34		
Port Royal in 1607	34		

CHAPTER V.

CANADA UNDER CHAMPLAIN.

	PAGE		PAGE
De Monts's New Field	39	In Search of a Northern Sea	46
Quebec founded	39	The Récollets arrive in Canada	47
Indian Tribes	40		
The Algonquins	40	Champlain visits the Hurons	47
The Iroquois	41	War with the Iroquois	47
The Hurons	42	Champlain among the Hurons	48
Champlain's Difficulties	44	Condition of the Colony	48
Better Prospects	44	The Company of New France	49
Foray against the Iroquois	44	Shattered Hopes	50
The Battle	45	Capture of Quebec by Kirk	51
Champlain's Purposes	45	Treaty of St. Germain	51
The Site of Montreal selected	46	Champlain's Death	51

CHAPTER VI.

THE RULE OF THE HUNDRED ASSOCIATES.

	PAGE		PAGE
Chief Features	53	Domestic Quarrels	62
Montmagny	53	Laval	63
Character of the Age	54	Liquor Traffic	63
Jesuit Missionaries	54	Heroism at Long Sault	64
The Three Marys	55	Close of the Rule of the Hundred Associates	65
Founding of Montreal	55		
Hostility of the Iroquois	56	Earthquakes	65
The Huron Missions	57	Rival Governors in Nova Scotia	65
The Huron Villages attacked	58		
St. Joseph	58	Fort la Tour captured	67
St. Louis	58	De la Tour and D'Aulnay Charnisé	68
The Hurons abandon their Country	59	Le Borgne	68
New England	60	Acadie seized by the English	69
Proposed Treaty	61	Treaty of Breda	69

CHAPTER VII.

ROYAL GOVERNMENT.

	PAGE		PAGE
Officers of Government	70	Obstacles to Progress .	74
Laval and Mézy .	71	The Liquor Traffic and Bush-	
Mézy's Recall	71	rangers	75
New Officers	71	Trade	75
New York taken by the English	72	Jesuit Missions . .	76
		Extension of Territory	76
Courcelle's Expedition against the Mohawks	72	Feudal Tenure in Canada .	76
		Duties of the Seignior .	77
The Mohawks chastised	73	Obligations of the Vassal	78
Improvements under Talon .	73	Doing Homage . . .	78

CHAPTER VIII.

CANADA UNDER FRONTENAC.

A New Governor .	79	Hudson's Bay Company organized	85
Discovery of the Mississippi	79		
Fort Frontenac founded	81	Dennonville . . .	85
La Salle	81	War against the Senecas	86
Frontenac recalled .	83	Prospect of Peace .	87
La Barre	83	The "Rat" kills the Peace	88
Rivalry between French and English	84		
		Massacre at La Chine .	89

CHAPTER IX.

BORDER WARFARE BETWEEN FRENCH AND ENGLISH.

Frontenac's Return .	90	Acadie under Villebon .	95
Raids against the English	91	Hannah Dustan . .	96
Retaliation . . .	91	Ravages of Ben Church	97
Phips takes Port Royal	92	Treaty of Ryswick .	97
Phips fails to take Quebec .	93	Death of Frontenac .	97
Expedition against Montreal	95	De Callières and the Indians	98

CHAPTER X.

QUEEN ANNE'S WAR.

How the War began .	100	Colonel March at Port Royal	103
Deerfield . . .	101	A False Alarm . .	104
Retaliation . . .	101	Capture of Port Royal .	104
Privateering . .	102	Sir Hovenden Walker ...	107
Restrictions removed .	102	The Treaty of Utrecht .	108

CONTENTS.

CHAPTER XI.
THE STRUGGLE CONTINUED.

	PAGE		PAGE
Vaudreuil	109	Annapolis besieged	114
Beauharnois	109	Capture of Louisburg	115
Rivalry between the French and English	110	D'Anville's Expedition	116
		Ramesay at Beaubassin	118
Louisburg founded	111	Massacre at Grand Pré	119
Nova Scotia	111	The Acadians between Two Fires	120
Acadian Settlements	112		
Treatment of the Acadians	112	Treaty of Aix-la-Chapelle	120
Government	113		

CHAPTER XII.
SETTLEMENT OF HALIFAX.

	PAGE		PAGE
A New Scene at Chebucto	122	Lunenburg settled by Germans	127
Making a Home	123		
The Acadians refuse Oath of Allegiance	124	Boundaries	127
		The Limits of Nova Scotia	128
Hostility of the Indians	125	Fort Beauséjour	128
Evil Influences	126	Fort Lawrence	129

CHAPTER XIII.
THE YEAR 1755.

	PAGE		PAGE
Summary of Events	130	Shirley fails to take Niagara	137
Governors	130		
The Ohio Valley	131	Capture of Beauséjour	137
George Washington	132	Expulsion of the Acadians	138
Reinforcements from England and France	132	Grand Pré and Canard	139
		A Sad Scene	140
Plan of the Campaign	133	Annapolis and Chignecto	140
Braddock's Defeat	133	Results	140
Dieskau at Lake George	136	Character of the Measure	141

CHAPTER XIV.
THE SEVEN YEARS' WAR.

	PAGE		PAGE
Parties, Places, and Conditions	142	Policy of William Pitt	146
Officers	142	Second Siege of Louisburg	146
Capture of Oswego	143	St John's Island taken by the English	149
Loudon and Holbourne at Halifax	144	The St. John River	149
		British defeated at Ticonderoga	150
Fort William Henry taken by the French	144	Frontenac and Duquesne	150

CHAPTER XV.

THE END OF FRENCH RULE IN AMERICA.

	PAGE		PAGE
Dark Days	152	A Bold Scheme	159
The British Plan of Conquest	153	The English on the Heights	160
Character of Officers	153	Montcalm's Decision	161
Lake Champlain and Niagara	154	The Battle	162
The Siege of Quebec	154	Death of Wolfe and Montcalm	163
The French Defences	156		
Policies of Montcalm and Wolfe	157	The Surrender	165
		Too Late	166
Fire-ships	157	The British occupy Quebec	166
Advance Movements	157	Efforts to recapture Quebec	166
Failure of July 31	158		
The English move up the River	159	The Closing Scene	167
		Surrender of Montreal	168

CHAPTER XVI.

LAYING NEW FOUNDATIONS.

Provisional Government	169	First Assembly in Nova Scotia	177
The Inhabitants of Canada	169		
Pontiac's Conspiracy	170	New England Colonists in Nova Scotia	177
Treaty of Paris	172		
Government of Canada	172	County of Sunbury	178
Privileges of the "New Subjects"	174	The Island of St. John	179
		The Island made a separate Province	180
French Canadians dislike English laws	174	An Alarm	181
The Quebec Act	175		

CHAPTER XVII.

THE AMERICAN REVOLUTION.

British American Colonies	182	Carleton's Narrow Escapes	187
Conditions	183	A Feeble Hold	188
Restrictions	183	Montgomery's Failure and Death	189
Taxes without Representation	183	Retreat of the Enemy	190
The Boston Tea Party	184	Privateers and Plunderers	191
The Continental Congress	185	Independence of the United States recognised by Great Britain	191
The War begins	186		
Invasion of Canada	186		
Seizure of Montreal	187		

CHAPTER XVIII.

THE UNITED EMPIRE LOYALISTS.

	PAGE		PAGE
Condition of the Loyalists	192	The Province of Cape Breton	196
Aid for the Loyalists	193	Lord Dorchester the Governor-General	196
The Loyalists in Nova Scotia	193	Desire for Change	197
The Loyalists in Ontario	194	The Constitutional Act	197
Loyal Indians	195		
New Brunswick a separate Province	195		

CHAPTER XIX.

THE BEGINNING OF PARLIAMENTARY GOVERNMENT.

Interest in Public Affairs	199	The Maroons	205
The Government and Legislature	200	New Brunswick	205
		Prince Edward Island	205
Parliamentary Customs	201	Lower Canada	207
Governor Wentworth	202	Upper Canada	210
Royal Visitors	204	Customs and Social Condition	212
King's College	204		

CHAPTER XX.

THE WAR OF 1812.

State of Affairs	215	Capture of the *Chesapeake*	231
Causes of the War	216	Defeat of British on Lake Erie	232
Officers	220		
Machillimackinac and Detroit	222	Battle of Moravian Town	232
		Battle of Chateaugay	233
Niagara Frontier	222	Battle of Chrystler's Farm	235
The Enemy along the Niagara	224	Towns burned	235
		Effects of the War	236
Battle of Queenston Heights	225	Effects of the War in the United States	237
The Army of the North	226		
Summary	226	The War in 1814	237
The War continued	227	Lacolle—Port Dover	238
The Capture of York	228	Oswego—Maine	238
The Niagara Frontier given up to the Enemy	229	Chippewa—Lundy's Lane	238
		Capture of Washington	240
Stony Creek	229	Plattsburg	240
Beaver Dams	230	New Orleans	241
Sackett's Harbour	231	Treaty of Ghent	241

CHAPTER XXI.

PROGRESS AND AGITATION.

	PAGE		PAGE
Hard Times	243	Cape Breton	249
New Settlers	244	Miramichi Fire	250
The Cholera	244	Grievances	250
Agriculture	245	The Clergy Reserves	252
Education	245	Lower Canada	253
Public Roads	248	Catholic Emancipation	253
The *Royal William*	249	Prince Edward Island	254

CHAPTER XXII.

BRITISH FUR TRADERS IN THE NORTH.

English and French Rivalry	257	Cook and Vancouver	262
The North-West Fur Company	257	Astoria	263
The Partners	259	Rivalry between the Companies	263
Headquarters	259		
Explorers	260	Red River Settlement	263
Fur Traders on the Coast	262	Union of Rival Companies	265

CHAPTER XXIII.

AGITATION FOR REFORM IN CANADA.

Tories and Reformers	266	Sir Francis Bond Head	271
Upper Canada	266	Lower Canada	272
Gourlay, MacKenzie, Baldwin	267	The Earl of Dalhousie	273
Leaders in the Government Party	270	Louis Papineau	274
		Redress	275
Sir John Colborne	270	The Storm Breaks out Anew	276

CHAPTER XXIV.

AGITATION FOR REFORM IN THE MARITIME PROVINCES.

New Brunswick	277	Changes in the Council	282
The King's Property	278	Unsuccessful Efforts	283
Important Concessions	278	Disputed Territory	284
Nova Scotia	279	Progress in Great Britain	285
Joseph Howe	280	Queen Victoria	287

CHAPTER XXV.

REBELLION.

	PAGE		PAGE
Lower Canada	290	Aid to the Rebels from the United States	296
Rebellion in Lower Canada	291		
The Earl of Durham	292	Navy Island	296
Renewed Insurrection	294	The End of the Rebellion	297
Upper Canada	294	Papineau and MacKenzie	298
Failure of the Plot	295		

CHAPTER XXVI.

RESPONSIBLE GOVERNMENT.

Earl of Durham's Report	299	Nova Scotia Government	307
Union of Upper and Lower Canada	300	Coalition Government	307
		The Coalition broken up	309
The New Constitution	301	Responsible Government	310
Lord Sydenham	302	New Brunswick	311
The First Reform Ministry	302	The Ashburton Treaty	313
Lord Metcalfe	303	Responsible Government in New Brunswick	314
Rebellion Losses	304		
Lord Elgin	304	Prince Edward Island	314
Immigration	305	Executive Council	315
Riot over Rebellion Losses	306	Responsible Government	316
Parliament Houses burned	306		

CHAPTER XXVII.

OLD QUESTIONS SETTLED AND NEW SCHEMES PROPOSED.

The Seat of Government	318	The Macdonald-Cartier Ministry	328
Progress in Canada	318		
Education	319	Representation by Population	329
Commerce	320		
Railways	320	Ottawa the Seat of Government	329
Clergy Reserves	321		
Seigniorial Tenure	322	The "Double Shuffle"	331
Reformers divided	323	Visit of the Prince of Wales	331
The Hincks-Morin Government	324	Death of Prince Albert	332
The Reciprocity Treaty	325	Mason and Slidell	332
The M'Nab-Morin Government	326	Defeat of the Cartier-Macdonald Government	333
Settlement of Burning Questions	327	Liberals and Conservatives unite	334

CHAPTER XXVIII.

THE MARITIME PROVINCES UNDER RESPONSIBLE GOVERNMENT.

	PAGE		PAGE
General Features	335	The Atlantic Cable	339
Railways	336	The Liberals again in Power	339
Conservative Government in Nova Scotia	337	Free Schools in Nova Scotia	341
		Prince Edward Island	343
Mines and Minerals	337	Landlords and Tenants	343

CHAPTER XXIX.

BRITISH COLUMBIA.

Oregon	345	British Columbia a Crown Colony	349
The Boundary Disputes	346		
Fort Victoria	346	The Boundary Question again	349
The Boundary settled	347	San Juan	350
Colonisation of Vancouver	347	British Columbia and Vancouver united	351
Discovery of Gold	348		

CHAPTER XXX.

CONFEDERATION.

Union Movement in the Maritime Provinces	352	Union accomplished	356
		The Canadian Constitution	357
The Charlottetown Convention	353	Difficulties between U. S. and G. B.	360
The Quebec Convention	354	Termination of the Reciprocity Treaty	363
Reception of the Scheme	354		
An Unexpected Change	355	Fenian Invasions	363

CHAPTER XXXI.

THE DOMINION ORGANIZED AND EXTENDED.

The Ministry	366	The Rebellion ended	375
The Opposition	366	Riel and Governor Archibald	377
First Parliament	368		
D'Arcy Magee	368	British Columbia enters the Union	377
Repeal Agitation in N. S.	369		
Acquisition of the North-West	370	The Washington Treaty	379
		The New Brunswick Schools	380
Rebellion in Red River Settlement	373	P. E. I. enters the Union	382
		Death of Cartier and Howe	383
Province of Manitoba	375	Ontario	383

CHAPTER XXXII.

THE MACKENZIE ADMINISTRATION.

	PAGE		PAGE
The Pacific Railway Scandal	385	Important Measures	390
Change of Government	387	The Scott Act	390
Alexander MacKenzie	387	Governor Letellier	391
The Pacific Railway	389	The National Policy	392
Dissatisfaction in British Columbia	389	Fire in St. John, N. B.	393
		The North-West	393

CHAPTER XXXIII.

THE DOMINION CONSOLIDATED.

A New Régime	395	The Canadian Pacific Railway	396
The Marquis of Lorne and Princess Louise	395	Rebellion in the North-West	398
		The Queen's Jubilee	403
The Boundary between Ontario and Manitoba	396	The Jesuits' Estates Act	403
		Death of Canada's Premiers	405

CHAPTER XXXIV.

RECENT EVENTS.

Premier Abbot	407	The Bowell Administration	417
M'Greevy and Mercier	407	Election of 1896	420
Sir John Thompson Premier	408	The Laurier Government	422
The Columbian Exhibition	408	Settlement of Manitoba School Question	423
Bering Sea Arbitration	410
Manitoba Schools	412	Changes in the Tariff	423
The Intercolonial Conference	414	The Queen's Diamond Jubilee	424
Death of Sir John Thompson	415	Klondike	424

CHAPTER XXXV.

THE PROVINCES SINCE CONFEDERATION.

Nova Scotia	425	Quebec	429
Education in Nova Scotia	427	Ontario	429
New Brunswick	428	Manitoba	429
Prince Edward Island	429	British Columbia	430

THE DOMINION OF CANADA

CHAPTER I

INTRODUCTION.

THE Dominion of Canada stretches from Ocean to Ocean. On the east, between it and Europe, lies the Atlantic; on the west, the broad Pacific separates it from Japan and China in Eastern Asia. On the south, it is bounded by the United States, from which it is separated in part by the Great Lakes: northward it loses itself in the islands of the Arctic Ocean. The sun, which makes the circuit of the earth in twenty-four hours, is five hours in crossing this wide land from east to west; so that when it is noon in Vancouver Island it is five o'clock in the evening in Cape Breton.

Extent.

This vast country has an area of 3,470,000 square miles, comprising nearly one-third of the territory in the British Empire and about one-fifteenth of the land surface of the earth. It includes several political divisions united under the central government at Ottawa. On the east, washed by the Atlantic Ocean, are the Atlantic Provinces, Nova Scotia, New Brunswick, and Prince Edward Island; farther west, lying along the River St. Lawrence and the Great Lakes, are the larger provinces, Quebec and Ontario; still more remote from the sea are the midland province Manitoba, the districts Assiniboia, Alberta, Saskatchewan, and Athabasca; in the extreme west, between the Rocky Mountains and the Pacific Ocean, is British Columbia; and on the north of these provinces are North-West Territory, Keewatin, and North-East Territory.

Four Hundred Years Ago. The history of some countries goes back for thousands of years into the shadowy past, until we find it hard to tell what is truth and what is fiction in the mingled story. But even the oldest of the provinces of the Dominion of Canada are comparatively new countries. Four hundred years ago nearly all this broad land was one unbroken forest, without roads, or cities, or cultivated fields. Save the wild animals which roamed through its forests, its only inhabitants were a race of savages scattered thinly over the country. How these people came here, whence they came, or how long ago, nobody can tell. They had no history or written language. They lived in rough dwellings formed of poles covered with the bark of trees. Some of them cultivated Indian corn, pumpkins, beans, and tobacco, in a rude way, but for the most part they lived by hunting and fishing. They were a roving people, remaining but a short time in one place. When they travelled they went on foot, or they glided along the rivers and lakes in light bark canoes. The different tribes were often engaged in war with each other. Their weapons were bows and arrows, clubs and stone hatchets. Before a battle they held a grand feast, followed by wild war dances, during which they filled the air with hideous shouts and yells. Prisoners taken in war they tortured to death and then feasted on their bodies.

There are indeed evidences that North America had earlier inhabitants than the Indians, a people of higher rank in civilisation, who had disappeared before the discovery of the country by Europeans. *Earlier Inhabitants.* Mounds of earth are found in various places, from which have been taken articles of pottery, tools made of stone and copper, and other articles fashioned with much skill and taste.

At the present time the Dominion of Canada is the home of about five millions of people, engaged in the various pursuits of civilised life. *The Present Inhabitants.* These people, with the exception of those in the Province of Quebec, are generally of British origin and speak the English language. The great majority of the inhabitants of Quebec are of French descent and speak the French language. There are many in the other provinces also whose ancestors came from France. The county of Lunenburg in Nova Scotia and several counties in Ontario are peopled largely by descendants of German settlers. Manitoba has a mixed population. When it was formed into a province its few inhabitants were principally half-breeds of French and Indian descent; but the older provinces, especially Ontario, have since contributed largely to the settlement of this new country. Indians are scattered through all the provinces, but they are most numerous in British Columbia and the North-West.

4 THE DOMINION OF CANADA.

The Mother Country. The British Islands, the ancestral home of so many Canadians, and hence often called the "Mother Country," lie eastward beyond the Atlantic Ocean, over three thousand miles away. These Islands are small compared with the Dominion, their united area being only about two-thirds the size of the Province of Quebec. They have, however, a population seven times greater than the whole Dominion.

The British Empire. The British Isles have a wonderful history. They were once the seat of many petty states which were almost always at war with each other. Finally they were united under a common sovereign and government, forming one strong kingdom. The inhabitants were enterprising and prosperous. They sent their ships abroad, discovered new lands, formed colonies, and made conquests, until they had established the largest and most populous empire that ever existed on the face of the earth. Thus the British Empire, of which the Dominion of Canada forms so large a portion, comprises about one-fifth of the land surface of the earth and about one-fourth of its inhabitants.

It is not on the land alone that Great Britain has established her power. Her ships sail on every sea, some for the protection of her scattered subjects, and others to carry from her shores her vast and varied manufactures to distant lands, or to bring from these lands the raw material for her busy artisans. The navy and the merchant ships of Great Britain far surpass those of any other nation. Canada may well be proud of her relationship to this great empire. The ancient Roman found safety in his citizenship.

INTRODUCTION. 5

In like manner the most humble British subject may rest secure under his nation's flag, knowing that he can invoke the whole power of the empire against any foe that may assail him.

On the south of the British Isles, across a narrow channel of water, lies the sunny land of France. From this land came the ancestors of many of our Canadian people. Like Great

THE BRITISH FLAG.

Britain, France ranks as one of the "Great Powers" among the nations of the world. It has vast foreign possessions, scattered over different parts of the earth, but principally in Africa and Asia. In former times England and France were keen rivals, and often waged war with each other. We shall see, in the following pages, how for a century and a half they struggled with each other, by sea and land, for the possession of Canada. It is pleasant now to realise that the memory of this great conflict stirs up no bitter strife or awakens no old feeling of hostility against each other among the children of these fatherlands. The sons of Englishmen and the sons of Frenchmen are alike true and loyal Canadians. As brothers of one great family, they live together in peace, and work harmoniously for the prosperity of their Canadian home.

CHAPTER II.

THE DISCOVERY OF AMERICA.

IN the early times, as now, the people of Norway, who are known in history as Northmen, were fond of the sea. They had a colony in that cold northern island called Iceland, which they visited frequently in the summer months. It happened on one occasion, as some of them were on their way to this island, that they fell in with an adverse wind, and were blown far from their destination. They were carried to Greenland. Then, it was not very long until they found their way to Newfoundland and Labrador. It is supposed that after this they visited various places on the coast farther south, including Nova Scotia and Massachusetts. They do not seem to have made any permanent home on this side of the ocean, and after a time, from some unknown cause, they ceased to visit America. *The Northmen.*

These discoveries do not appear to have been heard of in the countries of Central and Southern Europe. This is not very remarkable. The art of printing was not known at this time, and there was little intercourse among different countries. Besides, in their voyages across the ocean, the Northmen took a northerly route by way of Iceland and Greenland. The mariner's compass was not then known in

Europe, and long voyages out of sight of land were impracticable.

In the fifteenth century the people of Western Europe had their faces turned easterly towards Asia. For centuries they had carried on a lucrative trade with India, exchanging their woollens and other manufactures for the spices, silks, ivory, pearls, diamonds, and other products of that rich land. This trade was carried on overland by caravans between India and the eastern shores of the Mediterranean, and thence over this inland sea to Venice, Genoa, and other ports. The long-used route of trade was now obstructed by the hostile Turks, who had recently taken possession of Constantinople. The merchants of Italy, Spain, and Portugal were wishing for some new and safer route to India. Some of them were beginning to think that possibly the desired road lay around the south of Africa; but what were the difficulties and the perils of that way, if such a way existed, nobody knew.

The Route of Trade with India

In these early times the people of Western Europe, though they lived along the shores of the Atlantic, knew very little of the character and extent of this ocean. They spoke of it as the Dark Ocean. Mariners, dreading that some imaginary evil might befall them, were afraid to sail out upon it beyond sight of land. They had a superstitious notion that the remote and unknown parts of the world were peopled by Gorgons, Hydras, and all sorts of horrid monsters, ever ready to seize and destroy any human being who should be so unfortunate as to come within their reach. They believed

Strange Notions.

that far south there was a fiery atmosphere in which no human being could live, and that down in the southern seas there were steaming whirlpools, which would swallow up vessels coming within their influence. They had observed that when a vessel sailing out upon the ocean disappears from sight, it seems to be going down hill, and they feared to sail far along an unknown declivity, lest they might not be able to return.

One of the first and most noted explorers of this age was Prince Henry of Portugal, often called Henry the Navigator. This prince, who was a cousin of King Henry V. of England, erected an observatory and established a school at a seaport of Portugal near Cape St. Vincent for the instruction of noblemen's sons in mathematics, astronomy, and navigation. The mariners trained in Prince Henry's school were inspired with much of his enthusiasm. In 1418 they discovered the Madeira Islands, and later they explored part of the west coast of Africa, proceeding to a point much farther south than had been previously reached. Navigators had been for some time exploring this coast, very cautiously however, and not venturing very far on the downward road towards the burning zone and the boiling whirlpools which were supposed to lie in this direction. They thought it specially dangerous to pass Cape Nun, which was then regarded as the utmost limit of the earth. This cape always seemed to say "No farther" to the timid mariner. But in the year 1433 one of Henry's mariners, more daring than his predecessors, passed without harm the forbidden limit. At length, in 1487, Bartholomew Diaz, while exploring

Portuguese Navigators.

this coast, was driven southerly by a violent wind until he had passed the extreme limit of Africa. Not knowing where he was, he turned easterly, then northerly, and by lucky accident found himself on the east side of the Continent. On his way back he named the most southerly point of the land Stormy Cape; but on his return to Portugal, the King said the point should be called the Cape of Good Hope, as there was good reason to believe that a new route to India would be found to lie around that cape. And so it proved.

CHRISTOPHER COLUMBUS.

Columbus.

Meanwhile a bolder scheme had been suggested to the King of Portugal than sailing around the Cape of Good Hope. He was told that a shorter and better route to the Indies lay westward over the dark and unknown Atlantic Ocean.

THE DISCOVERY OF AMERICA. 11

It was Christopher Columbus who proposed this idea to King John II. of Portugal. Columbus was an Italian, born in or near the city of Genoa, but, with his younger brother Bartholomew, he had removed to Portugal. He was not of high birth, but he was one of nature's noblemen—a man of commanding presence, courtly bearing, and charming conversational powers. He was large-hearted, noble-minded, and energetic in action. What he undertook he gave his whole heart to, and he was not easily discouraged by the difficulties which lay across his path. Much of his life had been spent on the sea, in merchant voyages, in contests with the Mohammedan pirates on the Mediterranean, and in exploring adventures along the African coast.

The earth's spherical form had been known from the time of Aristotle by men learned in physical science. This truth had been established by various proofs, such as we at the present day are acquainted with. But while the earth's spherical form had been known for eighteen centuries or more, it required the genius of Columbus to make this knowledge an active force in directing the destiny of the world. He was a man of action; he could do as well as think. *The Earth's Spherical Form.*

Columbus had a very erroneous idea of the distance to India by a westerly route. He estimated the distance from Portugal to Japan at something less than 3000 miles. If he had known that it was four times as far, he never could have persuaded the men of his day to favour his enterprise. His error seems to have had its origin in the opinion favoured by a statement in the *The Circumference of the Earth underestimated.*

Book of Esdras, that the land surface comprises six-sevenths of the entire breadth of the earth. Taking the circumference of the earth in the latitude of Lisbon to be 18,000 geographical miles, and allowing one-seventh of this as the breadth of the ocean, he made the distance from Portugal to Japan about 2600 geographical miles.

Columbus had not means to carry out his cherished scheme. The recounting of all his difficulties in trying to secure the aid of some royal patron would be too long a story to tell here. For ten years his efforts were unavailing. He tried the republic of Genoa, then that of Venice; but without success. He offered his services to the King of Portugal. The council of wise men, called by this sovereign to consider the matter, pronounced the scheme visionary. Columbus then sent his brother Bartholomew, who had just returned with Diaz from that first voyage around the Cape of Good Hope, to the courts of England and France. Meanwhile he himself went to Spain, to seek assistance from Ferdinand and Isabella, the sovereigns of the two kingdoms into which that country was then divided. For a long time there seemed little to hope for here, but Columbus persevered. Finally, through the aid of Mendoza, Archbishop of Toledo, and other persons of influence, he secured the interest of Queen Isabella. This noble woman even pledged her crown jewels in raising money for the project.

Queen Isabella aids Columbus.

The means provided were very small for such an undertaking. The little fleet comprised three ships, the *Santa Maria*, the *Piata*, and the *Nina*. The first named was a fair-sized

Provision for the Voyage.

vessel, but the other two were very small, and were without decks. It was hard to find sailors willing to risk their lives on such a perilous adventure over the dark ocean. Debtors were released from their obligations, and criminals were pardoned, as an inducement to enlist in the service. In this way three motley crews, comprising in all ninety men, were obtained. After a solemn religious service Columbus set sail from Palos on Friday, August 3, 1492.

As the little fleet sailed out of the harbour of Palos, the friends of those on board, standing on the shore, gave them a sad farewell, never expecting to see them again. Columbus ran first to the Canary Isles, intending to sail thence due west to the coast of Japan. Until they reached the Canaries, all went well; for thus far the sea was familiar. But when the last of these Isles disappeared in the eastern horizon, there arose a wail of despair from the sailors. They wept and sobbed like children. Columbus thought it not prudent to allow his men to know the distance sailed. He accordingly kept two reckonings, a correct one for himself, and a false one, giving less distance, for his men.

The Voyage.

As they passed over the unknown waters, new grounds of fear added to the distress. First, there was an unaccountable change in the compass needle. It had been pointing a little to the right of the pole-star; but as they sailed westerly the variation became less, until at last, when they had crossed the line of no variation, it swayed to the other side and pointed to the left of the pole-star. When about 800 miles from the Canaries they entered a remarkable portion of the Atlantic Ocean, now known as the Sargasso Sea—a vast extent of ocean, overgrown with a mass of seaweed, presenting the appearance of a prairie. As there was but little wind to urge them on, the vessels were so impeded by the tangled weeds that they could make but little progress, and the sailors feared they would stick fast. But soon the freshening north-easterly breezes dispelled this fear and became themselves a source of alarm. Day after day the north-east wind kept blowing, and the vessels glided steadily onward. This was all very well to carry them to the shores of Asia, but how should they ever get back? They were in the North-East Trade Wind.

Two months had passed since Columbus sailed from Spain. There was no appearance of land, but only a wide waste of waters on all sides. The crews were becoming mutinous and almost unmanageable. Hitherto the course had been due west. Columbus thought he might be sailing past Japan on the north; he accordingly changed his course two points to the south. Five days after this there was the shout of "Land, land!" A few hours later the ships were lying at anchor on the shore of an unknown island, while Columbus and his men were making the acquaintance of its uncivilised inhabitants. This was on the morning of October 12, ten weeks after they left Palos. The island was one of the Bahamas, but which one of this numerous group is doubtful.

Land.

Columbus remained for nearly three months, exploring the islands which he had discovered. Besides several of the Bahamas, he visited Cuba and Hayti. Here he had a serious mishap. The *Santa Maria*

THE DISCOVERY OF AMERICA. 15

struck upon a sand-bank on the coast of Hayti, and soon became a total wreck. The captain of the *Pinta* had previously deserted him, so that Columbus had only the *Baby* (*Nina*) remaining. He could not carry all his men in this little vessel, so with their full consent he left a colony of forty on the island of Hayti.

On his return to Spain, Columbus was received at court with distinguished honour. He was allowed to sit in the presence of the King and Queen, a privilege not usually accorded to a subject. He found it easy enough now to obtain money and men, so that he was able to proceed on a second voyage with a fleet of seventeen vessels and 1500 men.

In all Columbus made four voyages across the Atlantic, but he died in ignorance of having found a New World. He simply believed that he had discovered a westerly route to India, and that the islands which he had visited were off the coast of Asia. Hence these islands were afterwards named the West Indies, and the aborigines of America were called Indians.

CHAPTER III.

EARLY EXPLORERS.

The Cabots. Tidings of the wonderful discovery made by Columbus soon set all Western Europe astir. Neither India, China, nor Japan had yet been reached, but they surely were not far from the newly discovered islands. So thought Columbus, and the leading men of his time were of the same opinion. These lands had the reputation of possessing unbounded wealth, and the navigator who should open up to them a new and easy route would be on the high road to fortune. Henry VII. of England was a prudent-going king, but like the sovereigns of more southerly climes, he could be dazzled by the prospect of adding the empire of these pagan lands to his dominion and their wealth to his treasury. And so he was not unwilling to become the patron of a voyage of discovery across the western waters. He found suitable navigators to carry out his project in John Cabot and his son Sebastian.

Like Columbus, John Cabot was a native of Genoa. From this place he had removed to Venice, and had finally settled in Bristol, then the chief seaport of England. Under royal charter, he set sail in the ship *Matthew* on his first voyage in May 1497, in search of a westerly route to China and India. All lands that he might discover were to belong to the English Crown. Cabot was to have sole right of trade with such countries, and he was to give one-fifth of the profits to King Henry. Ferdinand and Isabella of Spain, hearing of Henry's project, warned him that they had exclusive rights to the territories beyond the western waters; but Henry gave little heed to their remonstrance.

At the end of three months Cabot returned. He had discovered land which he thought was a part of the Chinese coast. It is matter of dispute as to the exact place visited by Cabot, the rival claimants being some point on the coast of Labrador, a headland on the east of Newfoundland, or some place on the Island of Cape Breton. King Henry is said to have rewarded the explorer with a gift of £10. In the following year he and his son Sebastian made a second voyage, during which they explored a large part of the Atlantic coast of North America. Nothing further is heard of John Cabot, and it is supposed that he died upon the voyage, leaving the command to Sebastian.

The glory of discovering the continent of North America thus belongs to the Cabots, though it seems probable that at the time these mariners believed they were sailing along the coast of Asia. Little gain, however, came to King Henry from these discoveries. His ships returned without gold or silver to fill his treasury, nor had they found the desired route to the Indies. The expedition involved large outlay and no profit, so that his ardour for discovering new lands soon cooled. England, however, afterwards based her claims to a large portion of North America on the discovery of the Cabots.

B

18 THE DOMINION OF CANADA.

Yet another Italian, best known by his Latin name Americus Vespucius, claims distinction as a noted early explorer. He crossed the Atlantic several times, and explored portions of the coast of South America. The early explorers, includ-

Americus Vespucius.

PART OF LEONARDO DA VINCI'S MAP, *cir.* 1514.
Earliest known Map with the name "America."

ing Vespucius himself, had little idea that the lands they had found formed one continuous continent. They supposed that these lands were islands or projecting points of Asia, and they eagerly sought for some channel between them, through which they could pass to India.

EARLY EXPLORERS.

The name America seems to have been first given to Brazil, which was discovered by Vespucius. Afterwards, when this country was found to be connected with other lands, forming the southern continent, the name America was applied to the whole territory. At a later date when it was discovered that the lands on the north also formed a great continent, the name was similarly extended so as to include the two great divisions of the New World. The earliest map showing the double continent under the name America, was published in 1541. The author of this map was the distinguished Kaufmann, a native of Flanders, better known by his Latin name Mercator.

The first foreshadowing of the knowledge of a great ocean between the newly discovered lands and Asia was the glimpse had of this ocean by Vasco Nunez Balboa from a mountain-peak in Darien. *Discovery of the Pacific Ocean.* This noted Spaniard introduced himself to the world in rather ignoble fashion. To escape his creditors, he had himself sealed up in a cask and smuggled on board a ship about to sail from San Domingo. Afterwards, while at Darien, he heard of the wealth of Peru, the land of the Incas, where gold was said to be almost as plentiful as the stones in the field. At the head of one hundred men he set out for this land. As already told, while crossing the isthmus he got his first glimpse of the Pacific Ocean. As the water he saw lay to the south, the whole ocean was long known as the South Sea.

But it remained for the Portuguese navigator, Ferdinand Magellan, one of the first navigators of his age, to demonstrate the vastness of the ocean that separated the lands dis- *Magellan.*

covered by Columbus from the Indies which he supposed he had reached. Magellan had visited India by way of the Cape of Good Hope. While there he determined to seek a westerly route from Europe to this country. Returning home he submitted his scheme to the King of Portugal. Receiving no encouragement, he offered his services to the young Emperor Charles V. of Spain, under whose flag he made his great voyage. The account of this voyage across the Atlantic, along the east coast of America, through the Strait which now bears his name, and thence across the wide and till then untraversed ocean, is a thrilling story. When he first entered this great ocean he found its waters so peaceful, compared with the stormy sea he had just passed through, that he named it the Pacific Ocean. In March 1521, Magellan reached the Philippine Islands. He did not live to complete the full round voyage. Engaged in a conflict with the natives of one of the islands, his men were put to flight and he was killed.

The rulers of Spain and Portugal seemed to think that all newly discovered and all undiscovered lands belonged to them, and to prevent quarrels between them over these lands, it was agreed that a meridian three hundred and seventy leagues west of the Madeira Islands should be "the line of demarcation." All those lands east of that line were to belong to Portugal, and all to the west of it to Spain. Francis I. of France thought otherwise. He is said to have asked the kings of those countries by what right they claimed the whole world. If father Adam had made them his heirs, they should at least produce the will. While they were looking up

Francis I. of France.

the document, he proceeded to take a portion for himself.

Indeed, before Francis came to the throne, the Baron de Léry had in a feeble way asserted the rights of France in the New World by trying to establish a colony on Sable Island. This little strip of land, with which the sea is ever waging war, is situated about one hundred miles to the south of Cape Breton Island. The dangerous sand-bars on its coast have wrecked so many ships that the island has been called the "graveyard of the Atlantic." A few wild cattle found on the island many years after seem to have been the most permanent remains of De Léry's colony. De Léry, 1518.

King Francis I. had in his service an Italian named Verrazano, who had made himself famous by seizing a Spanish treasure-ship on its way from Mexico to Spain. The King now sent him in search of that long-sought westerly passage to China. Verrazano failed to find China, but he is said to have explored the coast of North America from Cape Fear to the Gulf of St. Lawrence. He named this vast country New France, and took formal possession of it in behalf of the French Crown. Verrazano, 1524.

The disastrous wars of Francis with Charles V., who ruled over both Spain and Germany, prevented any immediate measures for building up this French dominion beyond the Atlantic. Ten years later, however, Jacques Cartier, a renowned mariner of the seaport town of St. Malo, was sent to make further explorations in New France. He came direct to Newfoundland, passed through the Strait of Belle Isle, and proceeded as far as Bay Jacques Cartier, 1534.

Chaleur. At Gaspé he erected a wooden cross thirty feet high, bearing a suitable inscription, showing that he claimed the country for Christ and the King of France. The Indians of the place told him of a great water-road by which he could sail far up into the interior of the country. But the season was too far advanced for further explorations and Cartier set out for France with high hope that he had found the long-sought route to India and China. Before leaving he kidnapped two Indians, whom he carried with him to France.

JACQUES CARTIER.

In the following year Cartier came again, and sailed up the great river which the Indians had told him of on his former visit. To this river he gave the name St. Lawrence. Where the city of Quebec now stands Cartier found an Indian village named Stadacona.

EARLY EXPLORERS. 23

Its old chief Donnacona gave him a kindly greeting, and told him of a larger village, named Hochelaga, farther up the river, which Cartier determined to visit. The beautiful island near Stadacona, now known as Orleans, he called Isle Bacchus, on account of the abundance of wild grapes which it produced. *(Cartier's Second Voyage.)*

Donnacona tried to dissuade Cartier from visiting Hochelaga. But leaving his larger vessels and part of his crew near Stadacona, Cartier set out for the distant Indian village, at which he arrived early in October. This place comprised about fifty dwellings simply constructed of poles covered with bark. They were of rectangular form, about one hundred and fifty feet in length. Each of these long houses was a sort of tenement house, being divided into several rooms, each room being occupied by a distinct family. The whole village was fortified after the Indian fashion by a palisade formed of the trunks of trees set upright in the ground. Around the inside, next the palisade, was a sort of gallery from which stones could be hurled upon a foe coming up from the outside. The Indians of Hochelaga received Cartier with great respect, even regarding him as possessed of superhuman powers, enabling him to heal the sick by the touch of his hand. Around the village Cartier saw fields of maize, from which the Indians derived part of their food. Before leaving Hochelaga, Cartier visited the beautiful mountain which tourists still so much admire. He named it Mont Royal, from which has come Montreal, the name of the great commercial city now occupying the site of the Indian Hochelaga.

Cartier spent the winter in a palisaded fort on the banks of the St. Charles, near Stadacona. It was a dreary winter, whose rigours those who had been accustomed to the genial climate of France were ill fitted to endure. A fell disease, known as scurvy, brought on by bad food, broke out, carrying off twenty-five men and prostrating many more. The Indians showed the French much kindness, which was ill requited. Early in the spring, when the frost had relaxed its hold of the river, Cartier sailed for France, carrying off by force Donnacona and other Indian chiefs.

The war with Spain again interrupted the French king's plans for colonising New France, so that five years passed before Cartier returned to the country. But now new interest was awakened in the far-off land. Sieur de Roberval, a nobleman of high rank, was appointed Viceroy of Canada. Cartier, second in authority, with the title of Captain-General, was sent out first with five ships, bearing colonists and supplies. Roberval was to follow. The object of the enterprise was discovery, settlement of the country, and the conversion of the Indians. In the royal charter Canada was described as forming "the extremity of Asia toward the west." The Indians of Stadacona, remembering how their chiefs had been carried away, were less friendly than formerly. Cartier and his colonists spent a miserable winter at Cap Rouge, a little above where Quebec now stands. Cold and disease and the hostility of the natives awakened in his people fervent longings for the home they had left beyond the ocean. There was no sign of the Viceroy whom they were anxiously

Cartier's Third Voyage.

EARLY EXPLORERS.

awaiting. So when spring came, Cartier, gathering the survivors on board his vessels, sailed for France.

Meanwhile Roberval had sailed for Canada with three ships and two hundred colonists. On his way he called at St. John's, Newfoundland. Imagine his surprise when, shortly after his arrival, he saw Cartier's ships entering the harbour, and his rage when he found next morning that, under cover of the night, Cartier had, in opposition to his orders, proceeded on his way to France. Roberval went on to Cap Rouge, where his experiences were similar to those of Cartier. He had made scant provision for the winter. Famine, disease, and mutiny were among the ills which he had to contend with, and before spring came death had swept off one-third of his men. The colony was short-lived. In the summer of 1543 the King sent Cartier to bring them all back to France.

France was now passing through stormy times. Some of its people were Roman Catholics and some were Protestants, or Huguenots, as they were called, and they had little love for each other. Religious strife, persecution, and civil war so distracted and weakened the kingdom that there was little spirit or energy for foreign enterprise. For over half a century no attempt was made to establish colonies in Canada. *Troubles in France.*

Meanwhile, however, every summer fleets of fishing-vessels sailed from the western ports of France for the banks of Newfoundland. Nor had the passion for discovery lost its power. Navigators were still exploring the bays and rivers on the eastern coast of America in search of some passage to China and India. *The Fisheries of Newfoundland.*

Soon, also, it became known that the forests of
New France possessed sources of wealth
in their fur-bearing animals even more
lucrative than the treasures of the ocean. The fur
trade with the Indians awakened the keenest rivalry
among the merchants of the seaport towns of France.
It was a barter trade. In exchange for furs, which
brought a high price in European markets, the traders
gave the Indians knives, hatchets, cloth, brandy, beads,
and various trinkets. They were not satisfied with
having the trade free and open to all, but some company or individual obtained from the King letters
patent, securing to the holder sole right of trade within
certain specified limits.

The Fur Trade.

Henry IV., who now held the throne of France,
gave the Marquis de la Roche a patent
of this kind. This nobleman was made
Lieutenant-General of Canada and adjacent lands, and
was granted exclusive right of trade within his territory. He set out to take possession of his dominion.
The enterprise did not look very hopeful. As colonists
could not be obtained from other quarters, the Marquis
was permitted to take convicts from the public prisons
to make up the required number. The vessel in which
they sailed was so small that those on board could, by
leaning over the side, wash their hands in the sea.
Having crossed the Atlantic, De la Roche left forty of
his convicts on Sable Island until he should find a
suitable place for settlement. Shortly after he encountered a violent storm, by which he was driven
back to the coasts of France. He returned home, to
find that through the influence of rivals his commission was cancelled, his power gone, and himself in

De la Roche, 1598.

disgrace. He was deeply in debt, and, unable to make payment, he was thrown into prison. For five long years, while De la Roche lay in prison, the wretched men on Sable Island strove with cold and hunger and disease and with each other, until only twelve remained alive. Then the King, learning how they had been left, sent Chetodel, De la Roche's pilot, to bring them home. It was a sorry spectacle the surviving convicts made when brought into the King's presence, with their swarthy faces, long beards, and shaggy clothing made of the skins of wild animals. The King was so touched with their wretched appearance and the story of their sufferings, that he pardoned their past offences and bestowed on each a gift of fifty crowns.

A naval officer named Chauvin, and Pontgravé, a merchant of St. Malo, now obtained a patent from the King of France, giving them exclusive right to the fur trade in Canada. <small>Chauvin and Pontgravé, 1599.</small> The charter required them to establish five hundred colonists in the country. Their principal trading post was Tadoussac, at the mouth of the Saguenay. Here they erected store-houses and a few rude huts. They derived large profits from the fur trade: but as regards colonists, they brought out only sixteen, and these they sadly neglected. Indeed, but for the help of the Indians, the poor fellows would have died of starvation.

Henry IV. of France, known as Henry of Navarre, had to fight his way to the throne. Aymar de Chastes, Governor of Dieppe, had rendered the King important aid in his struggle for the crown. <small>Aymar de Chastes.</small> Now an old man, he desired to round out his service of God and the King by planting the cross and the *fleur de lis* in Canada. Henry, willing to gratify him, gave him patent rights to the fur trade. De Chastes, having formed a company of leading merchants to carry out his plans of settlement and trade, selected Pontgravé to explore the country.

There was at this time at the French court a young man who stood high in the King's favour, and who during the next thirty years took a prominent part in the affairs of Canada. This was Samuel de Champlain. He had just returned from the West Indies and Mexico, whither he had gone to gratify his love of adventure. He now became a member of the new company, and with the King's permission accompanied Pontgravé to Canada.

SAMUEL DE CHAMPLAIN

Pontgravé and Champlain crossed the Atlantic with two small vessels, one of fifteen tons, the other of twelve. They visited the grounds which Cartier had occupied sixty years before. Things had greatly changed. The Indian towns of Stadacona and Hochelaga had entirely disappeared, and only a few wandering Algonquins were now found in the country. Having finished their explorations they returned to France. In the meantime De Chastes had died, and this led to a reorganisation of the company under Pierre du Guast, Sieur de Monts, the Governor of Pons. De Monts was made Lieutenant-General of Acadie, a vast territory extending from the fortieth to the forty-sixth degree of north latitude. The company's exclusive right to the fur trade within this territory was secured by royal charter.

CHAPTER IV.

THE FIRST CHAPTER IN THE HISTORY OF ACADIE.

In the spring of 1604 De Monts sailed for Acadie. His colonists formed a motley company. On board his vessels were men of all classes and conditions, from those of highest rank and character to the common labourer and the vilest criminal. Among the leading men who accompanied him were Pontgravé, Baron de Poutrincourt, and Champlain. As to religion, some were Catholics and some were Huguenots. The motives which took them over the seas were as varied as their character and condition. Some went for love of gain, some for love of God to carry the Gospel to the poor Indian; and yet others went for love of adventure. Some went to extend the power and glory of France; and again, others were dragged on board by force, to make the required number. Accompanying the expedition were Roman Catholic priests and Huguenot ministers. During the voyage these messengers of peace debated religious questions with such heat that they sometimes came to blows. De Monts was a Huguenot, but he gave pledges that the Indians should be instructed in the Catholic faith.

De Monts sails for Acadie, 1604.

Dreading the severe winter in the country bordering on the St. Lawrence, De Monts steered for a more southerly point. The first land he sighted was Cape la Have on the south of Nova Scotia. In the little bay now known as Liverpool Harbour he found a fellow-countryman engaged in buying furs from the Indians. As this was a violation of his rights, De Monts seized the vessel and cargo. Shortly after, Pontgravé, who had been exploring the coast farther east, arrived with the spoils of four traders whom he found trespassing near Canso. Pontgravé then sailed for Tadoussac to carry on the fur trade with the Indians, while De Monts proceeded westerly in search of a suitable place to establish his colony.

At St. Mary's Bay a party, including a priest named Aubry, and a Huguenot minister, went ashore for a stroll through the forest. On their return to the vessel the priest was missing. Search for the lost man was unavailing, and the Huguenot was suspected of having killed him. Sixteen days after an exploring party returned to St. Mary's Bay. While at anchor near the coast they heard a feeble cry as of one in distress. Looking towards the shore they saw a man waving his hat. It was Aubry. Stopping to drink at a spring, he had laid his sword on the ground and forgotten to take it again. Afterwards returning to get it, he lost his way. For over two weeks he had lived on berries, and he was now nearly exhausted from hunger.

The southern shores of the Bay of Fundy are for the most part guarded by high cliffs of trap rock. Sailing up the bay De Monts observed an opening in the rocky wall, through which the sea found an inlet. Passing through this narrow

Port Royal.

gateway, he beheld, stretching away to the eastward, the beautiful land-locked water now known as Annapolis Basin. The placid waters, glittering with silvery sheen, dotted here and there with an islet, and bordered all around with the leafy forests, like a mirror set in emerald, filled the beholders with delight. On the north shore near Goat Island, where land and water mingle all their charms, a site was chosen for a town. This place, honoured with the kingly name Port Royal, De Monts bestowed on Poutrincourt.

Leaving Port Royal, De Monts and his colonists continued their voyage up the bay. They sailed around Cape Blomidon into Minas Basin; then, returning, they entered a large river flowing into the bay from the north. It was the 24th of June, and in honour of the day they named the river St. John.

It was time to seek winter quarters. A place was selected on a small island in Passamaquoddy Bay, near the mouth of the St. Croix River. Here, at considerable cost, they erected dwellings, placing them around an open square or court. The site had not been well chosen, and the little colony suffered greatly during the winter. The cold was intense, wood and water were scarce, and the food was bad. Disease broke out, which carried off thirty-nine men before spring came. Pontgravé and Poutrincourt had returned to France in the autumn; but the stout-hearted Champlain remained, a source of strength and hope to the little colony.

St Croix.

Early in the spring De Monts and Champlain went farther west along the coast seeking a site for their colony, but no place pleased so well as Port Royal. Thither, accordingly, all returned,

Port Royal founded, 1605.

bringing with them the materials of which their houses were made. But scarcely were they well settled when bad news came from France. Rivals were plotting against De Monts, trying to persuade the King to cancel his charter. De Monts, therefore, at once proceeded to France, leaving Pontgravé, who had recently returned from that country, to take charge of the colony, and Champlain to explore new territory.

De Monts could do little to maintain his position in Acadie. His enemies, jealous of his monopoly, asserted that he had neglected missionary work among the Indians; his friends, dissatisfied with the small profits on their investments, failed to give him active support. Poutrincourt, however, was enthusiastic over his new estate, and, assisted by De Monts, he prepared to return to Port Royal. He sailed from Rochelle in May 1606. His arrival at Port Royal was opportune, for the little colony had been reduced to extremities. Two Frenchmen and an old Indian chief occupied the fort. Pontgravé had gone with the others to obtain supplies from fishing-vessels which they might find on the coast. Learning of Poutrincourt's arrival, he soon returned. It was a joyous reunion. To add to the good cheer, Poutrincourt placed a hogshead of wine in the open square, and invited all to drink at their pleasure. *Poutrincourt returns.*

Poutrincourt was accompanied by a young man named Marc Lescarbot, who proved an invaluable aid to the colony. Lescarbot was by profession a lawyer, but he was a man of varied talents and accomplishments. He encouraged the cultivation of the soil, looked after the public *Lescarbot.*

health, and superintended the building of a water-power mill for making flour in place of the hand mill previously used. He was the historian of the colony, and he also, after a fashion, wrote poetry, with which he was wont to amuse his friends.

The following winter passed pleasantly. There were fifteen principal men in the colony. At the suggestion of Champlain, they formed themselves into a club called the Order of the Good Time. Day about each held the office of Grand Master, whose duty it was to provide for the table and to furnish amusement for his day of office. Each, as his turn came to cater for the club, strove to outdo his predecessor, while stream and forest yielded their choicest luxuries of fish and game to enrich the bill of fare. At the appointed hour the Grand Master, wearing the insignia of office, entered the dining-hall, followed by the members of the order, each bearing a dish for the table. Welcome guests at the festive board were the Indian chiefs, most honoured of whom was the aged Membertou, whose head was now whitened by a hundred winters. After dinner the members of the club drank their wine, smoked their lobster-claw pipes, sang French songs, and listened to the old chief's Indian tales.

L'Ordre de Bon Temps.

When spring came, the colonists, stimulated and guided by the versatile Lescarbot, set about cultivating the soil. In this agricultural life of the colony lay its chief promise of permanence; but there was an element of weakness which even this feature could not overcome. The colonists had not come to Acadie to make a home for themselves and their families. They were simply

Port Royal in 1607.

dependents of a company whose interests all centred in the fur trade. The culture of the soil was a pastime and not a vocation.

And now came the day of trial. De Monts failed to withstand the clamour of his rivals. His charter was cancelled. The Company's monopoly of the fur trade having been taken away, the expenses of the colony would exceed the income. Poutrincourt was accordingly instructed to break up the settlement and return with all the colonists to France. And so, much to the grief of the Indians, especially of the old chief Membertou, Port Royal was abandoned. Reluctantly did Poutrincourt leave the place in which he had taken so much interest. *Port Royal abandoned, 1607.*

Poutrincourt did not lose his love for Port Royal. Three years elapsed, however, before he was able to return. The Indians of Acadie, ever friendly to the French, gave him a hearty welcome. In confirming his title to the place from De Monts, the King insisted that he should provide means for instructing the natives in the Catholic religion. Poutrincourt had brought with him a priest, Father Flèche, for this purpose. The Indians were very docile under their teacher. The old chief Membertou, his family, and his clan gave assent to the faith, and received Christian names at their baptism. Membertou was called Henry, after the King of France, and his squaw Mary, after the Queen. Biencourt, the youthful son of Poutrincourt, was sent to France to report to the King this success in missionary work. But before he arrived, King Henry had fallen by the hand of an assassin as he was driving through the streets of Paris. *Return to Port Royal, 1610.*

Troubles. The religious order known as the Jesuits at this time stood high in favour and influence at the Court of France. Many of the French people, however, were strongly opposed to the order. Poutrincourt shared in this feeling, and he used every available means to keep its members out of his colony. In spite of these efforts, two Jesuits, Biard and Masse, accompanied Biencourt on his return to Port Royal. Troubles now came thick upon Poutrincourt. He went to France to look after the interests of his colony, leaving Biencourt in charge. Rivals plotted against him. He was burdened with debt and was thrown into prison, where he fell ill. In the meantime affairs got on badly at Port Royal. Food was scarce, and the colonists had to forage in the forest to keep themselves from starving. There were constant quarrels between Biencourt and the Jesuit fathers. But now a new enemy, worse than all others, appeared on the scene.

Jamestown. The settlement of Jamestown, on the coast of Virginia, formed in 1607, was the first English colony in America. It was established by a company acting under authority of King James I. of England. The territory of the company extended northerly to the Gulf of St. Lawrence, and included Port Royal. The hero of the colony was Captain John Smith, whose adventures and hair-breadth escapes in various parts of the world give interest to the story of his life. He now added to his fame by abducting from her forest home an Indian chief's daughter, the beautiful and tender-hearted Pocahontas.

At Jamestown was one Captain Argall, a daring,

THE HISTORY OF ACADIE.   37

unscrupulous man, ready for almost any enterprise. He was sent north in an armed vessel by the Governor of Jamestown to expel any Frenchmen whom he might find within the limits of the Company's territory. *Port Royal destroyed, 1613.* He first attacked a little colony just established at the mouth of the Penobscot River, making prisoners of the colonists and seizing their property. Shortly after, the Governor of Virginia sent him against Port Royal. When he arrived at this place Biencourt and part of his men were absent; others were reaping their grain in the fields. Argall plundered the fort and then laid it in ashes, setting fire even to the grain in the harvest-field. Poutrincourt once more, in the following spring, visited Port Royal, to find it in ruins, and his son a homeless wanderer in the forests. Returning to France, he shortly after fell in battle. His son Biencourt remained in Acadie. He built a rude fort near Cape Sable, on the south coast, giving it the name of Fort Louis. There was with him a Huguenot of some note, named Claude de la Tour, who, together with his son Charles, had come to Port Royal in 1610 with Poutrincourt. On the death of Biencourt in 1623 Charles de la Tour succeeded as lieutenant, making his home at Fort Louis. Meanwhile Claude de la Tour proceeded to France to seek the royal favour for his son.

The kings of England at this time had much more power than belongs to the sovereign in our day, and they sometimes made liberal gifts to their friends. *Nova Scotia, 1621.* James I., who now held the throne, claimed, in virtue of Cabot's discovery, a large part of North America, including the French Acadie. This country he now bestowed on a Scottish knight named Sir William Alexander. In Sir William's charter, given in 1621, the country was called Nova Scotia. Four years later, to aid Sir William in settling the country, Charles I., who had succeeded to the English throne, created an order of knighthood for Nova Scotia. There were to be one hundred and fifty knights baronets of Nova Scotia, and each knight was to receive a barony in the colony on condition of taking thither a certain number of colonists. Through Sir William's efforts a small Scotch settlement was formed in the part of the country now called Granville. But Sir William's plans did not prosper, and he soon abandoned the scheme.

CHAPTER V.

CANADA UNDER CHAMPLAIN.

DE MONTS did not abandon his purpose of founding a colony. Leaving Port Royal to Pou-trincourt, he chose the country of the St. Lawrence as a field of operation. *De Monts's New Field.* He had sufficient influence at court to secure a renewal of his monopoly of the fur trade for one year. Accordingly, with the threefold object of founding a colony, making money by the fur trade, and exploration, he fitted out two ships for the St. Lawrence. Pontgravé, having command of one, proceeded to Tadoussac to carry on the fur trade with the Indians. Champlain, who, as lieutenant-governor, had charge of the other, was to care for the colony and explore the country. They left France in the spring of 1608.

A short distance above the Island of Orleans, a small river from the north, named the S. Charles, enters the St. Lawrence. *Quebec founded.* On the angle between the rivers is a rocky promontory, whose highest point, called Cape Diamond, rises to the height of 350 feet above the water. A narrow strand lies between the St. Lawrence and the cliffs. Here, under the shadow of the lofty Cape, on the site of the Indian Stadacona, Champlain erected a few wooden houses, which he protected by a strong wall of logs. On the outside of the wall was a moat, and on the inside a gallery, on which he mounted his cannon. Such was the rude beginning of the city and fortifications of Quebec, which in the course of years became, and still continues to be, the strongest fortress in America.

The story of Champlain's rule in Canada, as well as the succeeding history of the country, has much to do with the native Indian tribes. Hence, to make the story plain, it is necessary to give some account of these people. At this time the Indians of Canada and the neighbouring territories comprised three principal divisions – the Algonquins, the Iroquois, and the Hurons. More properly they may be included in two families, for the two last-named were of the same stock, and are often called the Huron-Iroquois. Each of these divisions included various tribes. At the time of Champlain's arrival the Indian villages of Stadacona and Hochelaga had entirely disappeared, nor were there in the country any Indians of that family which Cartier met seventy years earlier. Those of Cartier's time were of the Huron-Iroquois stock, and the country was now occupied by Algonquins.

The Algonquin family was widespread, being thinly scattered over a large part of the Atlantic slope of North America. It included the Indians on the Ottawa, on the Lower St. Lawrence, and in the territory now comprised in the Atlantic Provinces. Many of them, especially in the east, lived by hunting and fishing, wholly neglecting the cultivation of the soil. They were more roving in habits than the others.

The Iroquois occupied the territory now included in Central New York. In the early times they comprised five tribes—the Mohawks, the Oneidas, the Onondagas, the Cayugas, and the Senecas, from which they came to be called the "Five Nations." At a later period they were joined by the Tuscaroras from South Carolina, and they then

THE HURON MISSION.

became known as the "Six Nations." The Iroquois held a much higher position in the scale of humanity and the arts of life than the Algonquins. They had better dwellings, and cultivated the soil, though in a very rude sort of way. Their chief products were Indian corn, beans, pumpkins, tobacco, and sunflowers. They were also more skilful in war as it was practised by the Indians, and they were very cruel to such of their enemies as they captured, often putting them to death with extreme refinement of torture; and yet, to increase their own numbers, they sometimes adopted their captives as members of the tribe. Their habit was to make rapid incursions, by way of the rivers and lakes, into the country of the Algonquins and Hurons, swooping upon their unsuspecting victims, plundering and killing them, or carrying off those whom they could capture alive. Although the Algonquins were much more numerous than the Iroquois, yet such dread had they of this foe that they made their home far back in the depth of the forest, occasionally visiting certain points on the rivers for trade. The Iroquois usually entered the country of the Algonquins by way of the Richelieu River, which was at this time called the River of the Iroquois.

The Hurons The Hurons, as already stated, properly belonged to the Iroquois family, but they were separated from the other tribes of this family by a deadly feud. They inhabited the country between Georgian Bay and Lake Simcoe, now forming the northern part of Simcoe County in Ontario. In Champlain's time, and later, there were over thirty villages in this small district, with a total population said to be at least twenty thousand. As regards intelligence and mode of living they stood highest among the Indians of Canada.

The dwellings of the Hurons were long houses like those which Cartier found at Hochelaga, about thirty-five feet in length and the same in breadth, although some of them were over two hundred feet long. They were often constructed by planting two parallel rows of tall saplings, bending these inwards until they overlapped, and binding them together, thus giving the structure an arched form at the top. Cross-poles were then lashed to these uprights, and the whole was covered with bark, except an opening about a foot wide along the centre running the whole length of the dwelling. This opening served the double purpose of a window and a chimney. Each dwelling was occupied

GROUND-PLAN OF LONG HOUSE.

INDIAN LONG HOUSE.

by several families. The fires were on the ground along the middle of the house, directly under the opening at the top, one fire serving for two adjoining families. In winter, men, women, and children slept close packed around the fire. In summer their sleeping-place was a sort of scaffold along each side of the dwelling, made of poles covered with bark and skins of animals. The Hurons lived principally on Indian corn, which they stored up in large quantities, buried deep in the ground. They also cultivated tobacco, pumpkins, and sunflowers.

Matters did not at first run smoothly with Champlain. Scarcely was he settled when some of his men formed a plot to kill him. The conspiracy was discovered in good time, the ringleader was hanged, and his three chief accomplices were sent in irons to France. Scurvy, dread foe of the early colonists, broke out and sadly thinned the little colony. Before the winter was past only eight men out of twenty-eight remained alive.

Champlain's Difficulties.

But with the spring came health and renewed hope. Pontgravé, who had gone to France in the autumn, returned, bringing with him more colonists. Champlain was eager to begin his explorations, and a way now opened which seemed to favour his purpose. The Algonquins and Hurons, impressed with his superior equipments for war, invited him to join them in a foray against the Iroquois. Champlain accepted the invitation, and thus excited against himself and his countrymen the bitter and undying hostility of the fiercest and most warlike savages in America.

Better Prospects.

The allied forces comprised sixty Indians and twelve Frenchmen, including Champlain. The route lay by way of the waters now known as the River Richelieu and Lake Champlain. The Indians had canoes; the French went in a boat, as they had been told by the Indians that they could sail up to the headwaters of the lake without obstruction. All went well until they came to the rapids of the Richelieu. The boat could go no farther. Accordingly nine of Champlain's men were sent back with it to Quebec. The Indians, having carried the

Foray against the Iroquois

canoes on their shoulders over the portage to the smooth waters above, took Champlain and his two remaining men in with them.

At last, on the shores of Lake Champlain, probably near the site of Ticonderoga, sooner than they had expected, they met the foe they were seeking—a band of Iroquois two hundred strong. At first Champlain kept out of sight. When he stepped to the front, clad in the armour which warriors of that day were accustomed to wear, the Iroquois were filled with wonder, and when he fired upon them, killing two of their chiefs and mortally wounding a third, panic-stricken they flung down their weapons and fled. Champlain gained an easy victory; but it was a more difficult matter to restrain the fierce passions of his Indian allies. In spite of his remonstrances, they scalped their prisoners alive, and tortured them with every cruelty which their savage nature could invent. The victors now turned back—Champlain to Quebec, his Indian allies to their home on the Ottawa. *The Battle.*

Various French noblemen, for a short time, held in succession the office of Viceroy of New France. Champlain, however, acting as lieutenant under each, was the life of the colony, and he made several visits to France to awaken interest in its welfare and to secure means for its support. Two leading objects he kept ever before him—the conversion of the Indians and the discovery of a route to China. Except as it might provide means to carry out these objects, he cared little for the fur trade. To satisfy the merchants who cried out against monopoly, he offered them a share in the traffic. Some of them, however, preferred to carry on a rival trade in defiance of his charter. *Champlain's Purposes.*

The Site of Montreal selected, 1611

Champlain saw that the success of his Company required a fortified post at some point on the St. Lawrence, which would be of easy access both to the trading-vessels and to the Indians of the interior. The Island of Montreal, situated at the head of ship navigation at the mouth of the Ottawa, offered these advantages. With much good judgment Champlain chose for his post the site where Montreal, the great commercial capital of the Dominion, now stands. He cleared the ground, but for some cause failed to erect the fort. Little more was done at the place for thirty years. The Indians, however, were accustomed to gather here every year to sell their furs and to plan schemes of war against their enemies.

In Search of a Northern Sea, 1613

A Frenchman named Vignau, who had spent some months among the Indians on the Ottawa, then called the River of the Algonquins, reported, on his return, that he had visited a great northern sea beyond the headwaters of that river, and that he had seen the wreck of an English ship on its shores. Champlain believed that this was the long-sought route to India and China. Accordingly, accompanied by Vignau, four other Frenchmen, and an Indian guide, he made a long and perilous journey up the Ottawa in search of the sea. Finally the man confessed that his story was a hoax; he had found no such sea. Much disgusted with the impostor, whom he had promised to pardon in order to gain confession, Champlain made his way back to Quebec.

Champlain, returning from France, which he often visited, brought with him four monks of the order called Récollets, distinguished for the strictness of their rules and their self-denying manner of life. The arrival of these devoted men was an important era in the religious history of the colony. Two of them remained in Quebec, while the other two went among the Indians—one to the wandering Algonquins, and the other, Joseph le Caron, to the far-distant Hurons. *Récollets come to Canada, 1615.*

Champlain's Indian allies urged him to aid them again in a war against the Iroquois. Yielding to their entreaty, he set out for the country of the Hurons, where the forces were to be mustered. His route was long and arduous. He and a few companions, mostly Indians, went up the Ottawa, rowing against the strong current, and carrying their canoes around falls and rapids. Ascending the river to the Matawan, they struck across to Lake Nipissing, and thence passed down French River to Georgian Bay. There was great rejoicing among the Hurons over Champlain's arrival. Especially was he welcomed by Le Caron, the Récollet missionary. Nowhere among the Indians had Champlain seen such marks of intelligence. The dwellings were long houses occupied by several families, such as Cartier found at Montreal, and were surrounded by palisades in some cases thirty-five feet high. *Champlain visits the Hurons.*

The warriors assembled at their chief town, comprising two hundred dwellings, near where Orillia now stands. Having feasted and danced the war-dance, they shouldered their canoes and set out for the enemy's country. Their route was across Lake Simcoe and along the valley of the *War with the Iroquois.*

Trent by lake and stream to Quinte Bay. Thence they crossed Lake Ontario and marched inland to the country of the Iroquois. The enemy retreated from their fields and took shelter behind the palisades of one of their chief towns on the south of Lake Oneida. The Iroquois warriors occupied a gallery inside the palisades, where they were exposed to little danger from the besiegers. The Hurons, regardless of Champlain's counsel, exposed themselves to needless danger. Many of them were killed, and on the whole they had the worst of the fight. Champlain received a wound in the knee from an arrow, which so disabled him that for several days he had to be carried in a basket on the back of an Indian. Finally the Hurons became discouraged, and, in spite of Champlain's remonstrance, gave up the contest and set out for home.

Champlain winters among the Hurons. The failure of the attack on the Iroquois rather lessened Champlain's prestige among his Indian allies. He was not so powerful as they had supposed. When he asked them to send him to Montreal according to promise, they refused. Nor would they furnish him with boats for the journey. He was thus obliged to remain among them through the winter, which he spent in hunting and in visiting the different villages. In the spring, after a tedious journey of forty days, he returned to Quebec. There was great joy over his arrival, for his people had given him up for dead.

Condition of the Colony. Meanwhile the colony at Quebec was making little progress either as regards numbers or general prosperity. Its inhabitants did not exceed one hundred, and many of them spent their time in idleness or something worse. The cultivation of the soil was almost wholly neglected, and the few who engaged in this occupation did so rather for pastime than as a means of livelihood. The merchants set Champlain's authority at defiance, and the Company failed to supply the colonists with the necessaries of life. The Iroquois, in their turn, invaded the country, descending even to the very neighbourhood of Quebec. Indeed, some of Champlain's Indian allies showed by acts of violence that they could not be trusted. Changes in the viceroyalty brought no gain to the colony, and transferring the trade privileges from the old Company to two Huguenots, named Caen, only introduced religious strife. The policy was the same – to make as much money as possible out of the fur trade. A change was needed.

Cardinal Richelieu was now the real ruler of France. Through the influence of this great statesman a new company was formed. It consisted of one hundred associates, and was called the Company of New France, or the Company of One Hundred Associates. It had under its control a vast country from Hudson Bay to Florida, and from Newfoundland to the sources of the St. Lawrence. Within this territory it had a monopoly of the fur trade and of all other trade for fifteen years. During the period that the Huguenots had control of business affairs there arrived at Quebec three Jesuit priests, Lalemant, Brébeuf, and Masse, and two lay brothers of the same order. They were not very warmly received by the Huguenots, who regarded them with suspicion. The Company was under pledge to bring out immediately two or three hundred colonists, and to increase the number to four thousand within the next fifteen

The Company of New France, 1628.

D

years. All colonists must be French and of the Roman Catholic religion. Thus the Huguenots were excluded. These colonists the Company was bound to support for three years, and at the end of this time to give them such cleared lands as would enable them to support themselves. Richelieu himself was at the head of the Company. Champlain still had charge of the colony as lieutenant-governor.

The new Company began well. A fleet of transports, accompanied by four armed ships, bearing supplies and new colonists, was sent out from France. Safely it made its way across the Atlantic, and was now in the St. Lawrence, within a few hours' sail of Quebec. The starving inhabitants were eagerly watching for its arrival. Alas for their hopes! An enemy lay concealed at Tadoussac, also on the lookout. Civil war had broken out in France. The Huguenots, long persecuted, were in revolt, and Charles I. of England sent aid to the rebels. War between England and France awakened to new life Sir William Alexander's project of colonisation. Influenced by him, a company of London merchants, under authority of King Charles, sent out a fleet to drive the French from North America. The fleet was under the command of three brothers named Kirk—David, Lewis, and Thomas. They had made an easy conquest of Port Royal, and they were now ready for business in the St. Lawrence.

Shattered Hopes.

David Kirk, who was chief in command, sent a message to Champlain, demanding immediate surrender. Champlain was in sorry case for fighting. His fort was all out of repair, he had only fifty pounds of gunpowder, and his stock of provisions was low.

CANADA UNDER CHAMPLAIN. 51

But his courage was equal to the occasion. He would hold the fort. He placed each man at his post, determined to fight it out. But no foe appeared. The English were deceived by his boldness, and for the present let him alone. They captured all the French transports, however, and seized the supplies which Champlain so much needed.

There was great suffering in Quebec during the following winter. The colonists were on the verge of starvation. At last their only food was acorns and roots of Solomon's seal and other wild plants. One day in July, when all were out in search of food, Champlain alone remaining in the fort, three ships appeared ascending the river. Shortly after they dropped anchor before Quebec. The Kirks had returned. Resistance was useless, and the English flag was soon flying over the fort. Champlain was taken to England by his captors. *Capture of Quebec, 1629.*

Peace had already been made between England and France before the surrender of Quebec. The French Government accordingly claimed that the captured places should be restored. It is said that King Charles was influenced by French gold to respect the claim. However this may be, by the treaty of St. Germain-en-Laye, Quebec, Port Royal, and Cape Breton were given back to France. *Treaty of St. Germain-en-Laye, 1632.*

In the spring of 1633 the Company of One Hundred Associates took possession of their vast domain. At the same time Champlain, accompanied by a band of new colonists, returned to Quebec as governor. With his accustomed energy and unswerving integrity he devoted himself *Champlain's Death, 1635.*

to the building up of the colony. His care for the morals and the religious training of his people was most unwearied. Nor had his concern for the conversion of the Indians at all abated. The Récollet missionaries, who with so much devotion had begun the work, did not return with Champlain. The Jesuits, whose wonderful heroism will be described in succeeding chapters, came instead. But except as the influence of his life and character impressed itself on those who came after him, Champlain's work was done. On Christmas Day 1635 this greatest and best of the early explorers of Canada passed away. Over a quarter of a century had elapsed since Champlain planted his colony on the banks of the St. Lawrence, and yet, with all the fidelity and energy with which he had worked, he had done comparatively little to build up a French dominion in America. Save the little settlements at Quebec and Three Rivers, New France was still a vast unbroken forest. In all, the colonists did not exceed two hundred, and the prospect before them was by no means encouraging.

CHAPTER VI.

THE RULE OF THE ONE HUNDRED ASSOCIATES.

THE rule of the One Hundred Associates began in effect with the return of Champlain to Quebec. The Company obtained its charter five years earlier, as stated in the preceding chapter. Great things were expected of the Company in the way of colonisation and in strengthening the power of France in America. It really did little for either of these objects. The chief features of the period were missionary work among the Hurons and the troubles with the Iroquois. Chief Features, 1633.

Montmagny was Champlain's successor He belonged to a military-religious order called the Knights of Malta, noted for their courage and enthusiasm in the wars carried on in the Middle Ages by the Christian nations of Europe against the Turks. He was distinguished for his fidelity to the Roman Catholic Church and for his strictness in enforcing its rules. His first acts on landing at Quebec showed his great religious zeal. As he climbed the steep path which led to the fort of St. Louis, he fell devoutly on his knees before a cross which stood by the way; then, attended by priests and officers, he proceeded to the church, where a Te Deum was chanted for his safe arrival. He then Montmagny.

went to a hovel to act as sponsor at the baptism of a dying Indian.

Great religious zeal was characteristic of the age.

Character of the Age.
In France men and women were ready to give their money for the building up of the Church at home and abroad, and members of various religious orders were eager to devote their lives to mission work among the Indians of the New World. Much of this fervour was due to the activity of the Jesuits, a remarkable religious order which had its origin in Spain about one hundred years earlier. Under the rule of the new Company, members of this order were brought to Canada in place of the Récollets, the pioneer missionaries among the Hurons. The influence of the Jesuits in determining many civil and religious questions in Canada, as in most lands where they have obtained a foothold, has been a factor of vast potency.

The work of the Jesuit missionaries among the

Jesuit Missionaries
Indians in Canada commands the highest admiration. These self-denying men were impelled by a burning desire to bring the savages under the power of the Cross. To reach the remote abodes of the Indians, they travelled through pathless forests, paddled their canoes along the rivers, or bore them on their backs over portages. They lodged in smoky, filthy wigwams, suffered from cold and hunger and fatigue, and many of them, falling into the hands of the Iroquois, were tortured and killed in the most cruel manner. Very properly the Jesuits attached high value to the education of Indian children. They had been in Canada but a short time, when, through funds raised in France, they established a seminary

THE RULE OF THE ONE HUNDRED ASSOCIATES. 55

for the training of Huron boys. At this early period also the Jesuit College was founded at Quebec.

In this missionary work there were French women also no less distinguished for the ardour of their enthusiasm. Conspicuous among these were Madame de la Peltrie, Mary Guyard, better known as Mary of the Incarnation, and Mary of St. Bernard. In 1639 these devoted women came to Quebec to establish an institution for the instruction of French and Indian girls. In this way arose the Convent of the Ursulines, of which Madame de la Peltrie was the founder, and Mary of the Incarnation was Lady Superior. Another lady of high rank, the Duchess of Aiguillon, about the same time endowed a hospital for the care of the sick. This institution was called the Hotel Dieu. *The Three Marys.*

Montreal owes its origin to the missionary movement of the time. A few persons, men and women in France, burning with religious zeal, formed themselves into an association for mission work among the Indians. Having obtained a grant of the Island of Montreal from the One Hundred Associates, they resolved to make the place a centre of operation. The Company was called *La Société de Notre Dame de Montreal*. A hospital and a seminary were considered essential equipments. A large sum of money was raised to meet expenses, teachers were selected for the seminary, and Sieur de Maisonneuve, a man of great courage and piety, was appointed governor of the mission station. With a company of forty men and four women, Maisonneuve sailed for Canada. Conspicuous among them was Mdlle. Mance, a lady of good family who had from *Founding of Montreal, 1642.*

early years consecrated her life to the service of God, and who afterwards became head of the Hotel Dieu of Montreal.

Remote from any French settlement, and on the great highway of the Iroquois in their incursions into Canada, the place selected was a dangerous one. Montmagny pointed out its perils, and tried to persuade Maisonneuve to take instead the Island of Orleans. The reply showed the character of the man: "I have not come here to deliberate, but to act. It is my duty and my honour to found a colony at Montreal, and I would go if every tree were an Iroquois." And so Maisonneuve with his mission band proceeded on his way. Landing on the Island of Montreal, the devout leader and his companions fell on their knees and sang a hymn of thanksgiving. Then followed a solemn religious ceremonial, conducted by the Jesuit Vimont, ending with an invocation of Heaven's blessing on the colony. "You are a grain of mustard-seed," were the prophetic words of the priest, "that shall rise and grow till its branches overshadow the earth. You are few, but your work is the work of God. His smile is on you, and your children shall till the land." Thus on May 18, 1642, was founded Ville Marie de Montreal.

For some months the Iroquois did not discover the new settlement at Montreal. The colonists meanwhile made good use of their time in building fortifications. It was well they did, for when the Iroquois found them out they showed that their old enmity to the French was unabated. Having obtained firearms from the Dutch traders on the Hudson River, they were now a much

Hostility of the Iroquois.

THE RULE OF THE ONE HUNDRED ASSOCIATES. 57

more formidable foe than when they fled in terror before three armed Frenchmen on the shores of Lake Champlain. Their usual route into Canada was by way of Lake Champlain and River Richelieu, although they sometimes came across the east end of Lake Ontario. They seldom ventured on open war, but lay in ambush along the routes of travel, or lurked in the forests near the settlements, watching for defenceless Hurons or Frenchmen. The colonists of Montreal were in the greatest danger. If one ventured outside the fort, it was at the risk of his life. With horrid yells the savages sprang upon their victim, dragging him into the forest for cruel torture; or, striking him down, they hastily tore off his scalp and left the bleeding body where it fell. Sometimes only two or three Iroquois would be seen prowling around; but when the unsuspecting Frenchmen pursued them into the forest, suddenly hundreds of wild savages started up from their hiding-places.

The Hurons formed the most hopeful field of missionary work. The Jesuits had eighteen missionaries in their populous villages around the western lakes. They wrought unceasingly in faith and patience. The Hurons at first were slow to accept the doctrine of their new teachers. They even thought the missionaries a source of evil, bringing on them sickness, bad harvests, and ill-luck in war. Nor was the heaven described by their teachers such a place of bliss as the untutored savage felt he could enjoy. But the Jesuits never became discouraged or lost hope. Finally their labours were rewarded. Many of the Hurons embraced

Mission Work among the Hurons.

the Christian religion, and in various ways showed its power over their lives.

In the midst of promise came utter ruin. There was no good reason why the Hurons should not have been more than a match for their hostile kinsmen. They seem to have lost spirit. It is impossible to give here the full story of the savage warfare by which the Iroquois carried out their purpose of destruction—the burning of Huron villages, the cruel tortures inflicted on the captives, the shocking deaths to which they were subjected. The relentless foe was equally hostile to priest and people. One or two examples will suffice.

The Huron Villages attacked.

St. Joseph, a Huron village of about two thousand inhabitants, was situated on the borders of Lake Simcoe, near where the town of Barrie now stands. The Iroquois, taking advantage of the absence of the Huron warriors on a hunting excursion, rushed upon the defenceless people as they were assembling in their chapel for religious service. Père Daniel, who had for many years been their teacher and spiritual guide, could now only counsel them in their extremity with a few hasty words: "Fly, brothers," said he; "as for me, I must die here. We shall meet in heaven." And so it was. A shower of bullets and arrows pierced his breast and he fell dead. Having completed their work of murder, the savages set fire to the chapel and flung Daniel's body into the flames.

St. Joseph, 1648.

In the following year about a thousand Iroquois attacked the village of St. Louis, situated near the site of the modern Orillia. A fearful massacre ensued. Some of the victims the

St. Louis, 1649.

cruel savages reserved for torture. Among these were the Jesuits Brébeuf and Lalemant, who could have escaped, but who chose rather to die with their people. Unmindful of themselves, they encouraged those around them to endure their sufferings with patience. The fortitude of the priests only enraged the Iroquois and stimulated their ingenuity to invent new modes of torture. They hacked their bodies, pulled out their finger-nails, and hung collars of red-hot hatchets around their necks. Brébeuf, being more unyielding, excited their fiercest passions. Maddened by his words of comfort to his friends and of warning to themselves, they cut off his lips and thrust hot irons down his throat. Then, in mockery of the rite of baptism, they tore off his scalp and poured boiling water on his head. Finally they tore out his heart and devoured it, hoping thus to acquire the courage and heroism of their victim. The mangled bodies of the missionaries were afterwards found by their friends. The skull of Brébeuf was taken to Quebec, where it was enclosed in a silver bust sent out from France, and it is still preserved among the precious relics in the Hotel Dieu.

The once prosperous country of the Hurons was thus laid in ruins, and the persecuted remnant of its people fled in all directions. For a time many of them sought refuge on Isle St. Joseph, now known as Charity Island, at the entrance of Matchedash Bay; but everywhere they were pursued by their relentless foe. Those who escaped death from the hands of the savage were fast falling victims to famine and pestilence. Overwhelmed with despair, they besought the

The Hurons abandon their Country.

Jesuits to take them to some place of safety. In great perplexity the missionaries prayed in turn without ceasing during forty hours for Heaven's guidance. Then they gathered the scattered fragment of their stricken people and fled from the country. They brought about three hundred of them to Quebec and placed them on the Island of Orleans. The Hurons were afterwards removed to Lorette, near Quebec, where their descendants still live.

New England. Meanwhile the English had been forming colonies in North America. Jamestown has already been mentioned. The New England colonies were established a few years later along the Atlantic coast on the south of Canada. The early settlers came here seeking the enjoyment of religious liberty, which was denied them in Old England. King James I. tried to compel all his subjects to use a prescribed form in their church service. The Puritans, so called on account of their strict morals and severe manner of life, refused to comply with the laws for the regulation of public worship. They held their religious meetings secretly in private houses and other places where they could worship as they pleased. Often the secret meetings were discovered by the authorities, and then the worshippers were subjected to bitter persecution. Some of the Puritans sought refuge in Holland, where they were made welcome. But though badly treated these people had no desire to give up their connection with England, or have their children become aliens to the mother country and strangers to their native tongue. They accordingly conceived the plan of forming a New England in the wilds of America. Returning to

THE RULE OF THE ONE HUNDRED ASSOCIATES. 61

England, they, joined by a few others, embarked on the *Mayflower* to seek a new home beyond the Atlantic.

It was Christmas Day 1620 that this little band, known in history as the Pilgrim Fathers, landed on Plymouth Rock. They made what shelter they could against the winter's cold and storm. It was a hard struggle for life, and before spring half of the colonists found graves in the wilderness. But the little remnant did not lose heart. They were joined from time to time by others from the old home, and the colony, struggling with many difficulties, grew apace. In the course of a few years several little centres of civilised life were established. Thus sprang up the colonies of Massachusetts, Rhode Island, Connecticut, and New Hampshire. At the end of the first fifty years of their existence these colonies had a population of about fifty thousand.

The New England colonies proposed to the Governor of Canada that they should form an alliance with each other, agreeing to take no part in the wars of the mother countries, but to trade with each other and live in peace. *Proposed Treaty.* The French Governor refused to enter into such an alliance unless the Iroquois were held as a common enemy. To this condition the English would not agree; for the Iroquois were on friendly terms with them and lived along their borders. Thus the effort to secure a treaty proved a failure. When the Iroquois heard what the French had asked for, they were provoked to greater hostility. There followed a reign of terror. Montreal, being most exposed, escaped utter extinction as if by miracle.

Domestic Quarrels.

It was not the Iroquois alone that disturbed the peace of Canada at this time. The French quarrelled among themselves. The Governors of Quebec and Montreal were scarcely ever on good terms with each other. The Governor of Quebec claimed that as Governor-General his authority extended over the whole country; a claim which the Governor of Montreal was slow to recognise. There were unseemly disputes, too, between the Jesuits and the Sulpicians, who had taken charge of the mission at Montreal. Then, towards the close of the rule of the One Hundred Associates, a serious strife arose between the governors and the clergy.

BISHOP LAVAL.

The strife between Jesuits and Sulpicians grew hot over the choice of a bishop for Canada. Each party

THE RULE OF THE ONE HUNDRED ASSOCIATES. 63

wanted its man. In this matter, as in most others, the Jesuits finally triumphed. They did not indeed secure the appointment of a Jesuit; for the laws of their founder did not allow a member of the order to hold this office. But they got a man thoroughly devoted to their interests. This was the Abbé Laval. Although he bore the title of Bishop of Petræa, yet, for certain reasons which need not be stated, he was not made bishop till some ten years later; in the meantime he held the office of Vicar Apostolic. This distinguished prelate, who was of the noble family of Montmorency, was noted for his piety and austere manner of life. He was a man of strong will, and he held decided views as to the supreme authority of the Church over the civil ruler. For thirty years Laval controlled religious matters in Canada, and had much influence in civil affairs as well. His name has ever been held in honour by French Canadians, and it is perpetuated in the name of the Catholic University at Quebec. *Laval, 1659.*

There were frequent changes of governors at Quebec, but the changes added little to the welfare of the colony. Affairs went on from bad to worse. The liquor traffic became a serious evil. It was a source of profit to the traders, many of whom were men of influence. The Indians were fond of brandy, and when intoxicated they were like infuriated wild beasts. The clergy fought against the traffic, and finally succeeded in securing prohibition. The penalty for violation of the law was death, and two men were shot for selling liquor. Then there came reaction, and matters were worse than ever. *The Liquor Traffic.*

The French found safety nowhere outside the forts

of Montreal, Three Rivers, and Quebec. And now there was a rumour that twelve hundred Iroquois, who had wintered among the forests of the Ottawa, were descending upon these places to sweep them out of existence. Montreal would be the first point of attack. All hearts were trembling with fear. A little band of seventeen resolved to drive back the foe or perish in the attempt. Daulac, or Dollard, Sieur des Ormeaux, a young man of twenty-five, was the leader, and the others, like himself, were youthful. Maisonneuve gave his consent. The heroes prepared themselves as if for death—made their wills, confessed their sins, and received the sacrament. They bound themselves by an oath to stand by each other and by their purpose; then they bade their friends a solemn farewell. They ascended the Ottawa to the foot of a rapid known as the Long Sault, which the Iroquois would need to pass. Here they took up their position in an old palisade fort made by some Indian war party. While waiting for the Iroquois they were joined by about forty Hurons and Algonquins.

Heroism at Long Sault, 1660.

They had not long to wait. In a day or two the scouts brought in word that the enemy was descending the rapids. Soon the struggle began in all its fury. For eight days the heroes resisted their assailants, who outnumbered them twenty to one. The Iroquois were beaten back again and again, until they were well-nigh ready to give up the contest. They called to their aid five hundred of their warriors who were waiting for them at the mouth of the Richelieu. With the exception of five who remained faithful, all Daulac's Indian allies deserted to the enemy. Finally the Iroquois came up under thick wooden shields, cut their way into the fort, and shot down its valiant defenders. Every Frenchman was killed. The deserters gained nothing by their cowardice. With the exception of five, who escaped to tell the tale of the brave defence and of their own baseness, all were put to death. But Montreal was saved. The Iroquois saw how Frenchmen could fight; their victory had cost them too dear, and they retreated to the forests.

The rule of the Company of One Hundred Associates had utterly failed. Their colonists did not exceed two thousand, and the principal settlements were at Quebec, Three Rivers, and Montreal. Outside the forts of these places there was no safety. Indeed the Iroquois passed under the very guns of Quebec to attack the feeble remnant of the Hurons on the Island of Orleans. The King accordingly cancelled the charter of the Company, and established a new form of government under the direct control of the crown. *Close of the Rule of the One Hundred Associates, 1663.*

The year 1663 was remarkable for earthquakes in Canada. They occurred at short intervals from February until August. Loud noises were heard, the ground was violently shaken, the roofs of the houses fell in, the trees in the forests swayed to and fro, and other strange things occurred which greatly terrified the inhabitants. It does not appear, however, that any lives were lost. *Earthquakes.*

Meanwhile events were taking place in Nova Scotia which claim brief notice. For over twenty years following the treaty of St. Germain-en-Laye the French had undisturbed possession of the country. The history of *Rival Governors in Nova Scotia.*

the period relates chiefly to the quarrels of the French governors.

On board one of the French transports captured by the Kirks in 1628 was Claude de la Tour, of whom mention has been made. He had visited France and was returning with supplies to Acadie. Taken to London as a prisoner, he was soon on good terms with his captors and was ready to unite his fortune with theirs. He married a lady of the English Court, and received from the King the title of Knight-baronet of Nova Scotia. He also secured the same honour for his son Charles, promising on his behalf immediate submission to the Crown of England. Joining an expedition fitted out by Sir William Alexander for the support of his colony, Sir Claude, accompanied by his wife, set out for Acadie. He had, however, miscalculated his influence over his son. Charles could be moved neither by English honours nor by paternal entreaty, and when his father tried the power of shot and shell, Fort St. Louis proved as unyielding as its commander. The baronet was now in trouble. From England he could expect only disgrace; from France a traitor's punishment. Hard fortune compelled him to accept from his son a home at Cape Sable.

Meanwhile, the King of France had made Isaac de Launay de Razilly Governor of Acadie. Razilly made his headquarters at La Hève, on the Atlantic coast. He broke up the Scotch colony at Granville, and soon after his career was cut short by death. His successor was the Chevalier d'Aulnay, who made his home at Port Royal, which he rebuilt on the site of the present town of Annapolis, the original Port Royal having been farther west on the north side of the basin. Charles de la Tour also removed from Fort Louis to the mouth of the St. John River, where he built a fort, making it the headquarters of his fur trade. He and D'Aulnay were bitter foes, and in the petty warfare which they waged against each other, D'Aulnay had the advantage of possessing the King's favour. La Tour, however, gained such help from the English at Boston as enabled him to keep his rival in check.

Madame la Tour, who was a woman of much ability, went to France, hoping to influence the King in her husband's behalf. Failing in this endeavour, she crossed over to England. Here she took passage in a vessel bound for Boston, the captain agreeing to land her at her home. While cruising off the coast of Nova Scotia, D'Aulnay fell in with the Boston vessel. He came on board, but Madame la Tour escaped capture by hiding in the hold. The captain refused to call at Fort la Tour as he had agreed to do, and on arriving in Boston Madame la Tour brought an action against him and recovered damages to the amount of two thousand pounds.

Learning that La Tour, with many of his men, was absent on some trading expedition, D'Aulnay hastened to besiege his fort. *Fort la Tour captured.* Madame la Tour, with the small remaining force, for three days maintained a successful defence. When, betrayed by a Swiss sentry, she saw the enemy scaling the walls, she rallied her little band and showed so much strength that D'Aulnay, fearing defeat, proposed honourable terms of surrender. Thinking she dealt with a man of honour, Madame la Tour commanded her men to lay down their arms and open the gates of the fort. When D'Aulnay saw her defenceless condition, he charged her with having deceived him, and basely ordered all her garrison to be hung. One man alone purchased his life by acting as executioner of his comrades, while Madame la Tour, with a halter around her neck, was compelled to witness the scene. The wretched spectacle was too much for her, and she died broken-hearted before her husband's return. Ruined and hopeless, La Tour left the country. Nor did D'Aulnay long enjoy the fruits of his ill-gotten victory. Three years later he was accidentally drowned in the Annapolis River.

D'Aulnay left his estates greatly encumbered with debt. His principal creditor, Emmanuel le Borgne, a merchant of Rochelle, failing to secure payment of his claims, seized his debtor's effects in Acadie. He established himself at Port Royal and proceeded to enforce his claims to the whole country. He destroyed a little colony planted at St. Peter's in Cape Breton by Nicholas Denys, and carried off Denys to Port Royal. He seized the fort at La Hève and placed his son in command. About to extend his power still farther, he was himself compelled to yield to a stronger hand.

<small>Le Borgne.</small>

Meanwhile, La Tour has appeared again on the scene, and good fortune is smiling upon him once more. He is again in favour with the Court of France, and holds a royal commission as Governor of Acadie. He makes a romantic ending to the old feud by marrying D'Aulnay's widow, and he has his home again at the mouth of the St. John.

The Puritans, both in Old and New England, had **never been satisfied** with the giving of Nova Scotia to France in 1632. Oliver Cromwell, who now ruled over Great Britain, and who made his power felt both at home and abroad, sent out a fleet to attack the Dutch settlement of Manhattan. *Acadie seized by the English, 1654.* A portion of this fleet, under Major Sedgewick, was sent from Boston against Nova Scotia, of which it made an easy conquest; and now the English flag once more waved over the fort at Port Royal.

Charles de la Tour had now outgrown the patriotism which had led him to scorn the appeals of his father and to refuse English honours. He proceeded to London and petitioned Cromwell to reinstate him in his Acadian territory. His application was successful, Sir Thomas Temple and William Crowne being associated with him in Cromwell's commission. Shortly after La Tour sold his right to Sir Thomas Temple, reserving the fort at St. John, where he spent the remainder of his life.

Temple did not disturb the French colonists who were settled in the country. His chief concern was the fur trade, from which he *The Treaty of Breda, 1667.* expected large profits. To protect himself against intruders he spent a large sum of money in repairing the forts; but his hope of gain was not realised. Meanwhile, Charles II. succeeded to the throne of England. Setting little value on Nova Scotia, he was not unwilling to give it away for small consideration. The people of New England protested, and Sir Thomas Temple urged his claims, but without avail. By the treaty of Breda, Nova Scotia was once more ceded to France.

CHAPTER VII.

ROYAL GOVERNMENT.

Officers of Government. HITHERTO Canada had been governed by fur traders. The old order was now changed, and the country was made a crown colony. The government was vested in a Council of which the three principal members were the Governor, the Bishop, and the Intendant. The Governor had command of the forces and looked after the defence of the country; the Bishop had charge of all matters relating to the Church; and the Intendant had the oversight of civil affairs, including the expenditure of public money and the administration of law. Indeed, the authority of this last-named officer had a very wide range, giving him the power to interfere in matters which at the present time are regarded as belonging to the private rights of the individual. He was a general superintendent or overseer. Though in rank below the Governor, he had more to do in the management of public affairs. The respective duties of the different officers, however, were not very clearly defined, and this left room for unseemly disputes resulting in frequent appeals to the King. The general law adopted for the colony was the French code known as ' the Custom of Paris."

Bishop Laval had great influence with the King of France, and he was allowed to select a governor to suit himself. His choice fell upon Saffray de Mézy, a man in whose piety and in whose loyalty to himself he thought he could place the fullest confidence. For a time Laval had things pretty much his own way. But this state of matters did not last. By-and-by Mézy awoke to a sense of his dignity as the King's representative, and he then had a way of his own.

Laval and Mézy.

The Governor and the Bishop had joint powers in the appointment of the Council. But Mézy, becoming dissatisfied with certain members of this body, dismissed them and appointed others in their place without the consent of the Bishop. In other matters also he bore himself towards the Bishop in a most offensive and even defiant manner. He forgot that he owed his appointment to the Bishop, and that the power that made him Governor could unmake him. Laval deprived him of Church privileges and reported matters to the King. The unhappy Governor was forthwith ordered to France, but before he could obey the command he was taken suddenly ill and died at Quebec.

Mézy's Recall.

Mézy's successor was Daniel de Remy, Sieur de Courcelle. Jean Baptiste Talon, the first Intendant, came to Canada with the new Governor. Another distinguished officer arrived at Quebec about the same time. This was the Marquis de Tracy, who, with the title of Lieutenant-General, had the authority of Viceroy throughout the French possessions in America. He brought with him a regiment of veteran soldiers known as the regiment of Carignan-Salières.

New Officers.

An event occurred about this time which materially affected the subsequent history of Canada. The

English claimed the larger portion of North America in virtue of the discoveries of Cabot and of such later explorers as Henry Hudson. Charles II., the sovereign of England at this time, gave to his brother James, Duke of York and Albany, a grant of extensive territory on the Hudson River. Portions of this territory had been for many years occupied by the Dutch. The principal Dutch settlements, New Amsterdam, afterwards called New York, and Fort Orange, afterwards called Albany, were captured by an English fleet. Keen rivalry now sprang up between the English and French colonists, the former seeking to divert the fur trade from the St. Lawrence to the Hudson. In this way began a strife which continued for a century between the two peoples, culminating in the great struggle which resulted in the conquest of Canada by the English.

The English take New York.

The presence of regular soldiers in Canada had good effect on the Iroquois. Except the Mohawks and Oneidas, who kept up their warlike attitude, the Iroquois seemed disposed for peace. Courcelle, the Governor, determined on measures for improving the temper of the hostile tribes. Accordingly, at the head of five hundred men, he set out for the Mohawk villages, about five hundred miles distant. It was mid-winter. But with blankets and provisions strapped to their backs, and snow-shoes to their feet, Courcelle and his men pursued their long tramp. Their way lay along the St. Lawrence, the Richelieu, and Lakes Champlain and George, which were covered with a solid floor of ice. Day after day they strode on amid the driving storms and the biting frosts. At night they bivou-

March against the Mohawks.

acked in open air, lying close packed on beds of spruce around a central fire of logs. Striking across the country from Lake George to the Hudson, they lost their way, finally arriving at a Dutch village. Here they learned that the enemy they were after had gone off on some foray against another tribe. Courcelle was now in a bad case. The spring rains were setting in, and soon the way home would be impassable. His men were half-starved and were suffering from frost-bitten limbs. Then the English authorities, recently established in the country, were demanding his reasons for invading the territories of His Royal Highness the Duke of York. In no very comfortable mood he retreated as rapidly as possible and found his way back to Quebec.

In the following autumn a force of thirteen hundred men left Quebec for the country of the Mohawks; De Tracy, the Viceroy, had command. It was a tedious journey over river and lake and through wild forests. Food grew scarce, and the half-famished men were at times compelled to stay their hunger by feeding on chestnuts. Tracy, old and infirm, was seized with gout, and sometimes had to be borne along the way by his soldiers. But in spite of difficulties the French pushed forward. Panic-stricken the savages fled, leaving their strongholds and their stores of Indian corn to the invaders. De Tracy, having reduced the whole to ashes, returned to Quebec before winter set in. The Indians suffered greatly from the loss of their houses and corn. For twenty years they gave the French no further trouble.

The Mohawks chastised.

Canada now made much progress in the arts of peace. Talon, the Intendant, was energetic and un-

Progress.

wearied in his efforts to promote the welfare of the colony. He encouraged the cultivation of the soil, the domestic manufacture of coarse woollens and linens, the export of lumber and fish to the West Indies, and the importing of cattle, horses, and sheep from France. Every year new bands of colonists came to the country. Many of the soldiers were disbanded and settled on lands which had been allotted by the Government to their officers. To furnish wives for the unmarried colonists, ship-loads of young women of various social ranks were sent out from France. These girls, placed under the care of a matron, were taken to Quebec or Montreal. Men in want of wives came to one of these places and made choice according to their liking. Bounties were given by the King on early marriages and on large families, while fathers who failed to marry off their sons and daughters at an early age, and bachelors who obstinately refused to be enticed into wedlock, were heavily fined.

Obstacles.

Louis XIV. and his able minister Colbert, who then guided the affairs of state in France, meant to do the best they could for Canada. They did not, however, always fall on the wisest measures to carry out their good intentions. On the one hand there was too much coddling; on the other, too much restriction. Scarcely was the new form of government established, when the trade of the country was handed over to a great corporation known as the West India Company. Talon protested against this monopoly, and at length some of the Company's privileges were withdrawn. The people were allowed no part in making the laws by which they were to be governed, and they had little freedom of action. A public meeting, even, could not be held without leave of the Government. Trade with the English colonies was prohibited, nor was any one allowed to visit these colonies without a passport. Even the number of horses a man might keep was regulated by law.

Two gigantic evils marred the well-being of the colony: these were the liquor traffic and the bush-rangers. Stringent laws against the sale of brandy to the Indians seemed of little avail. There were then, as now, ways and means by which such laws could be violated with impunity.

Two Great Evils.

The other evil is one the force of which at the present day it is difficult to understand. Free, wild life in the forests had a fascinating power over young men of that day. Hundreds of them abandoned their homes and roamed through the distant forests, living with the Indians and adopting their modes of life. They threw off all restraint and became even more lawless than the savages themselves.

One of the most noted characters of the time was the Baron de St. Castine, who came from France with the Marquis de Tracy. After remaining in Canada a short time, he made his home at Pentagoet, on Penobscot Bay. He adopted the wild life of the Indians, married a squaw, and exercised the powers of a chief among the Abenaquis Indians.

All forms of activity in the colony seemed to revolve around the beaver. The trade in beaver skins kept everything in motion. A great annual fair was held in Montreal, to which gathered the Indians with their furs from all quarters. Hither also came the merchants from Quebec, bringing their

Trade.

various wares. The trade was carried on in booths. It was chiefly a barter trade, for there was little money in the country. The beaver skin was the chief currency.

Jesuit Missions. Meanwhile the Jesuits were pursuing their mission-work with unabated ardour. After the disastrous failure of the Huron mission, they chose a new field among the scattered tribes of the North and West. They had several stations along the borders of the Great Lakes, the chief of which were at Sault Ste. Marie, near the outlet of Lake Superior, and at La Pointe, near the western extremity of that lake.

Extension of Territory. Talon, the ever-active Intendant, was as energetic in his endeavours to extend the bounds of Canada as he was in developing its industries. His policy was to confine the English to the narrow coast country which they then occupied, and to hold the whole interior for France. To carry out this purpose, he sent agents to explore the northern and western territories and secure the good-will and homage of the Indians. At a grand council of chiefs held at the mission-station of Sault Ste. Marie, a royal commissioner, Sieur St. Lusson, received the various tribes of the West under the protection of Louis XIV. He also asserted the authority of his sovereign over the country by setting up on a cedar post the royal arms of France.

Feudal Tenure. A curious feature of the age was the manner of holding lands, known as the Feudal System. It had been the custom in Europe for several centuries, and it still prevailed in France. Shorn of some of its features the system was introduced into Canada. The King granted extensive tracts of land to military officers and other persons on certain specified conditions. These owners of land were called Seigniors, and they parcelled out their lands to others under them called vassals or habitants, who paid homage to the Seignior. The domain of a Seignior generally fronted on the St. Lawrence, the Richelieu, or other river, sometimes extending several miles along the river. It was cut up into narrow strips giving a river frontage to each tenant. As the farms were narrow, the houses in a settlement or Seigniory were not far apart. In the more exposed places, for purpose of defence against the Indians, the houses were built together and surrounded by a palisade, making a fortified village. In such places the habitants or tenants had to travel some distance to their farms. They had, however, a convenient, ready-made road in the river, which flowed past their lands. The Seigniory generally took its name from the Seignior or feudal chief. The names of many places in the Province of Quebec had their origin in this way.

The Seignior was required to render military aid in defence of the country. He was also required to clear a certain proportion of his lands within a definite time, and he was not permitted to sell any portion of his uncleared lands. He could, however, give these lands to subordinate seigniors for a small rental, who in turn parcelled them out to their tenants. It was his duty to build a fort, a chapel, and a mill. The mill was an important matter. It was usually built of stone and furnished with loopholes, so that it could serve the double purpose of a mill and a fort or blockhouse. In some cases the Seignior was too poor to

Duties of the Seignior.

erect a mill, and his people were then compelled to grind their grain in hand mills. The Seignior exercised the duties of a magistrate in settling petty disputes among his tenants.

Obligations of the Vassal. Under the Feudal System as it existed in Europe in the Middle Ages, the vassal was bound to render military service to the Seignior. This was not the case in Canada. The tenant paid a small rental for the lands he occupied. This rental was either in money or in produce or partly in both. A common rental was half a sou and half a pint of wheat yearly for each arpent of land—an arpent being about an acre. Live capons often formed part of the payment. In such cases on pay-day, which was usually on St. Martin's day, there was a lively scene in the Seignior's barnyard when the tenants brought in their fowls. The tenant was also required to labour for his Seignior a certain number of days in the year, to give one fish out of every eleven caught in the river, to grind his grain in the Seignior's mill, giving one-fourteenth in payment. An obligation seldom insisted on was to bake his bread in the Seignior's oven.

Doing Homage When a Seigniory changed owners, as at the death of a proprietor, the tenant was obliged to do homage to the new Seignior. This was a curious ceremony, and was performed according to a prescribed form. The tenant came to the door of the manor-house, and there, divested of sword and spurs, with bare head, he fell upon his knees before the Seignior, and, repeating his name three times, acknowledged in due form his faith and homage. On the death of a tenant, his land passed to his heirs. But in the case of sale by a tenant, one-twelfth of the price was given to the Seignior.

CHAPTER VIII.

CANADA UNDER FRONTENAC.

DE COURCELLE and Talon were recalled. The new Governor was Count de Frontenac. He was a man of much energy and force of character; he was an excellent soldier; and next to Champlain he was the greatest of the French governors of Canada. He had no equal in his ability to manage the Indians. In dealing with them he assumed an air of dignity, and bore himself in such manner as to impress them with a sense of his superiority. During his rule the Iroquois were kept well in check. But Frontenac had grave faults. He was hot-tempered, imperious, and intolerant of any rival authority. He treated the members of his council with scant courtesy, giving little heed to their opinions. He and Bishop Laval often came into collision, the chief cause of disagreement being the sale of brandy to the Indians, which the Governor rather encouraged, despite the Bishop's strong opposition and fearless protest. *A New Governor, 1672.*

The Indians from the Far West, who visited the mission-stations on the Great Lakes, told of a great river in their country, which flowed southerly for hundreds of miles through a vast plain. Two ardent explorers, Marquette, a Jesuit missionary, and Jolliet, a fur trader *Discovery of the Mississippi, 1673.*

of Quebec, accompanied by five or six men, set out in search of this river. From Lake Michigan they proceeded by way of small streams and lakes and portages to the Wisconsin River. Launching their bark canoes on this stream, they were borne onwards to the object of their search, the great Father of Waters, the Mississippi. As they descended the majestic river a rich prospect greeted their admiring eyes. Stretching away to the distant horizon were boundless prairies covered with tall grass and bright flowers, the feeding grounds of innumerable herds of buffalo.

FRONTENAC.

At the mouth of the Arkansas they turned back, leaving it for others to trace the river onwards to the ocean.

For the purpose of guarding the entrance of the

St. Lawrence against a foe from beyond the lakes, and of controlling the fur trade, Frontenac built Fort Cataraqui, afterwards called Fort Frontenac, near the site of the present city of Kingston. He superintended the erection of the fort in person, bringing with him an armed force of four hundred men. At the same time he summoned the Iroquois to meet him at this place. They came obedient to his call. In order to impress them with a due sense of his power, Frontenac drew up his men in martial array. He then harangued the assembled savages, calling them children, and telling them that he had not come to harm them, but that he would punish them if they were bad. Thus by stern threatening, duly attempered with judicious flattery and many presents, he awed them to submission and won their hearts.

Fort Frontenac.

Jolliet's story of the Mississippi awakened to new life the spirit of discovery. Some people believed that, in its lower course, the river turned away to the westward and finally flowed into the Gulf of California. At this time there lived in Canada a young Frenchman named Robert Cavalier, better known as La Salle, a name borrowed from his family estate in France. He was a man of strong will and great power of endurance, though not always noted for wise forethought in planning his schemes. For a short time La Salle held a Seigniory at the western end of Montreal Island, given him by the priests of the Seminary of St. Sulpice. In 1669 he went on an exploring journey, during which he discovered the Ohio and the Illinois rivers. A little later he obtained from the King of France a grant of Fort Frontenac, which

La Salle's Explorations, 1669-1684.

F

fort he rebuilt of stone and made it the base of a fur trade with the western Indians.

Late in the autumn of 1678, with a company of followers, among whom was an Italian officer named De Tonty, and the Récollet friar Louis Hennepin, La Salle set out for the west. He spent the winter at Cayuga Creek, a short distance above Niagara Falls, where he built a small vessel. Early in the spring, in this vessel, named the *Griffin*, the first to navigate the Great Lakes above the Falls, he sailed up into Lake Michigan. Here he loaded the *Griffin* with a cargo of furs and sent her back to Niagara. But nothing was ever heard afterwards of either vessel or crew.

La Salle now crossed the country from Lake Michigan to the Illinois River, where he built a fort which he named Crèvecœur. His purpose was to explore the Mississippi to its mouth, but his difficulties were only beginning. In order to obtain supplies, twice he was compelled to return to Montreal, distant a thousand miles or more. Sometimes he travelled on foot through the dense forests, sometimes he sped along lakes and rivers in light canoes. During his absence part of his men whom he had left at the fort, under the faithful Tonty, mutinied, stole his goods, and deserted. Finally, however, La Salle triumphed over all obstacles. Coursing down the Illinois in canoes, he and his party reached the Mississippi and continuing down this great river, they reached the Gulf of Mexico in April 1682. The country through which he had passed La Salle claimed for France, naming it Louisiana in honour of Louis XIV.

On returning to Canada La Salle proceeded to

France, where he was received with great distinction. And now, fitted out by the King, he sailed to the Gulf of Mexico for the purpose of exploring more fully the country which he had discovered, and of founding a colony. But the expedition ended in disaster, and cost La Salle his life. The vessel bearing his supplies was cast away. He failed to find the mouth of the Mississippi, and landed his colonists farther west, on the coast of the present State of Texas. He spent two miserable years wandering about the Gulf coast; and finally, reduced to great want, he set out by an overland route for Canada. But before he had gone far on the journey he was murdered by some of his men, and his body was left without burial, a prey to wild beasts.

In the meantime affairs had been getting on badly at Quebec. Frontenac quarrelled constantly with the Bishop, with the Intendant, and with other members of the Council. Besides, he gave great offence to the clergy by encouraging the sale of brandy to the Indians. Bishop Laval and others complained to the King, and the final outcome was the recall of Frontenac and the appointment of La Barre governor in his stead. *Frontenac recalled.*

When La Barre arrived at Quebec he found the colonists in trouble. A fire had just laid the whole of the Lower Town in ashes, leaving a large number of people homeless. There was much alarm also on account of a threatened invasion of the Iroquois. The hostility of these old enemies of the French was encouraged by Dongan, the Governor of New York. The English in this colony wished to secure the fur trade in the territories *La Barre, 1682.*

around the Western Lakes, occupied by the Indian allies of the French, and they used the Iroquois as their agents in carrying out their purpose. La Barre mustered a force of French and Indians for the purpose of chastising the Iroquois. But while he delayed at Fort Frontenac many of his men were taken ill of fever, and he thought it prudent to patch up a peace with the warlike savages. The treaty showed great weakness on the part of La Barre; and the King, on learning its conditions, ordered him to return to France, and sent out the Marquis of Denonville as his successor.

<small>Rivalry between French and English.</small>
The rivalry between the French and the English was becoming keener, and was assuming a wider range than the fur trade with the Indians. The struggle for the ownership of the continent was looming up in the not very remote distance. The French aimed to confine the English to the narrow Atlantic coast; the English, on the other hand, would restrict the French to the valley of the St. Lawrence. Dongan, the Governor of New York, claimed that the Iroquois were subjects of his master, James II. of England, and he covertly endeavoured through them to extend the power of England south of the Great Lakes westerly to the Mississippi. Then, through the same agency, he was working with the Indian tribes around the Great Lakes to draw them from their alliance with the French. Moreover, the New England colonists were extending eastwardly the limits of the scene of the coming struggle by their plans to drive the French from Acadie.

In the far North, too, the English had planted

themselves, and were tapping the fur trade at its sources. In 1668 the first English trading post was established, by a few merchants of London, on the shores of Hudson Bay. Two years later the great fur-trading company, usually known as the Hudson's Bay Company, was organised by a charter granted by Charles II. of England. According to the terms of its charter, the Company secured exclusive right of trade throughout the country watered by the rivers flowing into Hudson and James Bays. The country was called Rupert's Land, in honour of its first Governor, Prince Rupert, the King's cousin. The Company claimed that its territory extended westerly to the Rocky Mountains, including the valley of the Saskatchewan. It had the right to govern its domain by officers of its own appointment.

<small>Hudson's Bay Company organised, 1670.</small>

Within a few years the Hudson's Bay Company established five trading posts on the shores of Hudson Bay, of which York Fort, at the mouth of the Nelson River, was headquarters. To these posts the Indians, by boat and canoe, brought down their furs, which they bartered for various articles of merchandise supplied by the Company's agents. Once a year, when the ice had left the bay and strait, ships came from England to York Fort, bringing new supplies of merchandise, and carrying away the furs which had been collected by the year's trade.

For the first time in the history of the Royal Government there was domestic peace in Canada. Governor, Bishop, and Intendant were in accord, and the common aim was to humble the foe on their borders. Dennonville saw

<small>Dennonville takes Active Measures.</small>

that he must strike a blow at once. He knew well that in the hostility of the Iroquois, Dongan was behind the scenes; but as England and France were at peace, he could not make war on him. He resolved to deal the blow at his agents, the Iroquois. He ventured, however, to authorise an attack on the English fur traders in the far-off territory around Hudson Bay. A company of eighty or a hundred men set out for this northern territory with evil purpose against their rivals. A long toilsome journey it must have been up the Ottawa, and then through pathless forests, by lake and stream, to the traders' forts. The journey completed, however, they made an easy conquest of the English, and packed them off to England in one of the Company's vessels which had just arrived.

Denonville mustered a strong force for war against the Senecas. Besides regular troops and militia, he invited his Indian allies around the Western Lakes to join him on the southern shore of Lake Ontario. While halting at Fort Frontenac he took part in a measure which did him and the Intendant little credit. The King wanted strong men for oarsmen on the royal galleys, and he instructed Denonville to send him Iroquois for this service. The Iroquois in the neighbourhood of Fort Frontenac, who had been living on good terms with the French, were invited to a feast within the fort. Having accepted the invitation in good faith, the men, to the number of about fifty, were basely seized and sent to France as galley slaves.

War against the Senecas.

At the appointed place on the borders of the Seneca country, Denonville met the Indian warriors whom he had summoned from the West. He had now a force of nearly three thousand men. The Senecas, hearing of his movements, lay concealed in a dense wood through which he had to pass. Starting up from their ambush as the French approached, they fought with desperation; but they had not counted on so numerous a foe, and soon gave up the contest. When Dennonville came to their villages he found them deserted. He burned their stores of Indian corn which he found in their granaries, and cut down their growing crop, but he thought it not prudent to pursue the savages, who had fled to the forests. His victory was not worth what it cost. A friendly Indian is said to have told him before he set out, that it was dangerous to disturb a wasp's nest without killing the wasps.

By disturbing one wasp's nest Dennonville angered the wasps of the whole country-side. The Iroquois were all enraged over his treat- **Prospect of Peace.** ment of the Senecas, and they threatened vengeance. They made raids into Canada, and there was no safety above Three Rivers outside the forts. In this hostility they had the sympathy of the Governor of New York. Dennonville was greatly alarmed, and desired to pacify the savages. He sent delegates into their country, bearing presents and making overtures of peace. Among the terms demanded by the Iroquois was the restoration of the captives sent to the French galleys. Dennonville was forced to yield, and he wrote to the King, begging him to send back the prisoners. It was finally arranged that the Iroquois should send delegates to Montreal to conclude the peace.

The Iroquois were not willing to include in the

treaty of peace the Indian allies of the French around the Western Lakes. Among these tribes was a remnant of the Hurons, living at Mackinaw, near Lake Michigan. Their chief, Kondiaronk, known among the Indians as the "Rat," held a high position in the councils of his people, and he was mighty in war as he was wise in counsel. Coming down the lakes with a band of warriors to make a raid against the Iroquois, he called at Fort Frontenac, where he heard of the treaty between the French and the Iroquois. He saw that the treaty meant destruction to the Hurons, for they could no longer count on the French to protect them. "We shall see," he said, as he left Fort Frontenac, bent on breaking up the treaty. Intercepting the Iroquois delegates, he made them all prisoners, telling them that he was acting on Denonville's instructions. When the delegates told him that they were on an errand of peace, he assumed an air of indignation against the French for making use of him to carry out their base purposes. Detaining one of his prisoners, as he asserted, to supply the place of one of his men killed by the Iroquois, he set the others free, bidding them go home and tell the story of French perfidy. "I have killed the peace," said the "Rat" exultingly. But his work was not yet complete. He returned to the fort at Mackinaw, and handed over his prisoner as a spy to the French officer in command, who had not yet heard of the treaty between the French and the Iroquois. The captive asserted that he was a peace delegate on his way to Montreal, and appealed to Kondiaronk to confirm his story. But the wily "Rat"

The "Rat" kills the Peace.

shook his head, said that the story was pure invention, and that the fear of death had turned the fellow's brain. The poor Iroquois was accordingly shot as an enemy. There was still another scene in the "Rat's" acting. In the fort was an old Iroquois prisoner. Kondiaronk set him free, and told him to go home and tell his people how the French had treated their delegate. Dennonville sent explanations to the Iroquois. Months passed and all was quiet; but the savages were meanwhile nursing their wrath for a day of vengeance.

It was in the month of August that the revengeful Iroquois let loose their rage. The fearful blow fell on La Chine, at the west end of Montreal Island, six miles from the city. *Massacre of La Chine, 1689.* At the midnight hour, when deep slumber had hushed the disquietudes of life, twelve hundred savages rent the air with the war-cry, and with torch and tomahawk began their work of slaughter. The annals of the country tell no tale so sad. Many of the inhabitants were slain on the spot; others made captive were reserved for torture worse than death. For over two months the Iroquois ravaged the open country, killing, taking prisoners, and destroying property without opposition. The French seem to have been paralysed with fear. Dennonville had forces at his command which should have been able to drive the invaders from the country. Instead, to the great disgust of some of his officers, he strictly enjoined defensive measures only. By his orders Fort Frontenac was blown up with gunpowder and abandoned. Quebec, Three Rivers, and Montreal alone offered safety to the fear-stricken colonists. As winter approached, the Iroquois withdrew of their own accord.

CHAPTER IX.

BORDER WARFARE BETWEEN FRENCH AND ENGLISH.

AMID the gloom which overshadowed Canada there shone a ray of hope. Frontenac was again made Governor. The colonists hailed his arrival with delight, and the members of the Council, once so glad to get rid of him, were now ready to receive him with every mark of honour. His imperious manner and irritable temper were forgotten: his power over the Iroquois made him welcome. He at once set about repairing the ruined fortunes of the country. The task was a hard one. Seven years had passed since his recall, and he was now seventy years of age. Successes had made the Iroquois insolent, and the friendly Indian tribes had lost confidence and respect. Even the Hurons of the West were seeking alliance with the enemies of Canada. Frontenac first tried to make peace with the Iroquois. He had brought back the survivors of Denonville's captives, of whom but thirteen remained alive. These he sent home, bearing pleasant memories of his kindness. But the Iroquois were not easily won.

Frontenac's Return, 1689.

Not without reason, Frontenac believed that the English, not the Iroquois, were the chief obstacle to the tranquillity of the country. On the other side of

BORDER WARFARE. 91

the Atlantic, England and France were not on good terms at this time. James II. of England had recently been driven from the throne by his angry subjects, and William and Mary ruled in his stead. The King of France supported the cause of the dethroned monarch, and he instructed Frontenac to make war upon the English colonists in America; and so the Governor sent three war parties against his English neighbours. It was not open war on the battlefield that he planned, but the sudden irruption, the stealthy approach at midnight, and the indiscriminate slaughter of men, women, and children, characteristic of Indian warfare. In midwinter three bands of French and Indians, after many days of toilsome marching through forests, came stealthily by night upon the unsuspecting colonists of New York, New Hampshire, and Maine. They burned the dwellings, killed and scalped the inhabitants, or, what was worse, they dragged them into captivity. Schenectady, in New York, Salmon Falls, in New Hampshire, and the settlement at Saco Bay were among the places thus attacked. These measures, though worthy only of savages, were carried out with such vigour and success that the Canadian colonists were animated with new hope. *Raids against the English.*

The English colonists of New York and New England were deeply indignant over these massacres. A congress of delegates met at New York to consider what measures should be taken in the circumstances. It was arranged that a land force, raised by the different colonies, should proceed, by way of Albany and Lake Champlain, against Montreal, and that a naval force from New England should attack Quebec. The colonies asked England to help *Retaliation.*

them drive the French from America. At that time, however, King William was not very firmly established on the throne, and he needed all his forces at home.

<small>Phips takes Port Royal.</small> Meanwhile Massachusetts undertook a little military exploit on her own account. French cruisers, making their headquarters at Port Royal, had for some months been preying on her commerce, and she determined to rid herself of this annoyance by seizing their place of rendezvous. Seven or eight small vessels, and about eight hundred men, sailors and militia, were soon in readiness for the expedition. The command was given to Sir William Phips, a colonist of humble birth and little education, but possessed of great ambition and energy. Early in May, Phips appeared before Port Royal and summoned Menneval, the governor, to surrender. Menneval saw that with his small garrison and dilapidated fort he had little chance of resisting an attack, but by putting on a bold air he adroitly concealed his weakness, and thus gained better terms from the enemy. Phips agreed to send the garrison to Quebec, and to allow the inhabitants to hold their property. All the cannon, military stores, and money belonging to the King were to be given up to the English. When Phips entered the fort and saw its weak condition he was annoyed that he had granted such favourable terms of surrender. He was therefore well pleased to find some excuse for breaking the agreement. The French soldiers carried off some of the property which, by the treaty, had been given up to the English. Thereupon Phips charged Menneval with violating his part of the bargain, sent him and his garrison prisoners to Boston, and allowed his soldiers to plunder the town.

Having seized several other French settlements in Nova Scotia, Phips returned to Boston with his booty.

The martial spirit was now fully aroused in Massachusetts. Emboldened by the success at Port Royal, the colony resolved to undertake, single-handed, the capture of Quebec. *Phips fails to take Quebec.* Preparations were made with due secrecy, in the hope of taking the French by surprise. The force comprised thirty-two vessels, large and small, and about two thousand men, including sailors. As a matter of course, the command was given to the hero of Port Royal. Meanwhile a rumour of what was going on in Boston reached Quebec, and caused the wildest alarm. Frontenac was at Montreal. He came with all haste to the capital, and, with characteristic energy, set the town in order for defence. For the most part, nature had fortified the place on the south and east by the high cliffs along the St. Lawrence and its tributary the St. Charles. Barricades of timber were placed at three weak points in this natural wall. The rear of the town was protected by palisades, a ditch, and an embankment.

Phips was too long in getting ready, and after he set sail the winds were unfavourable. It was in the month of October that the fleet passed Orleans and came in sight of Quebec. An officer with a flag of truce was at once sent ashore from the admiral's ship to demand a surrender. Blindfolded, he was led through the city to the palace of the Governor. Admitted into Frontenac's presence, he handed him a letter from Phips, and, taking out his watch, he demanded in the name of King William the surrender of the town in one hour. Filled with rage, the haughty Count replied: "I will not keep you waiting so long. Tell your general that I acknowledge no King of England but King James. The Prince of Orange, who calls himself King, is a usurper of a throne which belongs to his father-in-law." When asked by the messenger if he would send Phips a written answer, Frontenac replied: "No, I will answer him by the mouth of my cannon." Phips then opened fire on the town, but with little effect. He landed thirteen hundred men on the Beauport shore, below the mouth of the St. Charles, with the view of crossing this stream and attacking the town in the rear. But the opposing force was too strong, and this hope failed also. The men hastily re-embarked, leaving five of their cannon in the mud on the Beauport shore. Phips called a council of war, in which it was decided to abandon the siege. Matters had been badly managed. It is said that if Phips had arrived a week earlier, or remained a week later, he might have taken Quebec. In the first case he would have found the French unprepared for defence; in the other he would have starved them into surrender, for there was little food in the town. Deeply chagrined, Phips sailed away to Boston, bearing the first tidings of his defeat. There was now great rejoicing in Quebec. In memory of the deliverance of the city, the King of France had a medal struck, with the inscription, "Francia in Novo Orbe Victrix Kebec Liberata A.D. MDCXC."

Meanwhile the force which was to proceed against Montreal had been mustered at Albany, under Winthrop. It was not a strong force at first, and it was weakened by lack of provisions, by the ravages of smallpox, and by want of harmony. Winthrop marched as far as Lake Champlain, when, becoming discouraged, he gave up the undertaking and returned to Albany. A small detachment of his men, however, proceeding down the lake and the Richelieu, made an attack, in true Indian fashion, on the settlement of La Prairie, killing and taking prisoners both men and women, burning houses, and destroying property of all kinds.

The Expedition against Montreal.

Acadie, which comprised Nova Scotia, New Brunswick, and the eastern portion of Maine, was the scene of much of the petty warfare between the French and the English. When Phips captured Port Royal, he left no garrison in the fort to hold the country, and the inhabitants soon came to regard themselves as French subjects again. A Canadian named Villebon was appointed governor of the country. Among the important French settlements in Acadie at this time, besides Port Royal, were Beaubassin, on the head waters of the Bay of Fundy; Grand Pré and Minas, on Minas Basin; and La Hève and Canso, on the Atlantic coast. Thinking Port Royal too much exposed to attack from English cruisers, Villebon made his headquarters on the Nashwaak, a tributary of the St. John. Here, in his forest retreat, he gathered around him bands of Indians whom he encouraged in acts of outrage against the English. Baptiste, a noted sea rover, who preyed on the commerce of New England, also found refuge for himself and sale for his plunder in Villebon's fort. As a protection against the French and Indians, Massachusetts had built a stone fort at Pemaquid, called Fort William Henry. After a short siege, the French,

Acadie.

under a famous French-Canadian named Iberville, aided by St. Castin and his Abenaquis Indians, took this fort and levelled its walls to the ground. Iberville then sailed to Newfoundland, which was claimed by the French. Here he made an easy conquest of St. John's, and laid it in ashes. He then proceeded along the coast, among the English fishing settlements, pillaging and burning as he went. Iberville now set sail for Hudson Bay, where he took Fort Nelson, the most important centre of the English fur company of that northern territory.

The Indians of Acadie and New England were not so cruel as the Iroquois; but yet they gave many proofs that they were true savages. One example will show their method of falling upon unprotected settlers. In the spring following the capture of the fort at Pemaquid, they came suddenly in early morning upon the village of Haverhill, Massachusetts, attacking the farm-houses on the outskirts. The men were absent at work in the neighbouring fields. The only occupants of one of the houses were Mrs. Dustan, her infant child, and the nurse. The savages set fire to the dwelling, killed the infant, and carried off the two women into the forests, a hundred miles or more from their home. From time to time they added to the terror of their captives by describing to them the tortures which they had in reserve for them. The women decided on bold measures, which they successfully carried out. In the middle of the night they and a boy, who was a fellow-captive, took each a hatchet and killed their captors to the number of ten, two only, an Indian woman and a boy, escaping. Mrs. Dustan

Hannah Dustan.

and her companions then made their way back to Haverhill.

On their part the English colonists of Massachusetts sought reprisals and retaliation in every possible way. A fitting instrument for this work of revenge was found in sturdy old Ben Church, who had many years before gained renown in the wars against the Indians. With a fleet of whale-boats, well manned by hardy New England fishermen, Church sallied forth like an angel of destruction, laying waste every Acadian settlement from Passamaquoddy Bay to Cumberland Basin. *Ravages of Ben Church.*

But there came a short breathing spell in this foolish and destructive warfare between the English and French colonists. England and France, after eight years of fighting with each other, arranged terms of peace by the Treaty of Ryswick, and they also directed their colonies in America to stop fighting. It was agreed that all places taken by either nation during the war should be restored to the original owner. There was great joy in Quebec when the news was received, and on the following Sunday the *Te Deum* was sung in the cathedral in the presence of the dignitaries of the land. There followed in the evening a formal dinner, at which were delegates from New York, and toasts were drunk in honour of the sovereigns of the fatherlands. *Treaty of Ryswick, 1697.*

Frontenac's last conflict soon followed. He died, in the seventy-eighth year of his age, in the autumn after the peace was concluded. He had been a man of war. The English and the Iroquois on his borders gave him little respite; the *Death of Frontenac.*

Intendant and the clergy within his dominion had contributed their full share to the strife which fell to his lot. He was self-willed and irascible; but his strong hand had upheld Canada during a period of weakness and peril. He left many ardent admirers and some bitter foes. His wife, who was a lady of the King's Court, never came to Canada. In his will he directed that his heart should be sent to her for burial in France.

Frontenac had laboured to make peace with the Indians on the borders of Canada, a task in which he would have been more successful but for the rivalry of the English. His policy towards them secured their respect, and did much to break down the enmity which his predecessors had aroused. De Callières, who succeeded him as Governor, wished to finish the work thus begun. He invited all the Indian tribes, far and near, to meet him in a grand council at Montreal. He wanted the tribes to make peace with each other as well as with the French, and he urged them to bring with them all their captives for restoration to their own people. They came at his call—deputies from the Five Nations, from the tribes of the North, and from those of the far West. Fleets of canoes, bearing chiefs and captives, came over the lakes and down the St. Lawrence to Montreal. Twelve hundred Indian warriors in their paint, their furs, and their feathers, came to the great council. The Governor and his Council were present, and a large assembly of the leading colonists. Long speeches were made by Indian orators; presents were given; the pipe of peace was smoked, the Governor

Treaty with the Indians, 1701.

taking the lead; and then followed feasting and hilarity. The council lasted several days. Old Kondiaronk, the "Rat," was present; but in the middle of his speech he took ill, and he died before the council closed. The treaty was duly signed, the chiefs making the symbols of their respective tribes —a spider, a calumet, a forked stick, a bear, a beaver, or something else.

CHAPTER X.

QUEEN ANNE'S WAR.

PEACE between Great Britain and France was soon broken. Louis XIV. had all along taken sides with James II., whom the English people had driven from the throne; and now, on the death of James, Louis recognised his son as the rightful King of England. The English were indignant that a foreign power should interfere with their freedom in choosing a king. This action of the French king, with some other causes which need not be spoken of here, led to a new war between the two nations which lasted about ten years. It does not seem that the colonies in America should have quarrelled on account of the renewal of hostilities on the other side of the Atlantic; but the old feeling of rivalry, which had scarcely been allowed to slumber, was easily aroused. Queen Anne was the sovereign of England at this time, and the war, which was carried on throughout the greater part of her reign, was known in America as "Queen Anne's War." The war between the colonies consisted chiefly of raids made by small parties on border settlements, and of privateering on the coasts of New England and Acadie. For some time the Iroquois remained neutral, taking side with neither English nor French.

How the War began, 1702.

The kind of warfare practised during this conflict was most barbarous, and was wholly unworthy of civilised nations. One or two examples will show its character. In midwinter a party of two hundred and fifty or three hundred French and Indians came suddenly by night upon the village of Deerfield, in Massachusetts. The carnage went on until about fifty persons were killed, over one hundred were taken prisoners, and a large part of the village was laid in ashes. Many of the prisoners were afterwards ransomed by their friends, some were got back in exchange for French prisoners held by the English, and others were never recovered. Among the captured were a clergyman and his family named Williams. The husband and his wife were soon separated by their Indian captors. Mrs. Williams was not able for the long tramp through the deep snow. Faltering by the way, she was struck down by a blow of an Indian tomahawk, and her lifeless body was left where it fell. Williams and his children were also separated. He was held a prisoner in Canada for about two years, when he was given up to the English in exchange for the noted sea rover Captain Baptiste. Thirty-five years after the capture, one of Williams's daughters, now the wife of an Indian chief, visited her relatives at Deerfield. No entreaty, however, could induce her to remain with them, but after a few days she returned to her wigwam and the wild life which she had adopted.

Deerfield.

It was not easy for Massachusetts to punish the real offenders. Between her borders and the Canadian settlements lay vast forests occupied by the Indian allies of Canada. She made

Retaliation.

reprisal, however, against the colony of Acadie down by the sea, which she could reach more easily and with less danger. Ben Church, the famous fighter of Indians, though now sixty-five years of age, was still full of fire and fury. With a force of over seven hundred militia and Indians, he proceeded along the shores of Acadie, avenging, in what measure he was able, the cruelties of Deerfield on the unoffending inhabitants of Passamaquoddy, Minas, and Beaubassin. He burnt their dwellings and barns, broke down their dikes and let the tide in upon their growing crops, killed their cattle, and made prisoners of such inhabitants as failed to escape to the woods.

The fishermen of Massachusetts in vast numbers invaded the coast waters of Acadie. Not content with a share of the rich harvest which these waters yielded then as now, they made such havoc with their privateers among the Acadian fishermen that they nearly drove them from their own grounds. But this was a business that both sides could take a hand in. French privateers, too, were generally hovering around the coast, on the lookout for merchant vessels of Massachusetts, pursuing them sometimes even into Boston harbour. Amid all this strife, however, there were times when trade was brisk between Boston and Port Royal; for it was found that an exchange of English goods for Acadian furs was advantageous to both colonies.

Privateering.

With a country of countless resources the colonists of Canada yet looked to the mother-country for food, clothing, and many necessaries of life which they could easily have provided for themselves. For this state of matters the

Restrictions removed.

blame was not theirs. In order to provide a market for home products, the Government of France would not allow the colonists to carry on manufactures, even forbidding them to make cloths of the coarsest kind. It happened, while the war was going on, that a fleet of merchant vessels, carrying supplies to Canada, was captured by the British. This left the colonists without clothing and many other necessary things. It was then seen that Canada should make these goods for herself. Accordingly, some of the unwise restrictions were removed by the French Government, and the colonists began the manufacture of cloth and many other needful things. They also gave more attention to agriculture and were able to export grain to other countries.

French privateers caused great loss to the merchants of Boston. They made their headquarters at Port Royal, dashing out as occasion offered to seize English trading vessels. Massachusetts determined to rid herself of these plunderers by taking from them their place of refuge. Aided by the other New England colonies, she sent a fleet with about a thousand men, under Colonel March, for the capture of Port Royal. The fort in the old Acadian capital was in weak condition and its garrison was small. The force sent against it should have been able to take it with ease. Indeed, the people of Boston were so sure of victory, that they made preparation for a great celebration. But the fort was under the command of an able and experienced officer, Subercase, the last French Governor of Acadie. On the other hand, the English officers were very incompetent, and the men were not well dis-

March's Expedition, 1707.

ciplined. The expedition failed wholly, and March, ashamed to return to Boston, sailed into Casco Bay. The Governor of Massachusetts ordered him to renew the attack; but feeling unequal to the task, he gave up his command. The fleet was sent back under another officer, but with no better success.

Startling news reached Quebec in the autumn of 1709. It was rumoured that the English were planning the conquest of Canada. An army of fifteen hundred men under Colonel Nicholson, the Lieutenant-Governor of New York, was reported to be near Lake Champlain, ready to advance against Montreal, and a naval force was to proceed from Boston against Quebec, as soon as expected help should arrive from England. Rumours of these warlike measures caused great alarm at Quebec. At the command of the Governor, the Marquis de Vaudreuil, the men in the neighbouring settlements came to help in defence of the city, while their women, children, and cattle were sent to a safe hiding-place in the forest. It was needless alarm. England, requiring all her forces for the war in Europe, failed to send the aid she had promised, and as the colonies did not feel able to go on alone, they abandoned the undertaking for the present.

A False Alarm.

The New England colonists were thoroughly in earnest in the matter of conquering their French neighbours. They resolved on another effort to take Port Royal. With all their population and resources they should not have thought this a very serious undertaking; and yet they went again to Queen Anne for help. At

Capture of Port Royal, 1710.

the same time, partly for effect on the people of Great Britain, and partly to impress the Five Nations with a due sense of her greatness, five Mohawk chiefs were sent over to England. The chiefs were given a grand reception. They were clad in fine attire and presented to the Queen. They were lodged and feasted, driven about London in coaches, and waited on by liveried servants—all at the public expense. The final outcome was a plan for the capture of Port Royal and promise of the help asked for. The Queen took great interest in the enterprise, and gave money from her private purse for the fitting out of four New England regiments. Nicholson was appointed commander-in-chief of the expedition, and Colonel Vetch, who had for some time taken an active part in colonial affairs, was second in command.

It was midsummer when the English ships for the attack on Port Royal arrived in Boston, and it was the middle of September when the equipments were completed. The force, comprising about two thousand men besides the sailors, was larger than the occasion required. The fort at Port Royal was greatly out of repair, the garrison consisted of only about three hundred and fifty men, and the stock of provisions was low. Subercase, the Governor of Port Royal, made a fair show of resistance, but he was humane as well as courageous. Early in the siege he sent a messenger with a letter to Nicholson, asking him to take under his protection some French ladies of the fort, who were alarmed by the bursting of shells thrown by the English. Nicholson sent a courteous reply, stating that his sovereign had not sent him to make war against women, and offering to provide comfortable quarters for the ladies whom Subercase might place under his care.

Subercase soon saw that resistance would be unavailing, and he proposed to surrender on honourable conditions. The terms of surrender were soon arranged. Two lines of English soldiers were placed before the gate of the fort, and the French marched out between the ranks, with shouldered arms, drums beating, and colours flying, saluting the English commander as they passed. An English garrison took possession of the fort, and Colonel Vetch, who had been appointed Governor of Nova Scotia, assumed command. Thus Port Royal, and with it Nova Scotia, passed finally into the hands of the English, its name being changed to Annapolis Royal, in honour of its new sovereign. The highest courtesy was observed by both English and French commanders. Nicholson attended carefully to the comfort of those whom he had conquered, and Subercase complimented the English commander on his bravery and kindness. It was provided that the French officers and soldiers should be sent to France in British transports. The Acadians living within three miles of the fort were allowed, on taking the oath of allegiance to Great Britain, to remain two years on their lands; those living outside this limit were declared prisoners of war. All, however, were left in undisturbed possession of their property, and in the full enjoyment of the freedom and the privileges which had been accorded to them under French rule.

In the summer following the capture of Port Royal, the war cloud again appeared above the horizon of Canada. Through the influence of the colonies, Great

Britain resolved on the conquest of the whole country, and made preparations which seemed fully equal to the object in view. A British fleet under Sir Hovenden Walker, and a land force of seven veteran British regiments under General Hill, arrived in Boston, where the force was increased by the addition of fifteen hundred colonists under the command of Colonel Vetch, the Governor of Nova Scotia. Thus there set out for Quebec nine warships and about sixty transports, carrying about twelve thousand men, including sailors. At the same time a land force of about two thousand men, colonists and Indians, under Colonel Nicholson, was proceeding against Montreal by way of Lake Champlain. Vaudreuil, the Governor of Canada, was informed of the movements of the English, and he made what preparation he was able to receive them. The expedition looked formidable, and might well excite alarm. In number it was equal to nearly one-half the entire population of Canada. It had, however, an element of weakness which brought dire disaster on its promoters. State affairs in England were at this time seriously mismanaged. The sovereign then had much more control over public matters than at the present time, and Queen Anne, who was rather weak-minded, was much influenced by favourites of her own sex. Hence it came about that men were appointed to important positions because they were the friends of the Queen's favourites, rather than on account of their fitness for office. Walker and Hill were wholly incompetent for the command entrusted to them.

Canada threatened again.

The fleet, having no pilot to guide it up the St. Lawrence, ran out of its course in a dense fog, and several of the transports were wrecked on the reefs of the Egg Islands. Nearly a thousand men, soldiers and sailors, were drowned. Hill and Walker were completely unnerved by the disaster, and could see nothing but destruction in any further attempt to reach Quebec. A council of war was called, and, though no warship had been lost, and the number of men left exceeded the whole population of Quebec, it was decided to abandon the enterprise. Thus ingloriously ended this attempt to conquer Canada.

The long war between Great Britain and France was brought to a close by a treaty signed at Utrecht, a small town in Holland. The treaty provided that Nova Scotia, Newfoundland, and Hudson Bay Territory should belong to Great Britain. France still retained possession of Canada, Cape Breton, then called Isle Royal, and St. John's Island. Louis XIV. gave up Nova Scotia very unwillingly. He offered in exchange for it two or three islands in the West Indies, and in addition he even proposed to give up the fishing privileges in Newfoundland waters, which Frenchmen had enjoyed for two hundred years. But Great Britain was determined to keep Nova Scotia.

The Treaty of Utrecht, 1713.

CHAPTER XI.

THE STRUGGLE CONTINUED

AFTER the Treaty of Utrecht, for over thirty years Canada had peace. Even the Iroquois, *Peace and Progress.* who since the time of Champlain had been the scourge of the country, now gave little trouble. Vaudreuil was Governor of the colony until his death in 1725, when he was succeeded by the Marquis de Beauharnois, who held the office for over twenty years. During this period the country made much progress in many ways. Agriculture, trade, shipbuilding, and domestic manufactures advanced greatly. Attention was also given to the construction of public roads, so that in 1734 wheeled vehicles passed from Quebec to Montreal. Among the important industries established should also be mentioned the ironworks at Three Rivers. On the other hand, there were lacking some things which, at the present day, are thought necessary to the well-being of a country. Education of the common people was neglected; there was no printing-press in all the land; and the people had no voice in the government. The seigniorage system of holding land was also unfavourable to the highest progress.

During this period the population of Canada increased to forty or fifty thousand. The chief settlements were on the banks of the St. Lawrence, here and there along the river, from below Quebec to Montreal. The principal places in the West were Forts Frontenac, Niagara, Detroit, and Mackinaw. Ambitious of extending their power over the whole continent, the French were at this time forming a colony in the vast country then called Louisiana, in the Mississippi Valley. Adventurers were also exploring the country between the Mississippi and the Rocky Mountains, with the hope of finding an overland route to the Pacific Ocean. Among the more noted explorers were the Vérendryes, father and sons, who made their way north of the watershed which divides the great central plain of North America, proceeding as far as the Forks of the Saskatchewan, and establishing trading posts in the territory now included in Manitoba and the North-West.

Although there was at this time no open war between the French and English colonies, they did not regard each other with very friendly feeling. There was still keen rivalry between them in the fur trade. The English of New York established a trading house and fort at Oswego, on Lake Ontario. The French erected forts at Ticonderoga and Crown Point, on Lake Champlain, to protect themselves from invasion by the English along that route. Meanwhile, also, the Indian allies of the French on the south, known as the Abenaquis, continued their attacks on the outlying settlements of New England.

Rivalry between the French and English.

French Canada was an inland country, and the St. Lawrence, its grand highway to the ocean, was blocked with ice several months in the year. On this account especially, the King of France had desired to regain possession of Nova Scotia, and, failing in this, he now set high value on Cape Breton, or Isle Royal as it was then called. English Harbour, on the south-east coast of the island, was chosen for a naval station, and the name of the place was changed to Louisburg, in honour of the reigning sovereign. To this place came many of the French colonists of Newfoundland, as that island had now fallen to the English. Some of the Acadians, also, removed from Nova Scotia to Louisburg; but most of them did not care to leave their fertile marshes, and, by hard toil, make for themselves a new home among the forests of Cape Breton. Louisburg was built on a tongue of land between the harbour on the east and Gabarus Bay on the west. The French Government spent over $7,000,000 on its fortifications, so that in the course of a few years it became, next to Quebec, the most strongly fortified town in America. It was protected on the land side by stone walls thirty feet high, on the top of which were parapets or towers. Outside the wall was a deep moat or ditch eighty feet wide. Seaward the town was guarded by a fortified rocky islet called Battery Island. So strongly fortified was Louisburg, built to guard the approaches to Canada, that it was called the Dunkirk of America. It was the chief American naval station of France, and the headquarters of her fishermen that thronged American coasts.

Louisburg founded.

Meanwhile affairs in Nova Scotia were not in a very satisfactory state. Great Britain claimed it as hers, and yet she did little to promote its welfare or to show that she thought it of any value.

Nova Scotia.

With the exception of a small fishing settlement at Canso and a few families at Annapolis, there were no English people in the country, and for some years there seemed little indication that any were intending to make it their home. The garrison at Annapolis was very small, the fort was much broken down, and supplies were scanty. Governor Vetch asked aid from Great Britain, but his application received little attention. Such neglect of the country on the part of its new owners led the French to believe that Acadie would soon be restored to her former sovereign.

Acadian Settlements. The Acadians showed much judgment in choosing their lands in Nova Scotia. Their chief settlements were in the most fertile parts of the country, along the Annapolis Valley, at Canard, Minas, Grand Pré, Piziquid (Windsor), Cobequid (Truro), and Beaubassin, at the head of Cumberland Basin. In these districts they cultivated the rich marshes which they had, by strong dikes, reclaimed from the sea. Their wealth consisted in cattle, horses, sheep, and swine.

The Acadians. Great Britain was disposed to treat the Acadians in a liberal manner. According to the terms agreed on when Nova Scotia was ceded to her, the Acadians could have been expelled from the country, but Queen Anne gave orders that they should be treated in all respects as British subjects. If they had been left alone there would have been little trouble. At first those in the neighbourhood of Annapolis seemed disposed to submit cheerfully to the new order of things. Soon, however, the French authorities at Quebec and Louisburg sent agents among them to dissuade them from becoming

British subjects. A few of the Acadians then removed to Cape Breton, and some went to Prince Edward Island, which, under the name of St. John's Island, still belonged to France. But as they were unable to sell their lands, and they had no means for moving their personal property, most of them still remained in the country. Thus, while the Acadians continued to occupy their lands in Nova Scotia, they refused to become British subjects. They said that in case of war between France and Great Britain, they would join neither side, they would be neutrals. Many of them, no doubt, honestly and faithfully kept their pledge of neutrality; but their refusal to take the oath of allegiance caused them to be regarded with suspicion. Moreover, the Indians in Nova Scotia, who were still openly hostile, were believed to be under the influence of the French, and to receive encouragement from them in their attacks on the English.

For nearly half a century after Nova Scotia came under British rule the government of the country was vested in a Governor and a Council of twelve members appointed by the Governor. As already stated, Colonel Vetch was the first English Governor. He was succeeded by Colonel Nicholson. In 1717 Colonel Phillips became Governor. He held the office for thirty-two years, though during the greater part of this time he resided in England, the duties of his office being discharged by a Lieutenant-Governor. The most noted of the Lieutenant-Governors was Paul Mascarene, a French Protestant, whose family had been driven from France by religious persecution.

Government.

The question as to who should rule over Austria

H

now brought on another war between Great Britain and France. The colonies in America probably cared very little about this matter; but the old feeling of hatred had only been slumbering, and needed but slight cause to awaken it to new life. Duquesnel, the Governor of Louisburg, heard of the war in Europe before the news reached his English neighbours, and he resolved to take them by surprise. He at once sent a force under Duvivier against the fishing settlement of Canso, at the east of Nova Scotia. Having captured the block-house and burned all the dwellings at this place, Duvivier sent the garrison to Louisburg. He then sailed to Bay Verte and marched overland to Annapolis, taking this route probably for the purpose of gaining recruits from the Acadians. The Acadians, however, were faithful to their pledge of neutrality, and gave Duvivier little assistance. At Annapolis Duvivier was joined by about three hundred Indians who had for some time been hovering about the place. As the fort was weak and the garrison small, Mascarene, who was in command, could not have withstood a vigorous siege. But Duvivier had no artillery, and his mode of warfare consisted of skirmishing and night attacks on the garrison. Failing to make any impression on the fort, he had recourse to stratagem. He informed Mascarene that he was expecting strong reinforcement from Louisburg, and that surrender before the arrival of this force would secure more favourable terms. The officers of the garrison were disposed to yield, but Mascarene remained firm, determined to hold his ground until compelled to submit to superior force. Finally Duvivier withdrew and marched back to Minas.

War again

As a place of refuge to privateers, Louisburg had become a source of much annoyance and damage to New England. It was thus regarded with no very friendly feeling by the English colonies. The recent attack upon Nova Scotia caused great irritation, especially in Massachusetts. Shirley, the Governor of this colony, convened the Legislature, and having bound the members to secrecy by a solemn oath, proposed a scheme for the capture of Louisburg. It is said that one of the members, at his private devotions, praying for guidance in giving his vote on the question, spoke so loud that he was overheard in an adjoining room. Either in this way or by some other means the scheme was soon made public. After much hesitation it was decided to enter upon the bold undertaking, and the other colonies were invited to join in the expedition. Four thousand volunteers, untaught in the art of war, but full of enterprise and daring, were enrolled in the different colonies, Massachusetts taking the lead. The command was given to William Pepperell, a colonel in the militia.

Capture of Louisburg, 1745.

Early in April the fleet arrived at Canso. Gabarus Bay was full of ice, and Pepperell had to wait three weeks before he could approach Louisburg. In the meantime his force was strengthened by Commodore Warren of the British navy, who arrived with a small fleet from the West Indies. The siege was carried on with much vigour from both sea and land while the defence was maintained with equal spirit. Meanwhile a warship from France, bringing recruits and supplies, was captured by the English. At the end of seven weeks Duchambon, the Governor of Louisburg, hung out the white flag. Next day terms were agreed on. The French garrison marched out with colours flying, and Pepperell took possession of the fort. The French soldiers and such of the citizens as desired it, about four thousand in all, were sent to France in British ships. For several days the French flag was kept flying at Louisburg for the purpose of decoying French merchant ships. Three ships of great value, thus deceived, sailed into the harbour and were captured by the English.

The news of the fall of Louisburg caused great rejoicing in Boston and in London. Colonel Pepperell was rewarded with the honour of knighthood, and Warren was raised to the rank of admiral. But all did not go well with the captors of Louisburg. The men of New England had conquered the French: but there remained a foe before which many of them fell. Among the supplies which came into their hands was a quantity of rum. Every day scores of drunken men staggered through the streets. Unbridled appetite was followed by deadly fever, and before spring twelve hundred of Pepperell's men filled graves in the conquered soil.

The French felt much chagrin over the loss of Louisburg, and they took immediate steps to get it back. They resolved also to inflict severe punishment on New England. A powerful fleet was sent out from Rochelle, under the command of Duc d'Anville. It was the grandest force that had ever crossed the Atlantic. With dismay the citizens of Boston heard of the preparations which had been made to invade their land and lay their homes in ruins. By fasting and prayer they

D'Anville's Expedition, 1746.

THE STRUGGLE CONTINUED.

sought the interposition of Heaven to save them from threatened destruction. Never was expedition more fruitless or ill-fated than that of D'Anville. Not a single victory did it gain; it did not even meet the foe it came to destroy. Disaster followed disaster, until there were left only scattered fragments of the once proud fleet. Two of D'Anville's ships were taken by the English while yet on the coast of France; some were cast away on Sable Island: others were driven by storms far off their course and never reached the place for which they sailed. After a three months' voyage D'Anville arrived at Chebucto Harbour with a helpless remnant of his great force. Disease had broken out during his long voyage, carrying off many of his men; others were ill and dying. His misfortunes weighed heavily on his spirits and he died suddenly. D'Estournel, the next in command, arrived on the day of D'Anville's death. Disheartened, he urged the abandonment of the undertaking and immediate return to France; but his advice was overruled by the other officers. Then he fell ill, and in the delirium of fever killed himself with his sword. La Jonquière, who had recently been appointed Governor of Canada, and was then on his way to Quebec, now took command. It seemed useless to attack Louisburg, but La Jonquière thought his force was sufficient for the capture of Annapolis. For this place accordingly he set sail; but off Cape Sable, where many a vessel has since been cast away, a violent storm so shattered the fleet that the last hope was abandoned. It was now resolved to return to France.

In the following year France sent out another

strong force for the recovery of her lost possessions in America. But while yet on the coast of Europe this force was intercepted by a British fleet, many of the French ships were captured, and the expedition was completely broken up. Among the prisoners taken by the English was Jonquière, the Governor of Canada.

Meanwhile a force of about seven hundred, under Ramesay, had been sent from Quebec for the purpose of co-operating with D'Anville's fleet. Ramesay landed at Bay Verte, and marched overland by way of Cobequid and Grand Pré to Annapolis. Having waited in vain for the fleet, he attempted to take the fort; but failing in this, he marched back to Beaubassin, where he resolved to spend the winter. Mascarene, who was then in command at Annapolis, fearing another attack, applied to Governor Shirley of Massachusetts for assistance. Five hundred men, under Colonel Noble, were immediately sent from Boston. Their orders were to sail up the Bay of Fundy and post themselves at Grand Pré for the purpose of intercepting Ramesay in case he should return. Before they reached Nova Scotia winter set in, and on account of the ice they were unable to enter Minas Basin. They accordingly landed on the shore, far down the Bay of Fundy, and marched overland to Grand Pré. They were quartered in private houses, a few in a place, among the Acadians of the settlement. Here they were remaining in the utmost security, little suspecting the approach of an enemy in the severe winter months.

Forces from Quebec and Boston.

Ramesay heard of the arrival of Colonel Noble,

THE STRUGGLE CONTINUED.

and resolved to take him by surprise. Soon, under the leadership of Coulon de Villiers, six hundred French and Indians, fitted out with snow-shoes and hand-sleds, were on the move for Grand Pré. The march occupied seventeen days. On approaching Grand Pré, Coulon divided his men into small companies for the purpose of attacking, at the same moment, the various houses where

The Massacre at Grand Pré, 1747.

MAGAZINE AT ANNAPOLIS.

the English were lodged. Then, under cover of night and a blinding snowstorm, the French, led by Acadian guides, crept stealthily upon the foe. Killing the sentinels, they rushed into the houses where the English, all unconscious of danger, were sleeping. Some were slain in their beds; others, and among them Colonel Noble, fell fighting in their night-clothes. At daybreak the French were masters of the place, and the carnage ceased. On the morrow the English buried their dead, about eighty in number, in one grave. Then, with six days' provisions on their backs, they marched off sadly for Annapolis, leaving behind over fifty of their comrades as prisoners of war.

Ramesay, much elated over the victory at Grand Pré, sent circular letters to the Acadians, announcing that, as Nova Scotia had been reconquered by the French, they were free from all allegiance to Great Britain, and commanding them under severe penalties to remain faithful to France. On the other hand the English showed little disposition to abandon the country. Governor Shirley of Massachusetts lost little time in sending another force to Grand Pré to take the place of those who had been driven out. The government of that colony, also, was already urging upon the British Ministry the propriety of expelling the Acadians from the country as rebels against King George. These unfortunate people, thus threatened by dangers on either hand, were much perplexed as to what measures of safety they could adopt, and their difficulty was all the greater from the fact that neither power offered them any protection against the other.

The Acadians between Two Fires.

For three years, while the war was going on in Europe, Great Britain held the island of Cape Breton: but her ownership showed itself in little else than in the military occupation of Louisburg. She did nothing in the way of colonising the island or in improving its condition. Both Great Britain and France were now tired of fighting, and, by a treaty signed at Aix-la-

Treaty of Aix-la-Chapelle, 1748.

Chapelle, each nation agreed to restore its conquests, leaving the ownership of places as it was before the war. Thus, to the great annoyance of Massachusetts, Cape Breton was given back to France. To pacify the offended colony Great Britain refunded the money which had been expended in the capture of Louisburg. The restoration of Cape Breton was regarded by many in England as a national dishonour, and especially so from the fact that two English noblemen were sent to the French Court as security for the fulfilment of the bargain.

CHAPTER XII.

THE SETTLEMENT OF HALIFAX.

A New Scene at Chebucto. THREE years have passed away since D'Anville's shattered fleet lay moored in Chebucto Harbour, and his soldiers who had escaped the perils of the sea lay dying on its shores. And now ships are again arriving from beyond the eastern waters, and joyously the strangers whom they have borne hither are taking possession of the land. These are not French soldiers sent for the capture of forts and the destruction of human life, but English colonists—men, women, and children—come to make homes for themselves in the forest country.

The British Government had now begun to see that the true policy for strengthening its power in Nova Scotia consisted in settling the country with English people. Accordingly, as a first step in this direction, measures were taken to establish a fortified town on the Atlantic coast. The Government advertised for colonists, offering free passage, free grants of land, a year's provisions, and various other things needful to new settlers. Two hundred thousand dollars were voted from the public funds to meet expenses. Those who responded to the invitation of the Government included many officers and private men, discharged from the army and navy at the close

THE SETTLEMENT OF HALIFAX. 123

of the late war; there were also farmers, mechanics, and merchants. Counting women and children, they numbered in all two thousand five hundred and seventy-six. The Hon. Edward Cornwallis was appointed Governor of Nova Scotia. The colony was promised a representative legislature as soon as it had grown populous enough to elect its members; in the meantime the civil government was placed in the hands of the Governor and a Council of twelve members to be appointed by the Governor.

Colonel Cornwallis arrived in Chebucto Harbour on the 21st of June 1749, and he was followed within a few days by transports bearing the colonists. *Making a Home.* The hillside on the west of the harbour was selected as the site of the new city, which was named in honour of the Earl of Halifax, the President of the Lords of Trade and Plantations. Soon after his arrival the Governor chose his Council, a leading member of which was Paul Mascarene, who for many years had held the office of Lieutenant-Governor at Annapolis. And now, through the summer and autumn, Halifax presented a busy scene. The forests, which grew to the water's edge, were cleared away, and dwellings were erected. A few frame houses were built of material brought from Boston; but most of the dwellings were rude cabins, formed of upright poles stuck in the ground and roofed over with the bark of trees. On the summit of the hill, now called Citadel Hill, a square fort was built. Two rows of palisades, constructed of trunks of trees, as a defence against the Indians, extended from the fort to the water.

According to some authorities there were at this

time between 12,000 and 13,000 Acadians in Nova Scotia. Their chief settlements were at Annapolis, Canard, Grand Pré, Minas, Piziquid (Windsor), Cobequid (Truro), Beaubassin, Chignecto, Bay Verte, Shepody, and on the St. John River. Shortly after his arrival Cornwallis addressed to them a proclamation, reminding them of the privileges which they enjoyed under British protection, charging them with disloyally aiding the King's enemies, and offering to condone all past offence if they would now take the oath of allegiance and become faithful subjects of King George. Delegates from some of the Acadian districts were sent to Halifax to explain their position and make inquiries as to the intentions of the Government. They reported that their people would refrain from all hostility against Great Britain, but that they would not take an oath which would bind them to fight against France. They asserted that such allegiance would subject them to outrage from the Indians, who were opposed to the occupation of the country by the English. They asked if the Acadians would be allowed to sell their lands and other property in case they removed from the country. Cornwallis assured them that he could accept no conditional or half-way allegiance, and he pointed out to them that it was not the oath of allegiance which made them British subjects. Many of the Acadians were born in the land, others had enjoyed the protection of the British Government for over thirty years, by virtue of which they were already bound under the strongest obligations of loyalty. Cornwallis told the delegates that the desire of the Acadians to leave the province gave him great pain. He did not wish to interfere with their freedom; a forced service was worth nothing, and a subject compelled to be so against his will was not far from being an enemy. They and their fathers had cultivated their lands, and they had a right to enjoy the fruits of their labours. This was the King's desire. Everything had been done to secure to them the occupation and ownership of their lands for ever, and every assurance had been given them of free and full exercise of their religion. But he assured them that according to British law nobody could possess houses or lands in the province who would refuse to take the oath of allegiance when required to do so. Then he told them that they themselves knew that there were ill-disposed and mischievous persons among them who, regardless of their best interests, were corrupting their minds. The course they were pursuing was the result of bad advice which through their inexperience they were unable rightly to estimate. He told them that he could not at that time give them permission to leave the province, because so soon as they crossed the frontier they would be compelled by the French and Indians to take up arms against the English. But whenever this danger was removed by the restoration of peace and order, he would allow them full freedom to go where they pleased. The delegates went back to their people for fresh instructions, and returned several times, but no agreement was arrived at.

The Indians were very hostile to the new colony, and kept it in constant alarm. They were ever lurking in the woods on the borders of the settlements, ready to kill and scalp, or to carry off

The Indians.

those who came within their reach. English captives were often taken to Louisburg and sold to the French, from whom they were afterwards ransomed by their friends. Dartmouth, which was settled in the year after the founding of Halifax, suffered most from their ravages. Six men belonging to this place were attacked while cutting wood in the forest: four of them were killed and one was taken prisoner. A few months afterwards, the Indians, creeping upon the settlement during the night, killed and scalped several of the inhabitants. The screams of the terrified women and children were heard across the harbour in Halifax. Similar outrages occurred at Halifax, Canso, and other parts of the province. The Governor and Council, unwisely adopting the barbarous customs of the savages, offered large rewards for Indian prisoners and scalps.

Evil Influences. The conduct of the Acadians and Indians was largely due to the influence of the authorities of Louisburg and Quebec. The settlement of Halifax cut off their long-cherished hope that Nova Scotia would yet be restored to France, and they too readily adopted any measure which seemed calculated to annoy the English. Through their agents they advised the Acadians to refuse the oath of allegiance, and they threatened them with severe consequences if they failed to follow this advice. They encouraged the Indians in their hostility to the English, and supplied them with arms and ammunition to carry out their evil purpose. Among the agents employed by the Government of Quebec in stirring up this spirit of opposition to English rule was the Abbé le Loutre, whose intense zeal for the ascendency of the power of France led him to pursue measures alike dishonourable to himself and ruinous to the Acadians.

The British Government, anxious for the more rapid colonisation of Nova Scotia, invited people to come from Germany, offering them the same privileges as had been conferred on English colonists. Many accepted the invitation, coming at various times, so that within two or three years nearly two thousand Germans arrived in Halifax. They were mostly farmers. Differing from the other colonists in language and customs, they chose to form a settlement by themselves. Accordingly, in the year 1753, most of them removed to Lunenburg. Here they underwent many hardships, and, like the English colonists, suffered greatly from the ill-will of the Indians. A few months after they went to Lunenburg, certain evil-minded persons spread a report that some of the supplies sent out for them from England had been withheld. This caused great excitement, and the place was for several days under mob-rule. Colonel Monckton went down from Halifax with a few soldiers, and soon restored order without using any harsh measures.

The Germans.

The Treaty of Aix-la-Chapelle settled nothing as regarded affairs in America: it simply left matters as they were. The question of boundary-lines between the British and the French possessions had long been in dispute. The treaty left the question for future adjustment, and commissioners were appointed for this purpose. They met in Paris, but, after debating the matter for three years, they failed to agree. In the meantime the Governors of

Boundaries.

Canada undertook to settle the question by right of possession. The dispute was not confined to any one portion of the boundary, but related to nearly the whole line from Nova Scotia to the extreme western limits of the adjoining territories of the two nations. The conflict which arose over the matter was, however, restricted chiefly to Nova Scotia, the Lake Region, and the Ohio Valley.

The Limits of Nova Scotia.
The French maintained that the territory ceded to Great Britain in 1713, under the name of Acadie, included only the peninsula. Indeed, at times, they conceded even less than this, asserting that it comprised only the western portion of the peninsula. This theory suited their wish to have a continuous land route between Quebec and Louisburg. On the other hand, the English claimed that the territory comprised not only the whole of the peninsula, but also the territory now forming New Brunswick, extending westerly to New England.

Fort Beauséjour.
The settlement of Halifax alarmed the French, and they determined on active measures to restrict the English within narrow limits. They asserted that a little river called the Missaquash, at the Isthmus of Chignecto, formed the boundary between their territory and that of Great Britain. On the south of this river was the large Acadian settlement of Beaubassin. Partly to assert French claims to the country on the north of the Missaquash, and partly to encourage disaffection in the Acadians and Indians towards the English, the Governor of Canada sent a small body of troops, under La Corne, to Chignecto. On a low ridge of land, within sight of Beaubassin, La Corne built a strong

fort, which he named Beauséjour. Here the Acadians and Indians were supplied with guns and ammunition. Regular communication was kept up between this place and Louisburg by way of Bay Verte. Influenced by Le Loutre, many Acadians left their homes in the peninsula and crossed the Missaquash, some remaining in the neighbourhood of Beauséjour, others going to Prince Edward Island or to Cape Breton. Le Loutre also encouraged the Indians in their hostility by paying them for English scalps, and he kept the Acadians under his influence by threatening that he would send the Indians to destroy their property if they did not obey him.

Governor Cornwallis sent a force under Major Lawrence to Beaubassin, to watch the movements of the French. Influenced by Le Loutre, the Acadians, at the approach of Lawrence, fled across the Missaquash to La Corne. Le Loutre and his agents then set fire to their dwellings, reducing the whole settlement of Beaubassin to ashes. Lawrence fortified his position with earthworks and palisades, and gave it the name of Fort Lawrence. La Corne and Lawrence, being thus near neighbours, were for some time on friendly terms with each other. But all good feeling was brought to an end by the treacherous shooting of Captain Howe of Fort Lawrence. Howe went out under a white flag to hold a parley with a man in the dress of a French officer, when he was shot down by Indians lying in ambush.

Fort Lawrence.

CHAPTER XIII.

THE YEAR 1755.

THE year 1755 is a memorable one in the history of Canada. Among its events are the struggle for the possession of the Ohio Valley, the conflict in the Lake Champlain district, the capture of Fort Beauséjour, and the expulsion of the Acadians. But before describing these events it will be necessary to speak of some things of an earlier date.

Summary of Events.

It has been already stated that the Marquis la Jonquière, on his way out from France to assume the office of Governor-General, was taken prisoner by the English. During an interval of two years which elapsed before his arrival in Quebec, the office was filled by Count Galissonière, who was a most energetic officer, possessed of much intelligence and sound judgment. Jonquière was charged with having used his office as a means of securing gain for himself. Holding a monopoly of the liquor traffic, he is said to have realised large profits from the sale of brandy to the Indians. He was, however, far surpassed in greed by Francis Bigot, who held the office of Intendant during the closing years of French rule in Canada. Having charge of the expenditure of public money in the colony, this officer robbed the Government in the most shameful

Governors.

manner. The Marquis Duquesne succeeded to the office of Governor-General in 1752. He was noted for the vigour with which he pushed the claims of France to the disputed territories, and for his development of the military resources of the country. With great care he organised and drilled the militia, and drew away the able men to defend the forts on the borders. The result of this military policy was neglect of agriculture and scarcity of food in the country.

Both French and English claimed the territory drained by the Ohio and its tributaries, usually known as the Ohio Valley. The French prized it as a connecting-link between Canada and their colony of Louisiana, and they based their claim to the country on its discovery by La Salle. The English claimed the territory on the ground that it belonged to their subjects the Iroquois; and they valued it chiefly on account of the fur trade which the Ohio Company, composed of English and colonial merchants, was now carrying on in the country. The French set up a boundary of their own from Lake Erie to the Ohio, marking the line by leaden plates with suitable inscriptions, which they buried in the ground at certain intervals, and by tin shields bearing the arms of France, which they attached to the trees. Still later the Marquis Duquesne asserted more decidedly the rights of France by placing detachments of soldiers in a chain of forts erected along the line. The French warned English traders not to enter the country west of the Alleghanies, and they seized the furs of those who disregarded the warning. On the other hand, the English gave similar warning

The Ohio Valley.

to the French, and they sent a military force to protect their traders. They began to build a fort at the junction of the Alleghany and Monongahela rivers, on the site of the present city of Pittsburg. The French came upon them with a stronger force, drove them away, and completed the fort, which they named Duquesne in honour of their Governor.

George Washington. The Governor of Virginia sent a small force, under George Washington, into the disputed territory. Washington erected a fort on the Monongahela, which he named Fort Necessity. Falling in with a French officer, named Jumonville, at the head of a small body of troops, Washington ordered his men to fire. Jumonville and several of his men were killed. The French asserted that Jumonville had no intention of making an attack upon the English, but that he was sent with a letter of warning to Washington, which he was about to deliver when he was shot. They now sent a stronger force, and compelled Washington to retire from the Ohio Valley.

Reinforcements from England and France. Without any formal declaration of war, and, indeed, while messages of peace were passing between the two Courts, warlike measures were thus being taken on both sides. It was the beginning of the final struggle on this continent between the two great powers. Both nations sent out reinforcements. In the spring of 1755 eighteen ships, carrying three thousand soldiers under command of Baron Dieskau, left France for America. There went also a new Governor for Canada, the Marquis Vaudreuil, the last of Champlain's successors in New France.

THE YEAR 1755.

About the same time warships were sent from England for the purpose of destroying the French fleet while crossing the ocean. In this hope they failed, for the French reached Quebec in safety. Great Britain also sent two regiments of soldiers, under General Braddock, to Virginia, to aid the colonists in the war they were waging in the Ohio Valley.

Braddock and several of the governors of the English provinces met to devise a plan of attacking the enemy. The expulsion of the French from the Ohio Valley was assigned to Braddock himself; Governor Shirley of Massachusetts was to proceed against Niagara; Colonel William Johnson was to attack Crown Point; and Colonel Monckton was entrusted with the task of expelling the French from the Isthmus of Chignecto. *Plan of the Campaign, 1755.*

Braddock was a good soldier of much experience in regular warfare as it was practised in Europe; but he knew nothing of fighting in the forests or of Indian tactics, nor was he disposed to learn of those who could have given him counsel. Both he and his men despised colonial officers and troops with whom they were to co-operate. Benjamin Franklin warned him that the French and Indians would not meet him in open field, but would lurk in ambush, and fire upon him under cover of trees and rocks. But Braddock thought his Majesty's troops easily a match for wild Indians and untrained French militia. For the military ability of George Washington he had some respect, and he invited him to join the expedition as an officer of his staff. *Braddock's Defeat.*

Early in June Braddock set out for Fort Duquesne, the headquarters of the French in the Ohio Valley. It was a tedious march of one hundred and twenty miles, through dense forests and across the Alleghanies.

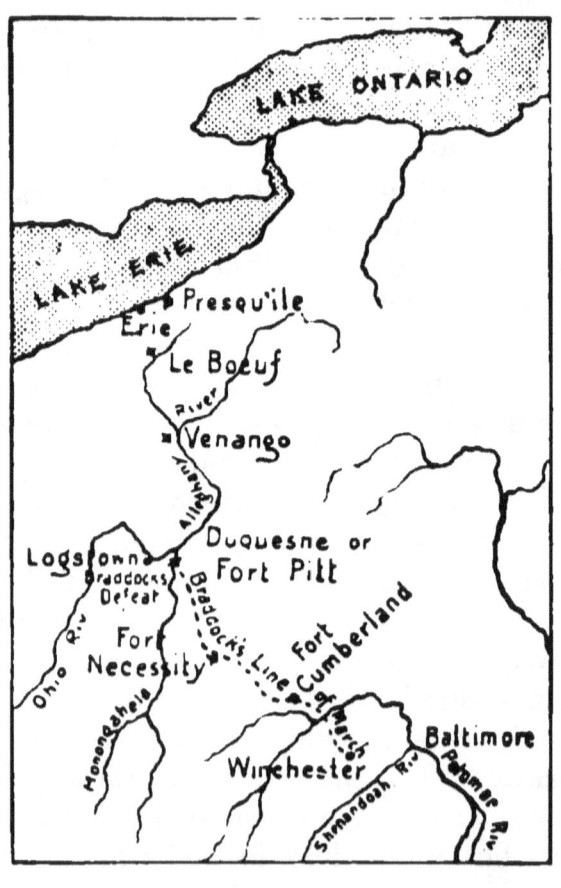

OHIO VALLEY.

Three hundred axemen led the way, felling trees, and clearing a road twelve feet wide for the pack-horses, artillery, and waggons laden with military stores, the whole forming a train four miles in length. The soldiers marched through the woods on either side of the waggon road. Progress was slow, sometimes not exceeding four miles a day.

The French learned from scouts, who were ever on the alert, that the English were advancing, and about nine hundred men, two-thirds of whom were Indians, set out from Fort Duquesne to meet them. On the 9th of July, when about eight miles from Duquesne, as Braddock was advancing with little thought of danger, the startling Indian war-cry and a shower of bullets revealed the presence of the foe. Skulking behind the trees, the French and Indians made deadly havoc of the English. Braddock's men fought bravely, but their valour counted for little. They could scarcely see an enemy, and their shot fell vainly on trees and rocks. Bewildered, they huddled together, and were mowed down with fearful slaughter. At length the survivors, flinging away their arms and abandoning their wounded companions, fled in disorder from the scene of conflict. Three-fourths of the officers and eight hundred men were either killed or wounded. Braddock had five horses shot under him during the engagement, and at last fell mortally wounded. Washington had a narrow escape: four bullets passed through his coat, but he came out of the battle without a wound. For the time the French were left in possession of the Ohio Valley, and hordes of savages were let loose upon the defenceless outlying settlements of Virginia and Pennsylvania.

William Johnson, who was elevated to the rank of major-general, and placed in command of the expedition against Crown Point, knew nothing of war, having neither military training nor experience; but he was one of those favourites of fortune who succeed at whatever they put their hand. He had great influence over the Iroquois. In fact, as he spoke the Mohawk tongue fluently, and as his wife, Molly Brant, was sister of a noted Mohawk chief, the Iroquois almost regarded him as one of themselves. But for Johnson's influence over the Iroquois they would have deserted the English in a body after Braddock's defeat. When Johnson was appointed to the command of the forces, before leaving his home, "Fort Johnson," near the Mohawk River, he called a council of the Mohawks. The assembled savages ate his beef, drank his whisky, made long speeches, and danced the war-dance. He had some difficulty, however, in persuading them to go on the warpath, so much had the English lost their confidence.

At the southern extremity of Lake George, Johnson

Dieskau defeated at Lake George.

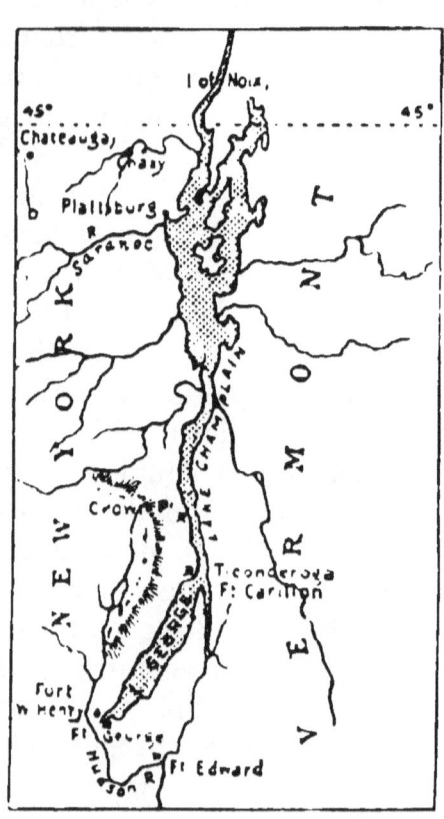

LAKE CHAMPLAIN DISTRICT.

was attacked by the French under Dieskau, whom he repulsed and forced to fall back on their fort at Ticonderoga. Dieskau was severely wounded and taken prisoner. As he was lying in Johnson's tent, after his wounds had been carefully dressed by an English surgeon, several Mohawks entered the tent. There followed a keen dispute in the Mohawk language between them and Johnson. After they had gone out, Dieskau asked what they wanted. "What did they want?" said Johnson. "They wanted to kill you, to eat you, to smoke you in their pipe. But never fear; you shall be safe with me, or else they shall kill us both." Johnson, feeling unable to dislodge the French from Ticonderoga, strengthened his position by erecting Fort William Henry near the place where he had gained his victory. The King of England rewarded him for his services by conferring on him the honour of knighthood. He failed, however, to take Crown Point, which was the object of his expedition.

Shirley's task was the capture of Niagara. He set out from Albany and proceeded as far as Oswego. Here he learned that his plans had become known to the French, through some of Braddock's papers which had fallen into their hands, and that the enemy had taken such measures as made further progress on his part inadvisable. He accordingly abandoned the expedition. *Shirley fails to take Niagara.*

Meanwhile the British had made an easy conquest at Chignecto. Early in June, Colonel Monckton, with a force of two thousand men, fitted out in Boston, landed near Fort Lawrence. Opposed by Acadians and Indians, he fought his way *Capture of Beauséjour.*

across the Missaquash and opened fire on Beauséjour. Vergor, who then held command of the fort, sent a hasty message to Drucour, the Governor of Louisburg, seeking aid, but a British squadron off the coast prevented the French ships leaving the harbour. He also called to his aid the Acadians of the surrounding country, who, having hidden their women and children in the woods, obeyed the summons. But they brought little strength to the fort. Seeing the English at close quarters, they became alarmed and began to desert. When the siege had lasted four days, Vergor thought it best to surrender. His soldiers were allowed to retire with the honours of war, and were sent to Louisburg. He was afterwards suspected of having given up the fort too readily, and was tried by court-martial for failure in duty, but the charge was not sustained. Monckton changed the name of Beauséjour to Fort Cumberland, and placed in it a small garrison. Le Loutre, who was in the fort when the siege began, fled in disguise before the surrender, and made his way to Quebec.

The conduct of the Acadians at Beauséjour aroused indignation on the part of the Government at Halifax, and this feeling was intensified by the joy they showed over Braddock's defeat. Major Lawrence, who had succeeded Cornwallis as Governor of Nova Scotia, called his Council together to determine on the line of action which should be taken with respect to them. The stern decision arrived at was the removal of the offending people from the province. But first one more chance of redeeming themselves was granted. The Acadians were called on to send delegates to Halifax, with

Expulsion of the Acadians decided on.

power to act for the whole people. The oath of allegiance was submitted to them, but they still refused to take any oath which would bind them to aid the British against the French. And now Lawrence sent instructions to the officers commanding the forts at Annapolis, Grand Pré, Piziquid, and Chignecto, directing them to seize all the Acadians and place them on board vessels provided for their removal. The Acadians were to be allowed to take their money and such household furniture as the vessels could carry; their lands, cattle, and other property were forfeited.

The task of removing the Acadians from Canard, Minas, and Grand Pré was entrusted to Colonel Winslow. He did his work thoroughly. Without making known his object, he commanded the men and boys to assemble in the church at Grand Pré on the 5th of September. When all were gathered the church was surrounded by armed soldiers. Then Winslow, standing at the altar, reminded the Acadians of the kindness which had been shown their people for half a century, and upbraided them with their ingratitude, closing his address with the startling announcement that they were the King's prisoners, and that vessels were waiting in the harbour to carry them out of the country. A guard was stationed around the church to prevent any from escaping. Their families were notified to send them food, and to get ready to leave their homes without delay. A few days later all were placed on board the transports in the mouth of the Gasperaux.

Grand Pré and Canard.

It must have been a wretched scene in the church at Grand Pré on that September evening, and many a sad household was there around the Basin of Minas.

A Sad Scene. The morning had dawned with bright prospects on those homes around which clustered many warm affections and happy memories. God's blessing had rewarded the hand of the diligent. The barns were bursting with the freshly gathered harvest, and the orchards were colouring with crimson and gold. A cloud of sadness, deeper and darker than evening shadows, now hung over every hearthstone and gloomed every heart. Imagine you see these poor people—men, women, and children—with funereal step and mien, wending their way to the vessels which would soon bear them to the land of exile. And now, when they are all gone, see the smoking ruins of houses and barns which complete the picture of desolation.

Annapolis and Chignecto. The work of expulsion was less successful in other parts of the country. At Annapolis, when the Acadians saw the vessels entering the basin, they fled to the woods. Some were brought back; others eluded pursuit. The prisoners on board one of the transports, having taken possession of the vessel, sailed into St. John Harbour and escaped. The worst scenes were enacted at Chignecto. Some of the men fled to the woods, leaving the women and children behind; others, joined by Indians, turned upon the soldiers, some of whom they killed.

Results. It is computed that at least three thousand Acadians were thus banished from Nova Scotia. They were scattered a few hundreds in a place, from Massachusetts to North Carolina—some even to Louisiana. In some cases families were broken up, and the children were bound out as apprentices or servants. Many, with ardent longing for their old homes, in the face of numerous difficulties found their way back to Nova Scotia.

It is not necessary to pronounce here on the absolute justice or injustice of the stern measure to which Great Britain resorted to secure for herself the permanent possession of Nova Scotia. *Character of the Measure.* The action should be viewed in its relation to a great and long-continued struggle then taking place between two powerful nations for the possession of a continent. The Acadians had little claim on the Government at Halifax. They had repeatedly refused to take the oath of allegiance to Great Britain—some of them had even given direct aid to the enemy. It should also be remembered that the English in Nova Scotia were not strong enough to deal generously with those on whose sympathies and aid they could not rely. The authorities at Halifax had several causes for alarm. The Indians were dangerous enemies, and there seemed little hope of their becoming friendly while the Acadians held themselves aloof. The French were strongly intrenched in Quebec and Louisburg, and they had recently gained important victories in the West. In event of their making another attempt to obtain Nova Scotia the Acadians might give them active support. On the other hand, it is no matter for wonder that the Acadians should be unwilling, by a direct oath of allegiance to Great Britain, to separate themselves formally from the great nation with which they were connected by race, language, and religion. The punishment inflicted on them was severe, and one may well regret that some milder method of securing the peace of the country was not considered practicable.

CHAPTER XIV.

THE SEVEN YEARS' WAR.

Parties, Places, and Conditions. THE great conflict known in history as the "Seven Years' War" began in 1756. Great Britain and Prussia were the allies on the one side; on the other were France, Austria, and Russia. War was waged simultaneously in Europe, Asia, America, and on the wide ocean. The story will be told here only as it relates to the conflict of Great Britain and France in America. The American colonies of Great Britain had at this time a population of about three millions, and they were comparatively prosperous. The French in Canada numbered only about eighty thousand, and their condition was one marked with hardship and suffering. War had taxed them severely. Their able-bodied men, from sixteen to sixty years of age, were often drawn away for military service, and the cultivation of the fields was left largely to the women. Crops had failed, and often transports bearing supplies from France had been captured by British cruisers. The people thus suffered from lack of food.

Officers. During the first two years of the war the French gained all the victories. This came mainly from two causes—centralisation of power and superiority of officers. Colonial militia formed an important element in the forces with which the war was carried on. In the English colonies there was no central authority to levy troops. The legislatures of the different colonies were suspicious of Great Britain and jealous of each other. They failed to act promptly or together, or they did not act at all. On the other hand, the Governor-General of Canada was not dependent on votes of popular assemblies, but he could call the colonists into service as he saw occasion, and send his forces where he pleased. The French had excellent officers in command of their forces. The Marquis de Montcalm, who was Commander-in-chief, was an experienced and able general; and the Chevalier de Lévis, the second in command, was scarcely less distinguished. At the beginning of the war the Earl of Loudon was Commander-in-chief of the British forces, and Admiral Holbourne was placed in charge of the fleet — two singularly incompetent officers. Referring to Loudon's activity without accomplishing anything, a wit said of him, "He is like the figure of St. George on a tavern sign, always on horseback and never riding on."

Montcalm's first success was the capture of Fort Oswego, an important position on Lake Ontario. With this fort there fell into his hand sixteen hundred prisoners and much booty, comprising cannon and other war material, provisions, and money. These supplies greatly aided the French, especially as food was scarce in Canada. The English felt severely the loss of Oswego. They had no other position on Lake Ontario, and they intended to make it the base of operations against Niagara and Duquesne. Montcalm burned the fort and every-

Capture of Oswego.

thing of value which he could not carry away. The captured flags he hung up in the churches of Montreal as trophies of his victory.

The capture of Louisburg was the first measure on the English programme. Early in the summer Loudon came from New York to Halifax, bringing with him about five thousand veteran troops. Shortly after Admiral Holbourne arrived from England with a strong fleet and additional troops. These officers had now a force of at least ten thousand troops and sixteen ships of the line. Still they hesitated. They learned that Louisburg had a strong garrison, and was guarded by a fleet equal to their own. Prudent counsels prevailed. Six weeks were spent in drill, naval review, and mock sieges. A wag remarked that they spent the summer in sham fights and raising cabbages: the last referring to the culture of vegetables by the soldiers as food to protect them from scurvy. Loudon returned to New York with his troops without seeing Louisburg. Holbourne spent the remaining part of the summer in sailing back and forth between Halifax and Louisburg, but had no engagement. Finally a violent storm overtook him, made a total wreck of one of his ships, and disabled most of the others. In the autumn he returned to England.

Loudon and Holbourne at Halifax, 1757.

Meanwhile the French had taken Fort William Henry, on the south of Lake George. Loudon drew away the best of his troops for the expedition against Louisburg, leaving the border defences weak. Montcalm saw his opportunity, and with despatch he collected his forces, regulars, militia, and Indians, to the number of

Fort William Henry taken by the French.

eight thousand, at Montreal. The savages of various tribes from far and near formed nearly a fourth of the whole. They were enthusiastic over Montcalm, and had been eager to see him. "We wanted to see the famous man who tramples the English under his feet," said one of their orators, addressing the General. "We thought we should find him so tall that his head would be lost in the clouds. But you are a little man, my father. It is when we look into your eyes that we see the greatness of the pine-tree and the fire of the eagle."

Fort William Henry was held by Colonel Munro, with a militia force of twenty-two hundred men. Before the siege began Montcalm sent a note to Munro, asking him to surrender, stating that he then had power to control the Indians in his ranks, which he might not be able to do later after some of them had been killed. But Munro, who had hoped for aid from Colonel Webb, of Fort Edward, on the Hudson, replied that he would defend the fort to the last. Webb wrote him that he had no men to send him, and told him to make the best terms he could. The Indian who bore the letter was captured and killed by Montcalm's Indians. The letter, found adroitly concealed on his person, was taken to Montcalm. After reading it Montcalm sent it to Munro, hoping it might lead him to lay down his arms, but the brave officer still continued the defence. Finally, however, seeing his inability to hold out, he gave up the fort. His men were to be allowed to march out with their guns, and were to be conducted to Fort Edward by an escort of French soldiers as a protection against the Indians. It is, however, sad to relate,

K

that this protection was not afforded. Little effort was made to restrain the savages, and a fearful massacre ensued. The bloodthirsty Indians fell upon the English as they marched from the fort, killing some on the spot, and reserving others for cruel torture, not even sparing the women and children.

Change at the Helm. A master mind in the councils of a nation is a tower of strength. Such was William Pitt, who now became Minister of War in the British Cabinet. Through lack of vigour on the part of those in command, the great military resources of the nation had been of little avail. Pitt's wise measures and splendid executive ability soon changed the aspect of affairs throughout the empire. Officers were not given positions of trust because of their rank, their politics, or the influence of their families, or even because of their long service; but men were placed in command over the army and navy on account of their ability, energy, and such other personal qualities as fitted them for the grave duties entrusted to them. The result of this distinguished Minister's administration was the complete overthrow of French power in America. The details of his scheme comprised the capture of Louisburg, Ticonderoga, Niagara, Duquesne, Quebec, and all Canada.

The Second Siege of Louisburg, 1758. Louisburg was the chief naval station of the French in America, and its position enabled it to guard most effectively the ocean approaches to Canada. The capture of this "Dunkirk of America" was the first part on the programme. For its conquest came a large fleet of warships and transports, bringing over twelve thousand

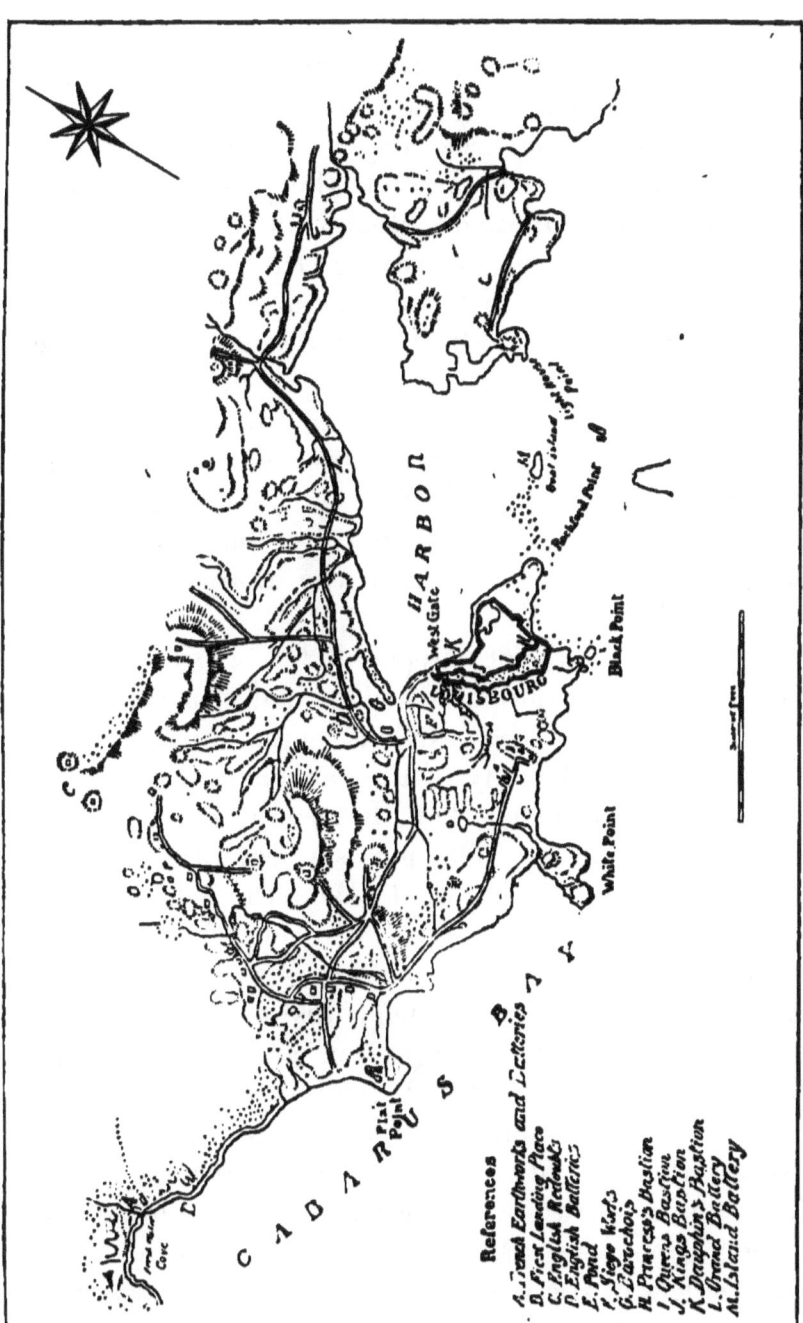

MAP OF SIEGE OF LOUISBURG, 1758.

troops. General Amherst was commander-in-chief, and under him were the brigadiers Lawrence, Wentworth, and Wolfe. On the 2nd of June 1758 the fleet arrived in Gabarus Bay. A wild storm was raging, and for nearly a week the angry surf kept the troops from landing. Meanwhile the French at Louisburg were busy fortifying the shore. With the first lull the British soldiers, arranged in three divisions, advanced boldly in their boats in the face of a brisk fire from the enemy. Wolfe, now only thirty-two years of age, distinguished himself throughout the siege. As the boats drew to the shore he leaped into the water, and was the first to gain the land. The French fought bravely, but they were forced to take refuge behind the ramparts of the town.

Louisburg was not prepared for a siege. The stonework of the ramparts had in many places fallen into the ditches, the earthen embankments were broken down, and many of the cannon were mounted on carriages so rotten that they could not bear the shock of discharge. The garrison comprised about three thousand five hundred men; the harbour was guarded by several warships. Drucour, the Governor of Louisburg, gathered all his forces within the ramparts, and resolved to defend his post. For over seven weeks the siege went on, and Drucour saw with dismay the widening breaches in his walls. The terror-stricken inhabitants of the town urged him to give up the contest. He proposed to surrender with the honours of war, but General Amherst would grant no conditions, and Drucour was compelled to yield. The soldiers of the garrison marched out as prisoners of war — their arms, ammunition, and provisions having been given up to the victors. The citizens who desired it were allowed to remove to France. The captured flags were sent to England, and placed in St. Paul's Church, London.

At different times after the Treaty of Utrecht, Acadians who were unwilling to submit to British authority had sought a home in Isle St. John (Prince Edward Island). The largest emigration to the island was in 1755, on the capture of Beauséjour and the expulsion of the Acadians. In 1758 the population was estimated at about four thousand. There were many well-tilled farms, yielding large crops of wheat, and well stocked with cattle. After the taking of Louisburg, General Amherst sent Lord Rollo with a detachment of soldiers to take possession of the island. Fort le Joye, near the present Charlottetown, readily submitted, and the soldiers of the garrison were made prisoners. Many of the inhabitants left the island, some crossing over to Gaspé, near the mouth of the St. Lawrence, others going to France. *Prince Edward Island.*

Another small force under Monckton was sent to the River St. John, where the French still held a small fort. Monckton took possession of the fort, and then sailed up the river to a French settlement on the banks of the Jemseg. At his approach the inhabitants fled to the woods, Monckton seized such property as he could carry away, and burned the dwellings. Similar measures were taken against the French settlement on the Peticodiac. *The St. John River.*

Meanwhile the British had been defeated at Lake

Champlain. General Abercrombie, an officer of the old regime who had been allowed to remain in command, marched from Albany with the largest army yet seen in America — between fifteen and sixteen thousand militia and regulars — to attack Montcalm, who guarded the gateway of Canada at Ticonderoga. Montcalm's force comprised only about three thousand five hundred men. His intrenchment was formed of squared beams of wood pinned together, in front of which were placed rows of fallen trees with their larger branches sharpened and pointing outwards. The defence was good against musket shot, but it could have been easily swept away by cannon. Abercrombie had made the fatal mistake of leaving his artillery at Fort Edward, on the Hudson, and he now rashly ordered an attack on the fort. His men advanced boldly and fought well; but unable, in the face of the enemy's fire, to force their way through the trees, they were repulsed with terrible slaughter. Finally they retreated, leaving nearly two thousand dead and wounded before the fort.

The British defeated at Ticonderoga, July 1758.

The easy capture of Frontenac and Duquesne was an offset for the disaster at Ticonderoga. Fort Frontenac, though a position of great importance to the French, was protected by a very small garrison. After the defeat at Ticonderoga, Abercrombie sent Colonel Bradstreet with three thousand men to invest the place. After two days' siege and without losing a man, Bradstreet took the fort and burned it to the ground.

Frontenac and Duquesne.

Later in the season, Duquesne, prized so highly for its command of the Ohio Valley and of the western country beyond, fell to the English. At the head of six thousand men, the gallant General Forbes, though so ill that he was borne on a litter, led his army across the Alleghanies to the distant fort. At his approach the French abandoned the place without a struggle. In honour of the Minister of War, the name Duquesne was changed to Fort Pitt, which was afterwards changed to Pittsburg.

CHAPTER XV.

THE END OF FRENCH RULE IN AMERICA.

Dark Days. AFFAIRS in Canada now wore a gloomy aspect. The men were drawn away so much to serve as soldiers that the farms were neglected, and supplies sent from France were often seized on the way by British cruisers. Thus food became very scarce, and there was great destitution in the country. The militiamen had their rations given them, but, unlike the regular soldiers, they received no pay for their service. Indeed, they were often given short allowance of bread, and had horse-flesh in place of beef. Worst of all, the officers sent by the King to govern the country, who lived in luxury, plundered and robbed the people. The Intendant Bigot and his agents enriched themselves at the public expense. They bought supplies for the troops, forcing the persons from whom they purchased to sell for less than value, and charging the King exorbitant prices. In like manner, when Bigot employed men to convey troops from one part of the country to another, he paid them much less than he received for the service.

Pitt was determined to wrest Canada wholly from France, and so with the return of spring he set his machinery of war in motion. In arranging the campaign for this year he made a threefold division of the work—the expulsion of the French from Lake Champlain, the capture of Fort Niagara, and the conquest of Quebec. *(The British Plan of Conquest.)* General Amherst was appointed commander-in-chief of the army, which consisted of regular troops and colonial militia. In the further distribution of the work, operations on Lake Champlain were entrusted to General Amherst; the expedition against Niagara was given to General Prideaux, Sir William Johnson being second in command; and the siege of Quebec was entrusted to General Wolfe. Under Wolfe the most important officers were Generals Monckton, Townshend, and Murray. The fleet sent to Quebec, comprising about fifty sail, warships and transports, was under the command of Admiral Saunders, who was ably assisted by Admiral Holmes.

Pitt generally chose his men wisely. The chief officers just named were able men. Amherst was energetic and cautious, though perhaps rather slow. *(Character of Officers.)* The hero of the campaign, the man one always thinks of as the chief instrument in the conquest of Canada, was General Wolfe. Not yet thirty-three years old, he was the youngest of the leaders named. He was not inexperienced, however, in the art of war, having entered the service when he was fifteen years of age. It is said that he did not look much like a hero. His bodily frame was not built for strength or endurance, nor did the features of his face indicate great power. Only his clear, keen eye revealed the inextinguishable fire of his spirit.

Marching from Albany, at the head of eleven thousand men, Amherst sought to seize the "Gateway of Canada." Remembering the defeat of Abercrombie, he advanced cautiously upon Ticonderoga. After a vigorous defence for three or four days, the French abandoned the fort and also Crown Point, retreating to a strong position on Isle-aux-Noix, at the northern end of Lake Champlain. Through lack of transports, Amherst was unable to follow them. He accordingly stayed at Crown Point during the remainder of the season, which he spent in building vessels, strengthening the fort, and making roads.

Lake Champlain and Niagara.

Meanwhile Niagara had been taken by the English. Early in the siege Prideaux was killed by the premature bursting of a shell fired by his own men. Sir William Johnson succeeded to the command, and though not a very skilled soldier he soon gained possession of the fort.

The siege of Quebec was the chief feature of the campaign. It was towards the last of June when the British fleet anchored off the west end of the Isle of Orleans in full view of the city. Wolfe landed his troops, numbering about eight thousand five hundred, on this island, which he made his headquarters. Before proceeding with the story we may pause for a moment and with him survey the scene of his exploits during the next eleven weeks. Before him, about seven miles distant, on the northern banks of the St. Lawrence, two hundred feet above water, is the city of Quebec, perched like an eagle's nest on the rocks. Up and down for several miles the coast is protected by a rocky wall, in many places too steep to climb, and in all places so difficult that a few men could guard effectively against the approach of

Wolfe before Quebec.

END OF FRENCH RULE IN AMERICA. 155

an army. Immediately below the city on the east is the river St. Charles, which here joins the St. Lawrence. About eight miles farther down, the Montmorency, after swirling through its deep chasm and making its great leap of two hundred and fifty feet over the rocks, contributes its waters to the main river. Between the St. Charles and the Montmorency is the curved and elevated shore of Beauport, and

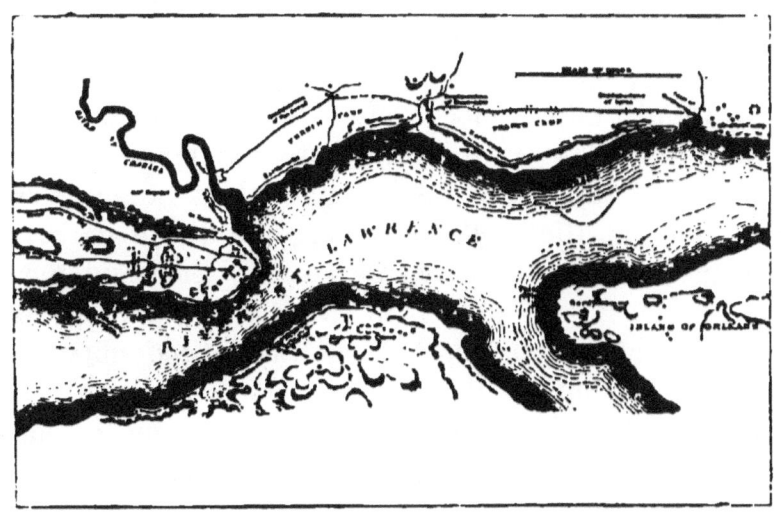

MAP OF THE SIEGE OF QUEBEC, 1759.

along the river are mud flats and shallows known as the Shoals of Beauport. From Wolfe's standpoint on the Isle of Orleans the shore above Quebec was hidden by the promontory on which the city stands; but for another eight miles, to Cap Rouge, it is high and rocky. On the heights behind the city, less than a mile distant, are the Plains of Abraham, where the great conflict which determined the destiny of Canada took place. Nearly opposite Quebec, on the south side of the river, is the headland called Point Lévis.

When Wolfe looked up and down along this great natural fortress, he saw that the French had not been negligent in taking advantage of the favourable position in which they were placed. Except the forces on Lake Champlain and at Niagara, the whole available strength of Canada was concentrated at Quebec. All the men from sixteen to sixty years of age had been summoned for the defence of their homes and their hearths, their country and their religion, and they had come at the call. There joined the camp even lads under sixteen and old men of four score. Over a hundred cannon were mounted on the walls of Quebec, and the garrison within the city comprised nearly two thousand men. The whole line of river-bank from the city to Montmorency was a succession of earthworks, redoubts, and batteries, defended by fourteen thousand men. In addition to this force, about one thousand Indians had come with their scalping-knives to lend their aid. Gunboats, floating batteries, and fire-ships occupied the harbour. The mouth of the St. Charles was protected by a boom of logs chained together, and by heavy guns placed on sunken vessels. As to guarding the banks above the city, that was at first deemed unnecessary, for it was not supposed that any British ship would venture to pass the guns of the fort. Later, during the siege, a strong force under Bougainville was sent to guard these heights. Directing all this machinery of war were the distinguished officers Montcalm, Lévis, Bougainville, and the Governor-General Vaudreuil, with others of less distinction.

The French Defences.

Montcalm, secure in his munition of rocks, quietly yet closely watched the enemy, but he would not come out of his fastness to risk a battle. Wolfe wanted to fight, but he could not get at the foe. He was greatly perplexed by the difficulties of his position, at times almost despondent. He wrote to his mother: "The Marquis of Montcalm is at the head of a great number of poor soldiers. I am at the head of a small number of good ones that wish for nothing so much as to fight him; but the wary old fellow avoids an action, doubtful of the behaviour of his army." *Policies of Montcalm and Wolfe.*

The chief offensive action of the French was an attempt to destroy the British fleet by means of fire-ships. On a dark night six ships filled with all sorts of combustibles and explosives, with slow matches attached, were set adrift in the river, that they might float down among the British ships and set them on fire. The explosion occurred before the fire-ships reached the neighbourhood of the fleet. The thundering crash of the explosion and the glaring flames that lit up the darkness startled the British tars; but they launched their boats and with grappling-hooks and poles turned away the fire-ships so that no damage was done. *Fire-ships.*

A few days after his arrival Wolfe obtained possession of the heights of Point Lévis, opposite Quebec. From this important position he could command the harbour and bombard the city, which was only about a mile distant. General Monckton with a body of troops was placed in charge. By shot and shell he soon laid much of the city in ruins, utterly destroying the Lower Town, so that *Advance Movements.*

most of the inhabitants not engaged in the defence fled to the country.

Wolfe's next movement was to land three thousand men at the Montmorency, below the point where that river joins the St. Lawrence. His object was to lead them across the Montmorency higher up, and thus come upon the French from the rear. The landing was effected with no great difficulty; but Lévis, who occupied the right bank of the Montmorency, guarded the fords so closely that Wolfe was unable to carry out his purpose.

Wolfe now took a bolder course and determined to fight the enemy from the front. The point of attack was General Lévis's camp on the west of the Montmorency. While the cannon of the British warships, of the batteries of Point Lévis, and of the battery on the east of the Montmorency stormed the French redoubts, a flotilla of boats bore the troops to the flats on the Beauport shore. At the same time two thousand men from the east of the Montmorency were crossing over by the fords below the falls to act in concert with those landing from the boats. Those who first gained the land, eager for the contest, instead of waiting for the others coming up to join them, rushed forward. Struggling up the bank, which, difficult at best, was slippery from a sudden shower of rain, they were met by the destructive fire which the enemy poured down upon them from the heights. For a time they buffeted the storm, and then, giving way, they retreated to their boats, leaving over four hundred of their number dead on the rugged bank. Wolfe was of feeble physical constitution; his sensitive and

Failure of July 31.

END OF FRENCH RULE IN AMERICA. 159

ambitious spirit chafed under this disaster, and brought on a raging fever, of which he lay ill for days.

With the view of seeking a more favourable point of attack, Admiral Holmes, passing the batteries of Quebec without much damage, conducted a portion of the fleet above the city. *The English move up the River.* To co-operate with him, a land force of twelve hundred men under General Murray was taken up along the south shore of the St. Lawrence. Murray was also able to intercept supplies of food for Quebec, which came by the river from Montreal and Three Rivers. For the purpose of guarding the banks above the city, Montcalm sent Bougainville with fifteen hundred men taken from the camp at Beauport. Admiral Holmes drifted with the tide up and down the river, between Cap Rouge and Quebec, and Bougainville, who had been commanded to watch his movements, was compelled to follow him along the shore in order to defeat any attempt to land his forces at some undefended point. Meanwhile the Canadian militia, many of whom were farmers, whose crops were ready for harvesting, began to desert in large numbers. The defences of Quebec were weakened too by the loss of the able officer General Lévis, who was sent to Montreal for aid against any attack on that place that might be made by General Amherst.

At a council of war held near the end of August, General Townshend proposed that an attempt should be made to land troops a *A Bold Scheme.* little above the city and take them up the steep bank to the Plains of Abraham. The scheme seemed rash and one that might end in utter defeat; but only desperate measures were available, and Wolfe adopted the proposed plan without hesitation. The troops of the Montmorency encampment were placed on board Admiral Holmes's ships, which were in the river above Quebec; others marched up from Point Lévis along the south shore to a spot agreed on, from which they could be taken across the river. Nearly five thousand men were then ready for the movement. The place selected for the ascent was that now known as Wolfe's Cove, where a rugged pathway was found leading up the almost precipitous banks. Twenty-four volunteers were readily obtained to lead the way up the difficult and dangerous path. The early morning of the 13th of September was chosen for carrying out the bold scheme.

During the night succeeding the 12th of September barges laden with British soldiers dropped down the river to the landing-place. As they floated along silently with the current, Wolfe, who was in one of the boats, quieted his mind by reciting Gray's "Elegy in a Country Churchyard," then recently published, remarking as he finished, "I would rather be the author of that poem than the conqueror of Quebec." Little thought he at the time that the end of his own career would so soon illustrate the verse—

The English on the Heights.

"The paths of glory lead but to the grave."

The time chosen for the landing was fortunate. A convoy of boats bearing provisions for the French army at Beauport was expected to pass down the river that night, and the sentry on the shore mistook the English boats for their own. Moreover, Wolfe so artfully concealed his purpose that his principal object was not suspected. While his troops were stealthily landing and clambering up the steep pathway, the cannon of the battery at Point Lévis and of the ships in the harbour were blazing away at the city and the Beauport shore, as if the whole event were to be determined at these places. Wolfe's success was in part due to lack of vigilance in the French. A guard was stationed on the heights near the end of the pathway; but its chief officer, Vergor, who gave up Beauséjour to the English, was asleep, and, on being aroused by the sudden appearance of the enemy, made slight resistance. Thus when the sun rose, Wolfe with four thousand eight hundred men, formed in line of battle, stood on the Plains of Abraham.

General Montcalm, who was at Beauport, could scarcely believe the messenger who came in hot haste to tell him that the British had gained the heights. *Montcalm's Decision.* With all despatch he crossed the St. Charles and entered the city, followed by a portion of the army. Vaudreuil and the troops of his division remained at Beauport; Bougainville and the troops under his command were at Cap Rouge. Montcalm, however, was able to muster a force of about seven thousand five hundred men, and he resolved to fight the enemy on the open field. He has been blamed for not remaining within the city and acting on the defensive behind his ramparts. The question was a difficult one. Every hour's delay enabled Wolfe to fortify himself and bring up more troops from the river: besides, the English could now cut off all supplies from Quebec.

L

The Battle. The French troops were eager for the fray, and they rushed forward rapidly, firing as soon as they came within range. The English stood firm as a wall, wasting no shots, and moving only to fill the gaps made by the fallen; for they had been ordered not to fire until the enemy were within forty paces. But when the word "Fire!" ran along the lines, every gun was levelled as by a single arm, and one simultaneous and overwhelming volley swept across the opposing columns. Fearful was the havoc among the French. The dead and wounded strewed the plain, and the broken ranks were completely disorganised. Then came the order "Charge!" at which some of the English rushed forward with fixed bayonets; others kept firing as they advanced;

WOLFE.

while the Scottish Highlanders with their broadswords fought their way through the ranks of the foe. The French militia fled in disorder. The regulars, animated by the gallant Montcalm, strove manfully; but they could not withstand the impetuous charge of the column which bore down upon them. The battle was short and decisive. Some of the French were driven across the St. Charles; others took refuge within the city walls. Their loss was between twelve and fifteen hundred men. The loss of the British in killed and wounded was about six hundred.

MONTCALM.

The two commanders threw themselves into the struggle with whole-souled valour, and both fell mortally wounded. Wolfe realised that he had staked everything on the issue of

Wolfe and Montcalm.

the day. It was victory or ruin. In the early part of the engagement he moved here and there among his men, cheering them by his presence and his words. He was soon seriously wounded in the wrist, but he tied his handkerchief around the wound and made no complaint. When he gave the order to charge, placing himself at the head of his grenadiers, he led the attack. Pressing on in the thickest of the battle, he received a fatal wound in the breast. He asked for the support of the officer near him, that the soldiers might not see him fall. As he was borne to the rear he heard the words, "They run!" "Who run?" eagerly asked the dying hero. "The enemy, sir," was the reply. Then, after sending a messenger with orders to one of his officers, Wolfe uttered his last memorable words—"God be praised! I die in peace." In the autumn, when the British fleet sailed away, one of its ships bore the embalmed remains of Wolfe to the mother-land. Montcalm was still trying to rally his fugitive soldiers, when he received a fatal wound. Supported on his horse by two soldiers, he was borne into the city. The surgeon who attended him pronounced the wound fatal, and told Montcalm that he had but few hours to live. "I am glad of it," said the patriot soldier; "I shall not live to see the surrender of Quebec." Before the morning dawned he had passed away. Coffined in a rough box, he was buried with little ceremony under the floor of the chapel of the Ursuline Convent.

In Montcalm's last moments, when his thoughts were turned chiefly to the objects which were dear to his heart—his beautiful home far away in France, with its unfading vision of mother, and wife, and

END OF FRENCH RULE IN AMERICA. 165

children—and to the great concerns of the future life, he did not forget those who had been his companions in arms, and the Canadian people, whom he could no longer serve. Their place in his latest thoughts is shown by the following note which he sent to General Townshend:—

"MONSIEUR,—The humanity of the English sets my mind at rest concerning the fate of the French prisoners and the Canadians. Feel towards them as they have caused me to feel. Do not let them perceive that they have changed masters. Be their protector as I have been their father."

General Monckton stood next to Wolfe in rank, but he being seriously wounded, the command fell to General Townshend. Before making an assault on the town, this officer proceeded to strengthen his position, and bring up such supplies from the ships as would enable him to carry on the siege. But no further blow was needed. Quebec was a mass of ruins, and had little means of defence. The greater part of the defeated troops had retired to Jacques Cartier, some thirty miles distant, whither the Governor and the Intendant had also betaken themselves. Thus there were but few regular soldiers in the city, and the militia could not be depended on. War material was nearly exhausted, provisions within the city sufficed for only a week on half rations, and further supply was cut off. Accordingly, four days after the battle, Ramesay, the commandant of the garrison, sent an officer bearing a white flag to the English camp, to ask for terms of surrender. Matters were soon arranged, and Quebec was given up to the

The Surrender.

English. The soldiers were allowed to march out with the honours of war, and the citizens were assured of protection for themselves and their property, and of the enjoyment of their religion.

<small>Too Late.</small> Meanwhile De Lévis, who had been at Montreal, hearing of the disastrous battle, hastened to the rescue. On his arrival at Jacques Cartier he rallied the army, inspired Vaudreuil with new resolution, and woke up Bigot, so that they were soon on the march for Quebec to retrieve their lost honour. On the way they learned that Quebec had surrendered.

<small>The British occupy Quebec.</small> The British flag now waved over the citadel in the capital of New France. Quebec was a mass of ruins; disorder prevailed: the inhabitants were famished and destitute. General Murray was chief in command, Townshend having returned to England. The severe Canadian winter which followed was keenly felt by the British soldiers, especially by the kilted Highlanders, whose costume gave them scant protection. The French nuns showed them much kindness, knitting long hose to cover their bare legs, and nursing the sick with great care and tenderness. Indeed, the friendly feeling and kind offices shown in Quebec during the winter by French and English towards each other afforded an earnest of that harmony with which, for the most part, the two races have since occupied their Canadian home.

<small>Efforts to recapture Quebec.</small> Early in the following spring De Lévis, at the head of eight or nine thousand men, attempted to retake Quebec. In this effort he was very nearly successful. Murray was young and impulsive. Disease had greatly weakened his

army, and he could bring only three thousand men into the field, yet he imprudently marched out to meet the enemy. In explaining his action afterwards he said, "Our little army was in the habit of beating that enemy." The struggle was a severe one, and in the end Murray, after losing over a third of his men, was forced to take refuge in the city. He now did much to make amends for his blunder by the wonderful energy he showed in placing the city in a state of defence. Order and confidence were thus restored, and the enthusiasm and spirit of the soldiers revived. Lévis was also an able general, and he was making preparations for a vigorous siege. It was difficult to predict the issue. Both sides were expecting reinforcements from Europe, and the one first to receive help from the mother-country seemed likely to win the prize. So when a ship was seen coming up the river, it was with feverish anxiety that all eyes watched her approach. When she unfurled the red cross of St. George, cheers of exultation rang out from behind the ramparts. A British squadron arriving a day or two later, the fate of the city was decided. De Lévis made a hasty retreat, leaving behind him his cannon, ammunition, baggage, and all the sick and wounded of his army.

The British forces now set out from three separate points, widely distant from each other, for Montreal, where the French, under Vaudreuil and De Lévis, had made a final stand. General Amherst, collecting an army of ten thousand men at Oswego, crossed Lake Ontario and proceeded down the St. Lawrence. Haviland, with three thousand men, advanced from Crown Point by way of Lake Cham-

The Closing Scene, 1760.

plain and the Richelieu, and Murray came from Quebec, receiving the submission of the inhabitants as he passed through the country. The only hope for Vaudreuil and De Lévis was in fighting these divisions separately before they concentrated their strength at Montreal. This they failed to do. Indeed, they had little fighting ability. Their army consisted largely of Canadian militia, who had lost all spirit for war, and were thinking rather of their homes and their starving families. And now, when the Canadians saw an army of from fifteen to twenty thousand men, including Indians, encamped before Montreal, they deserted almost to a man. Indeed, many of the regulars went with them. There remained only about twenty-four hundred men.

Surrender. Thus reduced, Vaudreuil and De Lévis offered to surrender. General Amherst demanded that they give up their arms and standards. Vaudreuil and De Lévis thought this too hard, and they pleaded for terms less humiliating; but Amherst, charging them with having encouraged the Indians in their acts of outrage, would abate nothing. De Lévis stood out decidedly against complying with the conditions, and secretly burned his colours rather than submit to the dishonour of giving them up to the enemy. According to the terms of surrender, the troops were to be sent to France under pledge of not serving again in the existing war; the inhabitants who chose to remain were assured of protection for their persons, their property, and their religion. Amherst especially enjoined on his men to refrain from all inhumanity and plunder, and to treat the Canadians in every respect as British subjects.

CHAPTER XVI.

LAYING NEW FOUNDATIONS.

PEACE was not concluded between Great Britain and France for over two years after the surrender of Montreal. Meanwhile Canada was placed under the rule of military officers. It was divided into three districts, each having its own Lieutenant-Governor:— *Provisional Government.*

 The District of Quebec, under General Murray.
 The District of Three Rivers, under Colonel Burton.
 The District of Montreal, under General Gage.

The inhabitants of Canada, at this time estimated at sixty-two thousand, were settled chiefly along the St. Lawrence, between the Gulf and Montreal; from this to Detroit the country was a wilderness without inhabitants. For the most part the peasantry remained in the country after the conquest. They, no doubt, were to some extent suspicious of the English, and felt a certain degree of discomfort under the rule of those whom they had been wont to regard as bitter enemies; but generally they accepted the new order of things with good grace. They could, indeed, scarcely grieve very much over the removal of a power which kept them under such rulers as the avaricious Bigot. The severe exactions *The Inhabitants.*

of the government had reduced them to the lowest poverty. The men had been drawn away from their usual occupations for military service, and the scanty products of their farms which they were able to dispose of had been sold to the Government for paper money, which was now worthless, or at least of very doubtful value. The English governors, especially General Murray, treated them with much consideration, and sought to reconcile them to the change which had come upon them so suddenly. In some important ways the condition of the common people was greatly improved. They were no longer called upon for service in war, and they could cultivate their farms without fear of disturbance.

The officers of the civil government, some of the French noblesse, and many of the merchants removed to France. Vaudreuil, Bigot, and several others, on their return to France, were thrown into the Bastile, and were afterwards brought to trial for fraud against the Government. Vaudreuil was acquitted. Bigot, who had enriched himself by shameless plundering, was compelled to give up his ill-gotten wealth. All his property was confiscated, and he was exiled for life.

Indian wars had not yet wholly ceased. Shortly **Pontiac's Conspiracy.** after the conquest of Canada the tribes of the West formed a great conspiracy against the English. The French had gained their goodwill by living amongst them, adopting their wild life, and giving them presents. The agents of the French Government now told them that the English would drive them from their hunting-grounds and seize the whole of their lands. This plot, which was a most serious affair, has been known as "Pontiac's Conspiracy," so called from one of its principal actors, Pontiac, a noted Indian chief of the Ottawa tribe. The forts around the Great Lakes and in the Ohio Valley had all passed into the hands of the English, and were held by small garrisons. Pontiac sent his messengers through all the tribes, and arranged for a simultaneous attack on these forts. The story cannot be fully told here. It must suffice to say that, by cunning stratagem or by open assault, the savages seized nine forts, and cruelly put the English to death or dragged them into captivity.

At Mackinaw, on Lake Michigan, they invited the officers to witness a game of La Crosse. The gates of the fort were left open, and when all were excited over the game, at a given signal the Indians seized the hatchets which the squaws had concealed under their blankets, rushed into the fort, killed part of the garrison, and made prisoners of the rest. At Detroit the stratagem was less successful. The wily Pontiac, accompanied by sixty warriors, each with a short gun concealed under his blanket, sought admission to the fort to smoke the pipe of peace. But the English had received timely warning, and, to Pontiac's surprise, he was met by soldiers ready for battle. This Indian war lasted for many months, when, largely through the good management of Sir William Johnson, the savages were pacified. Many of those who had been dragged into captivity by the Indians were now restored to their friends, while some, having become attached to wild Indian life, refused to return to their old homes.

Due in large measure to the wise policy of William

Pitt, the last part of the reign of George II. was a brilliant period in the history of England. The Seven Years' War brought success to the arms of Great Britain and glory to her flag. George III., who came to the throne in 1760, was very different from his grandfather, whom he succeeded. His mother had always been saying to him, "George, be a king!" and when his turn came to rule, he had high notions of a king's rights. He did not want a Minister who had a policy. It thus happened that Pitt was not in power when the war closed, otherwise some things would have been done differently. The treaty which settled affairs, known in history as the Peace of Paris, ceded to Great Britain all Canada, Nova Scotia, Cape Breton, the Island of St. John, and Newfoundland; in fact, all the French possessions in America east of the Mississippi except New Orleans. France was allowed the right of fishing in Newfoundland waters, and of drying fish on certain parts of the coast of that island. She also retained the islands of Miquelon and St. Pierre as fishing stations. Pitt strongly opposed this concession of fishing privileges, as he foresaw that some day it would be a source of trouble; but his opposition was of no avail.

The Peace of Paris.

In 1763 Canada, under the name of the Province of Quebec, was, by royal proclamation, declared a British possession, and General Murray was made Governor of the whole country. The Governor was authorised to call a representative assembly for the enacting of laws whenever he thought the province ready for this step. As Roman Catholics were at that time not

The Government of the Province.

allowed to vote, an assembly would have represented a comparatively small portion of the inhabitants. In the meantime, accordingly, the laws were made and the government of the province was carried on by the Governor and a Council chosen by himself. The power of levying duties on imported goods, and of imposing general taxes, was reserved to the British House of Commons. Town authorities, however, were allowed to tax citizens for the repair of the streets and for other local objects. The rights of the Indians to their hunting-grounds were carefully guarded in the King's proclamation. No private person was allowed to buy their lands. Purchase could be made only by the Governor or other high official, and the purchase could not be made in any private way, but only from the Indians assembled in council. English-speaking people were encouraged to settle in the province by the offer of free grants of land. Among the noted features of progress was the introduction of a printing-press in the city of Quebec. On the 21st of June 1764 was issued the *Quebec Gazette*, the first paper published in Canada.

Governor Murray found the English settlers very troublesome. Although they did not exceed five hundred in number, they insisted that he should call an assembly, by which they would have gained full control of the country. Failing to secure their object, they petitioned King George III. to remove him from office. Murray proceeded to England to meet the charges brought against him. He did not return to Canada, but for a year and a half, while residing in England, he held his office of Governor.

Privileges of the "New Subjects."
Although the "New Subjects," as French Canadians were called, were promised the same treatment as other British subjects as far as the laws of Great Britain would allow, they had not equal privileges with the English people who had come into the province. The laws of Great Britain at that time excluded Roman Catholics from all important public offices. Candidates for these offices were required to take what was called the test oath, denying certain doctrines of the Roman Catholic religion. The French Canadians were quite willing to take the oath of allegiance to the Sovereign of Great Britain, but they would not disown their religion for the honours or emoluments of office. They were allowed full freedom in religious matters, but their priests were forbidden to take any part in political affairs.

The Laws.
The French and the English could not agree at all as regards the laws which they desired. The French did not like the English custom of trial by jury, but preferred the simple decision of the judge. Trial by jury, in which the agreement of all was required before a verdict could be given, seemed to them a contest to try the jurymen's power of holding out, rather than a suitable means to decide the merits of a cause. Then the French laws relating to the ownership and transfer of lands were very unlike those of England. It will be remembered that the feudal system of holding lands was introduced at an early period into Canada. The peasant paid an annual rent for his land to the Seignior, and when he sold his land he had to give one-twelfth of the price to the Seignior. This tended to hinder improvement, for the

more valuable land became, the greater was the tax. But the *habitants*, being illiterate and unacquainted with business, could look to the Seignior as protector. Their lands, being under the guardianship of the Seignior, could not be seized for debt. Another peculiarity in the French system was the absence of registration of deeds and mortgages. The people were much opposed to the English custom, thinking that it involved needless expense; and as they could not read, they were suspicious that written records might be used as a means of concealing fraud. Their system, however, often led to bad results. One could mortgage his land to different persons, one mortgagee not knowing that it was mortgaged to another. The owner could thus realise more on his land than it was worth, or he might sell mortgaged land for its full value, and the purchaser not know of the encumbrance at the time of purchase. The laws relating to husband and wife were also unlike those of the English. In the matter of property the marriage relation was a sort of partnership in which each had equal interest. If the wife died before the husband, her heirs were entitled to her half of the property.

In 1768 Sir Guy Carleton succeeded General Murray as Governor of Canada. He found matters in a very unsatisfactory condition. The French inhabitants did not understand the English laws, and they disliked these laws so much that it was difficult to enforce them. The courts had in some matters adopted the old French laws, which gave offence to the English people. There was much confusion as well as murmuring. Governor Carleton went to England for the purpose of securing some better

The Quebec Act, 1774.

basis of government for the province. Accordingly, after some delay, the British Parliament, in 1774, passed what is known as the Quebec Act, which came into force in the following year. This Act extended the bounds of the province to the Mississippi on the west, to the water-shed of Hudson Bay on the north, and to the Ohio on the south. It established the use of French civil law and English criminal law. It removed all civil disabilities from the French inhabitants arising from their religion, and it secured to the Roman Catholic clergy the tithes from their own people, which they had been accustomed to collect under French rule. The Act did not give the province a representative assembly, but left the government, as before, with the Governor and a Legislative Council appointed by the Crown. The first Council comprised twenty-three members, eight of whom were Roman Catholics. It had power to make laws, subject to the approval of the Governor. The French were well pleased with the Act. Not so the English. They objected to the French civil code and to the provision made for the support of the Roman Catholic religion. The extension of the bounds of Canada gave offence to some of the other provinces.

Meanwhile some important events had taken place in Nova Scotia. The colonists in that province had been promised a representative legislature, and the laws made by the Governor and Council were considered by legal authorities to be of doubtful validity. Governor Lawrence was accordingly instructed by the British Government to call on the people to elect a House of Assembly. Fearing that such a body might assume

The First Assembly in Nova Scotia, 1758.

too much power and cause him trouble, the conservative Governor obeyed the order somewhat unwillingly. The first Assembly, consisting of twenty-two members, met in the Court House in Halifax on the 2nd of October 1758. Roman Catholics were not allowed to sit as members or to vote at elections. By the death of King George II., in 1760, the House was dissolved.

Better days now began to dawn on Nova Scotia. Governor Lawrence invited colonists to come from New England, offering free grants of the best land in the province. Many families of old Puritan stock from Connecticut and Rhode Island accepted his invitation, and settled on the fertile farms in Annapolis, Cornwallis, Horton, Windsor, Truro, Onslow, and Cumberland, from which the Acadians had been expelled. The Lords of Trade in England were not pleased with the action of the Governor in this regard, as they thought to reserve these lands for such officers and soldiers as might wish to settle in the country on the close of the war in Canada. Lawrence assured them that there was abundance of land equally good on the St. John River and elsewhere, but at the same time he frankly told them that soldiers did not make good colonists for a new country. Many of the soldiers who had come to Nova Scotia soon went away, and a large number of those who remained resorted to the liquor traffic for a livelihood. There came also a few families from Philadelphia, who formed the first English settlement in Pictou. These people endured great hardships, getting much of their food for a year or two by hunting and fishing. A few years later, in

New Colonists in Nova Scotia, 1760-1773.

1773, there came to Picton a small Scotch colony. These hardy pioneers had time only to build rude cabins before winter set in. To prevent their families from starving, the men went to Truro, forty miles distant, and dragged home flour and potatoes on hand-sleds. It thus happened that there was established in the western part of the province a population of New England origin, while in the east the people are generally of Scottish origin. These colonists in the east and west, differing from each other in many ways, but alike intelligent, moral, and thrifty, made a marked impress for good on the subsequent character of the province.

In 1755 many of the Acadians fled to the north side of the Bay of Fundy, some of them settling near Fort La Tour at the mouth of the St. John, others at St. Anne's and Jemseg. Acadian settlements were also formed on the Miramichi, Nepisiquit, and the Restigouche. During the late war attempts were made to expel them. Fort La Tour was captured, and its name was changed to Fort Frederick. The poor Acadians were greatly harassed, and in some cases they were driven from their settlements, but for the most part they still remained in the country. In 1765 an important colony of about eight hundred people from Massachusetts settled on the St. John River. Three years after, their settlement was formed into the County of Sunbury, with the privilege of sending one member to the Assembly at Halifax.

The County of Sunbury, 1765.

As already stated, the Island of St. John (Prince Edward) formed a part of the territory ceded to Great Britain by the Treaty of Paris. As the island

now comes into prominence it demands a place in our story. The name St. John is said to have been given to it by Champlain. *The Island of St. John.*
For a hundred and fifty years the island received little attention. In 1663 it was granted to a French captain named Doublet, who made it headquarters of his fisheries in the Gulf of St. Lawrence. But the fishermen had no thought of settling here; they simply had little huts at certain harbours where they cured their fish, and they came and went as suited their business. Not until the Treaty of Utrecht had given Nova Scotia to Great Britain was the island regarded as a suitable place for settlement. Some of the Acadians, preferring their old flag, now crossed the strait and made their home here. As the soil was found to be fertile and the climate agreeable, the French people were attracted to the island from time to time as the years went by. But the great accession to the population was in 1755, on the occasion of the capture of Beauséjour and the expulsion of the Acadians from Nova Scotia. The population was now increased to about four thousand. The island had its Governor, whose headquarters were at Fort La Joye, near the site of the present city of Charlottetown. As already stated, this fort was taken by the English after the second capture of Louisburg, and the whole island then fell to Great Britain. Shortly after the Treaty of Paris the island was placed under the Government of Nova Scotia. But in the meantime nearly all the French people had moved away, so that there were now only about one hundred and fifty inhabitants remaining.

By order of the British Government the Island of

St. John was divided into Townships or Lots, of which there were sixty-seven. These townships were given to certain officers of the army, and other persons, who were thought to have claims on the Government for some service rendered. To prevent disputes and charges of partiality, the distribution was made by drawing numbers from the ballot-box, thus determining by lot the division each should have. Certain conditions were specified on which the lands were to be held. The grantees were, within ten years, to settle at least one inhabitant for every two hundred acres of land. These settlers were to be Protestants, and they were not to be taken from the British Isles. Thus did the Government guard against depleting the population at home. After the first five years the proprietors were to pay to the Government a rental or tax known as quit-rent. The conditions were in very few cases carried out. At the end of ten years forty-eight of the sixty-seven lots had no settlement. This disposal of the island resulted in a system of non-resident landlords, which afterwards caused much trouble.

Very soon the proprietors, many of whom were men of influence, began to petition the King for a separation of the Island of St. John from the Government of Nova Scotia. This was done in 1770, when it was formed into a distinct province, with Walter Patterson, one of the proprietors, as its first Governor. At this time there were but five resident proprietors in the province, and the total number of inhabitants was about two hundred. The first Assembly was elected in 1773.

The Island made a separate Province. 1770.

In the summer preceding the restoration of peace

LAYING NEW FOUNDATIONS.

the French took St. John's, the capital of Newfoundland, and held it about three months.
When the news of the capture reached Halifax, the wildest alarm seized the people lest the enemy should attack Nova Scotia. Councils of war were held, forts were repaired, martial law was proclaimed, and the militia were brought from the country to defend the capital. The panic extended to the country. Many Acadians who were employed in repairing the dikes in Annapolis, Cornwallis, and Horton, were seized and sent to Halifax as prisoners. These, together with other Acadians brought from different parts of the province, were sent to Boston. The Governor of Massachusetts would not allow them to land, but ordered that they be sent back to Nova Scotia. They were kept some time as prisoners in Halifax, when some of them were sent to the West Indies. Suspicion of the Acadians, however, gradually died away, and in 1764, by order of the King, they were permitted, on taking the oath of allegiance, to settle on lands granted to them in various parts of the province. Many descendants of the old Acadians now live in Nova Scotia, and they are as loyal to the British Crown as are their neighbours of other races.

An Alarm, 1762

CHAPTER XVII.

THE AMERICAN REVOLUTION.

AT the close of the war with France, Great Britain had an unbroken territory along the Atlantic from Newfoundland to Georgia.

British American Colonies in 1763.

There were in all seventeen colonies, each having its own government: Newfoundland, St. John's Island, Nova Scotia, Quebec, Massachusetts, New Hampshire, Rhode Island, Connecticut, New York, New Jersey, Pennsylvania, Delaware, Maryland, Virginia, North Carolina, South Carolina, and Georgia. The "Peace of Paris" seemed to have settled the long-disputed question of empire in North America and to have made Great Britain mistress of the Continent. But George III. had not ceased to rejoice over his conquests when the last-named thirteen colonies rose in rebellion and claimed their independence. In fact it was the completeness of his victory which opened the way for rebellion and made the independence of these provinces possible. With hostile French and Indians beside them, ever ready to invade their homes, they could rightly value their connection with Great Britain; but now when there was no enemy to fear, they could lightly cut themselves loose from the mother-land.

At the time of the rebellion, or the "American

THE AMERICAN REVOLUTION. 183

Revolution," as it is called, the Government of Great Britain was not wisely directed. George III. was honest and wanted to do his duty; but in his narrow-mindedness and obstinacy he had surrounded himself with ministers who were ready to advise the course which he desired. Moreover, by some means, perhaps not always honest, his ministers found parliaments foolish enough to carry out their measures. One blunder followed another, until half a continent was lost to the empire. *Conditions.*

Principles of government were not then so well understood in Great Britain as they are at present. The policy of the times favoured restriction. Especially were the colonies hampered in matters of trade and manufacture. They were prohibited from trading directly with foreign countries, but were required to import tea, sugar, spices, and other articles of foreign production from Great Britain. This not only caused delay, but greatly increased the cost of the goods. It also led to smuggling, and this again to seizure of merchandise and vessels by Government officers. The owners of smuggled goods often resisted the officers, and unseemly riots occurred. In order to protect the industries of England the colonists were not allowed to manufacture certain articles. *Restrictions.*

The indignation of the colonies was aroused most of all by the taxes imposed on them by the British Government. Perhaps they did not fully consider the fact that Great Britain had spent vast sums of money for their protection and defence, or that the people of the British Isles were now heavily taxed to raise money for the payment of the nation's debts thus incurred. To some *Taxes without Representation.*

minds it did not seem unreasonable that the colonists should bear a portion of the burden. The tax in itself was not oppressive, but the colonists objected to the authority through which it was imposed rather than to the amount. They held that British subjects should not be taxed by a legislature in which they had no representation. The principle was an important one and was worth contending for, but perhaps with a little more patience the colonists could have secured their rights without rushing into civil war. Many people in England, including distinguished statesmen, disapproved of the tax.

The first burden of this kind was that imposed in 1765 by the Stamp Act, by which it was provided that certain legal documents, as drafts and notes of hand, must be written on paper with a Government stamp affixed to render them valid. The excitement was not at first very general. A few hot-headed men made a great ado. They said this was only the thin end of the wedge; more oppressive measures would follow; soon they and their children would be reduced to slavery. The feeling was most intense in Boston, New York, and Philadelphia. The church bells were tolled, flags were hung at half-mast, and in some instances those appointed to sell stamped paper were so roughly treated that they were forced to resign their offices.

The British Parliament repealed the Stamp Act, **The Boston Tea Party.** but passed another Act equally offensive. A small duty was placed on tea, glass, paints, and some other articles, and the amount thus raised was applied to the payment of the salaries of judges and other public officers. The colonists now resolved that they would not use articles on which duty was imposed by the British Parliament. King George's ministers would gladly have got out of the difficulty, but they had asserted the right of the Government to impose taxes on the colonies, and it seemed humiliating to recede from the position they had taken. They accordingly removed the duty from everything but tea, on which five cents per pound were required to be paid. People then, as now, were fond of tea, and they would use it so long as they could obtain it. But the leaders of the opposition were determined. A ship laden with tea arrived in Boston, and they decided that the cargo should not be landed. Accordingly about fifty men, disguised as Indians, went on board and threw the tea into the harbour. The British Government retaliated by closing the port of Boston, allowing no vessels to load or unload in its harbour. The custom-house was removed to Salem.

A convention, called the "Continental Congress," composed of delegates from the disturbed provinces, met at Philadelphia to discuss their grievances and to resolve on some course of action. *The Continental Congress, 1774.* A memorial was sent to the King, expressing loyalty, recounting grievances, and asking redress. The Congress also sent letters to the Provinces of Quebec and Nova Scotia, asking them to unite in the movement against the British Government. The letter addressed to the people of Quebec tried to excite ill feeling by showing the injustice of the Quebec Act in not giving them a representative Assembly.

There was little thought in England of any general

rising in the colonies, and no measures were taken against such an emergency. The first hostilities occurred near Boston. The Governor of Massachusetts, learning that arms and ammunition had been stored at Concord by opponents of the Government, sent a body of men by night to seize these military stores. The movement was to be kept secret, but in some way knowledge of it got abroad. As the soldiers returned to Boston they were attacked all along the way and many of them were killed. A little later in the same year the historic forts of Ticonderoga and Crown Point, on Lake Champlain, were seized by a small body of colonists collected in Vermont under Ethan Allen and Seth Warner. Thus began the Revolutionary War, which lasted six years.

<small>The War begins, 1775.</small>

The letter addressed to the people of Quebec failed to secure the desired result, and it was determined to try the effect of armed forces. There was probably little thought that much fighting would be required. The Congress believed that Canada would be ready to make common cause with the other provinces if a little encouragement were given to start the movement. Two invading forces were accordingly sent into the country by different routes. Benedict Arnold set out from Casco Bay, proceeding through the forests by way of the Kennebec, Lake Megantic, and the Chaudière, to Quebec. General Schuyler advanced against Montreal by way of Lake Champlain. Schuyler soon retired from the command, and was succeeded by General Montgomery. The movement against Canada was bold, even rash, and yet there were conditions which warranted some hope of success. The French

<small>Invasion of Canada, 1775</small>

inhabitants at this time could not be supposed to have any great love for Great Britain or for British institutions; the English-speaking inhabitants were mostly from the revolting provinces, and being dissatisfied with the Quebec Act, many of them were disposed to favour the rebellion. The regular troops in the province, on whom alone Great Britain could depend, did not exceed eight hundred men.

Montgomery proceeded along Lake Champlain and down the Richelieu. Two strong positions, Chambly and St. John's, were on his route. Chambly should not have been easily taken, but for some cause not very clear it soon surrendered. St. John's held out nobly for a time, but was forced to yield. Governor Carleton was in command at Montreal. He had both courage and ability, but he lacked means of defence, and he saw that effort to hold the place would be useless. He accordingly decided to withdraw with the few troops he had to Quebec. He had eleven vessels. Embarking with his men, he proceeded down the river. On the following day Montgomery took possession of Montreal. A few days later the inhabitants, learning that Montreal had been abandoned by Carleton, sent delegates to Montgomery, placing themselves in his hands. *Seizure of Montreal.*

Arriving at Sorel, on the St. Lawrence, Carleton found his way blocked by batteries of provincial forces on the Island of St. Ignace. Whatever might befall his vessels, or even his men, it was of the utmost consequence that he should reach Quebec in safety. On him chiefly depended the defence of the province. Accordingly, under cover of the night, he moved down the river *Carleton's Narrow Escapes.*

in a small boat propelled by muffled oars. As he approached the island, his men dropped their oars and used instead the palms of their hands, and thus softly he stole past the batteries. At Three Rivers he learned that another danger lay in his way—a provincial force was encamped at Point-aux-Trembles. He hastened forward, however, reaching Quebec in safety. His vessels and men that he left at Sorel fell into the hands of the enemy. Much excitement was prevailing in the city when Carleton arrived. After six weeks' march through the forests, Arnold had unexpectedly made his appearance before its walls and demanded its surrender. His summons had received no answer, and he had thought it advisable before taking further action to wait for Montgomery. It was Arnold's encampment which Carleton had passed at Point-aux-Trembles.

Great Britain now held Canada by a slender thread. **A Feeble Hold.** The English-speaking inhabitants were for the most part disloyal; the French peasantry were disposed to be neutral, scarcely knowing on which side were their friends. As a rule the higher classes of the French people and the clergy were loyal. Of the chief places in the province the city of Quebec, which was defended by a garrison of less than three hundred men, alone remained under British rule. There was disloyalty even here, and some of the inhabitants were urging surrender. Carleton promptly expelled all such persons from the city. He then strengthened his position in every possible way. The men of a war vessel in the harbour were brought in for the support of the garrison, and the crews of merchant vessels were impressed into service.

Volunteers from the French and English population increased the defending force to fifteen or sixteen hundred.

Embarking his soldiers in the vessels captured at Sorel, Montgomery proceeded to Quebec. He met Arnold near the city. It was now the month of December, and winter was setting in. The work demanded despatch. But Montgomery expected little trouble in taking the city. Indeed, he thought he had only to show himself before its walls and the joyful citizens would open their gates to receive him. He was surprised to find that his friends were all outside, and that the gates were locked against them. By the hands of an old woman he sent an impudent letter to Carleton, stating what evils would befall the city if resistance were attempted. His threats had no effect. Through the month of December, from the batteries which he had erected in the suburbs, he continued to bombard the Upper Town. Finally, on the morning of New Year's Day, before dawn, amid a driving snowstorm, an attempt was made to take the city by assault. While the batteries on the heights made pretence of attack on the Upper Town, Montgomery and Arnold tried to force an entrance into the Lower Town. Those who defended the city were ready to meet their assailants. Montgomery was killed, and his men fled in disorder, leaving his body to be covered by the falling snow. Arnold was wounded and was borne from the field. Some of his men, having forced their way into the city, after sharp fighting in the streets, were overpowered, and three hundred and forty of their number were taken prisoners.

Montgomery's Failure and Death.

Retreat of the Enemy. The besiegers remained before Quebec during the winter, but they made no further attempt to take the city. They suffered much from the severe cold, and many of them died of smallpox. Throughout the winter Carleton kept close within his walls. On the arrival of reinforcements in the spring he made a sortie on the enemy, who fled in confusion, leaving behind them their artillery, ammunition, and provisions. Congress, greatly desiring to hold its position in Canada, sent new relays of troops into the country. Three delegates from this body, one of whom was the distinguished Benjamin Franklin, came to Montreal for the purpose of gaining the friendship and co-operation of the Canadians. It was a fruitless mission. By the arrival of more troops under General Burgoyne early in the summer, the British forces in Canada were increased to between nine and ten thousand men. As this strong army ascended the St. Lawrence the invaders retreated, abandoning one post after another, until they made a final stand on Lake Champlain. At St. John's, on the Richelieu, through lack of means of transport, Carleton's progress in the pursuit was arrested for three months. Having built several vessels at this place, he followed the retreating foe to Lake Champlain, where, in a naval engagement, he gained a complete victory. Arnold abandoned Crown Point, and gathered all his forces at Ticonderoga. In the following summer he was compelled to yield this fort also. Thus ended the attempt to force Canada to join the revolting provinces.

During the war the coast settlements of Nova Scotia were kept in constant alarm by privateers from New England. Yarmouth, Annapolis, Cornwallis, Lunenburg, and the settlements at the mouth of the St. John were plundered by these freebooters. At Annapolis the invaders seized the block-house, spiked the cannon, and carried off whatever they found of value in the shops and dwellings. **Privateers and Plunderers.**

On the 4th of July 1776, the Congress at Philadelphia declared the revolting colonies independent of Great Britain, assuming for their country the name of the United States of America. But the struggle continued for several years. The leader in the revolution, and the man on whom its success largely depended, was George Washington. During the war he was commander-in-chief of the forces, and at its close he became the first President of the Republic. France was avenged on her great rival by sending aid to the rebellious colonies. King George III. was so resolutely set on subduing his disobedient subjects that for a long time he rejected all advice in favour of recognising their independence. But he finally yielded to public sentiment in England as expressed by the House of Commons. It has been estimated that Great Britain expended in the war $500,000,000 and lost fifty thousand men. **Independence of the United States recognised by Great Britain, 1783.**

CHAPTER XVIII.

THE UNITED EMPIRE LOYALISTS.

Condition of the Loyalists. THE treaty of peace between Great Britain and the United States was not very carefully drawn up. As we shall see later on, it left room for disputes in the matter of the boundary-line between the adjoining territories of the two nations. By some strange oversight, also, it failed to secure the rights of those persons in the United States who had throughout the war remained loyal to Great Britain. These people, who, on account of their desire to keep the empire from being broken up, were known as "United Empire Loyalists," were very badly treated by their fellow-countrymen. While those who rebelled against Great Britain took for themselves the name of patriots, they called the Loyalists Tories and traitors. The feeling against the Loyalists was even more bitter than against the British soldier who was sent into the country to put down the rebellion. For while the soldier was regarded as a tyrant's instrument of oppression, the Loyalist was treated as a despicable traitor to his country. His property was confiscated, and he was looked upon as an outcast. The great sacrifice made by these people rather than violate their sense of right entitles them to high rank on the roll of honour. Homeless, destitute, and per-

THE UNITED EMPIRE LOYALISTS.

secuted, they could now only turn for help to Great Britain. Among them were clergymen, judges, and others who had held high official positions before the war.

The British House of Commons voted a sum of money equal to about $16,000,000 for the relief of the Loyalists. Free grants of land were made in the Provinces of Nova Scotia and Quebec, two hundred acres being given to each Loyalist, and the same to each son on coming of age, and to each daughter on her marriage. The British Government also gave them farming tools, food, clothing, and other necessaries, and sent ships to convey to their new homes those who travelled by water. About thirty thousand people were thus provided for. Poor and dependent as they were, yet through their intelligence, social rank, and moral character they exercised an important influence in shaping the destiny of the provinces to which they emigrated. Sir Guy Carleton, the former Governor of Quebec, who commanded the British forces in New York at the close of the war, showed much interest in the Loyalists, and aided them greatly in their removal to Canada. Notwithstanding the care taken to provide for them, many of these people suffered greatly while making for themselves a new home in the wilderness

Aid for the Loyalists

About twenty thousand of these "Refugees," including disbanded soldiers, came to Nova Scotia. It is estimated that five thousand settled on the St. John River on the north of the Bay of Fundy. Of these the first arrived on the 18th of May 1783. The settlement at the mouth of the river was called Parrtown, in honour of Governor

Loyalist Settlements in Nova Scotia.

Parr of Nova Scotia. The largest colony of Loyalists in Nova Scotia was at Port Razoir, on the Atlantic coast. Previous to their arrival this place had few inhabitants; but it now suddenly became a city with a population of twelve thousand. Governor Parr visited the place and gave it the name of Shelburne, in honour of a British statesman of that name. Other Loyalists settled in various parts of Nova Scotia. Many also found homes in Cape Breton and in the Island of St. John.

With the exception of a few trading posts and forts here and there, the territory which now forms the Province of Ontario had up to this time remained unsettled. About ten thousand Loyalists, disbanded soldiers, and half-pay officers now made it their home. They settled chiefly along the Upper St. Lawrence, on the north of Lake Ontario, on the Niagara River, and on the Detroit. Some also made their home in that portion of the Province of Quebec now known as the Eastern Townships. Many of them came from New York, which, being held by Great Britain until the close of the war, became a place of refuge for the persecuted Loyalists. Their common route of travel to their new homes was by the Hudson River and its tributaries, some of them coming to Oswego and crossing Lake Ontario, others taking the lake at Sackett's Harbour, opposite Kingston. Thus the "Pilgrim Fathers" of Ontario, in the spirit of sacrifice for principle, laid the foundation of this great province. They still further showed their loyalty to George III. by naming their settlements for his children.

Loyalists in Ontario

Nor did Great Britain fail to provide for her faithful Indians of the "Six Nations." The Mohawks, who, with their distinguished chief, Joseph Brant, had been especially loyal, received large grants of land on the Bay of Quinte and on Grand River, where many of their descendants still reside. The Mohawk Church, built here in 1786, is said to have been the first church erected in Ontario.

Loyal Indians.

The Loyalists on the St. John soon became dissatisfied. They complained to Governor Parr that their lands had not been surveyed, and that they had not proper representation in the Assembly at Halifax. The Governor, in turn, blamed them for unwillingness to assist the surveyors, and he stated that his instructions from England disallowed any increase of members in the Assembly. Parr hoped to silence the grumbling by removing a few of the leaders to the south side of the Bay of Fundy. But the agitation went on until, in 1784, the British Government set off the territory on the north of the bay as a separate province, giving it the name of New Brunswick. The first Governor of the new province was Colonel Thomas Carleton. For two years he governed the province, with the aid of a Council of twelve members selected from the prominent Loyalists. In 1786 the first session of the representative Assembly of New Brunswick, consisting of twenty-six members, was held at Parrtown, the name of which had been changed to St. John. The second session also was held here, and then the seat of government was removed to St. Ann's (Fredericton).

The Province of New Brunswick, 1784.

The Island of Cape Breton also, having been a county of Nova Scotia for twenty years, was made a separate province. Its first Governor was Major Desbarres, who had fought under Wolfe at the siege of Quebec. Louisburg had hitherto been the capital of the island, but Desbarres founded a new capital on the east coast, naming it Sydney, in honour of Lord Sydney, the Colonial Secretary.

The Province of Cape Breton, 1784.

We left Sir Guy Carleton on Lake Champlain in 1776. To the surprise of almost every one, he was shortly after superseded in the command of the British forces by General Burgoyne. He was justly indignant at this mark of distrust, but he held the position of Governor until 1775. On his resignation at this date he was succeeded by General Haldimand. And now (1786), ten years after his faithful service in expelling the invaders of Canada, having been raised to the peerage as Lord Dorchester, he was appointed Governor-General and commander-in-chief of the British forces in North America. On his arrival at Quebec he was greeted with addresses of warmest welcome. Trusted by his Sovereign, and greatly admired by the people over whom he was placed, he continued for ten years to use his personal and official influence for the benefit of Canada. Previous to this date the governors of the different provinces held equal rank and authority. Lord Dorchester, as Governor of the Province of Quebec, was now given first rank, while the head-officers in the other provinces took the title and position of Lieutenant-Governor.

Lord Dorchester the Governor-General. 1786 1796.

The English inhabitants of Canada had never been satisfied with the Quebec Act. They wanted the English system of holding lands, of trial by jury, and of protection from imprisonment without trial secured by the old English Habeas Corpus Act. **Desire for Change.** Above all, they wanted the British system of making laws by a representative parliament. No doubt there was wisdom in retaining, for a while, in the Province of Quebec, the French laws and system of government. These laws were better suited to the condition of the French people, who, unaccustomed to independent action, trusted to the guidance and protection of their Seigniors. Now, as the English population had greatly increased, and the French people had become somewhat familiar with British institutions, there was a strong desire for change.

Another William Pitt, son of the War Minister of George II., was now Prime Minister of Great Britain. For the settlement of Canadian difficulties, he carried through Parliament a measure known as the "Constitutional Act." **The Constitutional Act, 1791.** This Act divided the old Province of Quebec into two provinces, called Upper Canada and Lower Canada. For the most part the Ottawa River formed the boundary between them. Each province was provided with a Governor, an Executive Council, and a Legislative Council, all appointed by the Crown, and also an Assembly elected by the people. A most important feature of the Act was the doing away with the test oath in Lower Canada, so that now Roman Catholics in that province were allowed to vote and hold public office. One-seventh of the public lands was set apart in both provinces for the support of the Protestant clergy. English criminal law was established in both provinces. In Upper Canada freehold tenure of lands was introduced; while in

Lower Canada French civil law, the seigniorial system of holding lands, and the old law of tithes and "accustomed dues" for the support of the Roman Catholic religion still remained in force. On the whole, the Constitutional Act was a great improvement on the Quebec Act, and for the time it gave fair satisfaction. Some of its provisions were, however, very ill-suited to a free people, and it cost much agitation and a disastrous civil war within the next half century to get rid of them. At the time, indeed, the English people in Lower Canada were strongly opposed to the Act, for it obliged them to submit to French laws and customs.

At the date of the division (1791), Lower Canada had a population of one hundred and thirty thousand; Upper Canada, of twenty-five thousand, a large proportion being United Empire Loyalists, or of Loyalist stock.

CHAPTER XIX.

THE BEGINNING OF PARLIAMENTARY GOVERNMENT.

HAVING no foreign enemies to fight and no external dangers to guard against, the people of the various provinces were able to give more attention to the development of the resources of the country. Many of the Loyalists, possessing intelligence and culture, exerted a good influence on public affairs and social life. Some of those who were elected to the Legislative Assemblies would have graced the parliaments of much older countries. There were among them men of thought and action, who were not disposed to let things drift. A natural result of increased intelligence and interest in public matters was frequent disturbance of the regular and placid movement of the machinery of government. The people began to think that they did not exist simply for the purpose of being governed, and their representatives began to claim their rights against governors and councils. There followed a state of unrest, a struggle of the new with the old. *Interest in Public Affairs.*

In all the provinces the form of government, modelled after that of Great Britain, was virtually the same. It comprised three departments—the *legislative* or law-making body, the *executive* or law-enforcing body, and the *judicial* department for trying and punishing law-breakers. The governor, appointed by the Government of Great Britain, represented the Sovereign. The parliament or legislative body comprised two houses, the legislative council and the house of assembly. The governor appointed the executive council, whose duty it was to advise him in regard to his official acts, although he was not bound to accept the advice of his council. The governor also appointed the legislative council, the judges, the sheriffs, the magistrates, and various other public officers. The members of the legislative council were usually selected from the most wealthy and influential class, and they held office for life. In most of the provinces the Anglican bishop and the chief justice were members of this council.

The Government and Legislature.

In the Maritime Provinces there was but one council with a double function, legislative and executive; that is, the members at one time acted as a part of the law-making machinery, and at another time as the governor's advisers. In Nova Scotia, at this early time, the assembly was elected for no definite period, but continued during the pleasure of the governor. The Assembly elected in 1770 was not dissolved until 1785, and is known as the "Long Parliament" of Nova Scotia. In 1792 an Act was passed limiting the term to seven years.

The revenue or public money of the provinces was derived from three principal sources — duties on certain classes of imports imposed by the Government of Great Britain, from the sale of Crown lands and royalty on minerals, and from duties on imports im-

BEGINNING OF PARLIAMENTARY GOVERNMENT. 201

posed by the provincial legislatures. The money arising from this last-named source was voted by the legislature for roads, bridges, and other public objects. The revenue of the two first-named sources, regarded as Crown funds, was expended by the governor and council, and was used chiefly to meet the expenses of government. When the fund was not sufficient for this purpose, the Government of Great Britain made up the deficit out of the imperial treasury. As the public officers were appointed by the governor, and drew their salaries from the Crown revenues, they were quite independent of the people and their representatives.

As reference will be made from time to time to the proceedings of legislatures, it may be well to explain some of the common rules of action in such bodies. **Parliamentary Customs.** When a House meets after an election it chooses one of its members to preside and maintain order. This officer is called the Speaker. After such election the choice is submitted to the governor for approval. A record of all business transacted is carefully written in books kept for the purpose, called the Journals. Care is used that business be done with due regard to system and with becoming deliberation. When a member wishes to introduce a measure, he asks leave of the House. Before a measure is agreed to by the House, it must come up and be voted on three several times, known as the first, the second, and the third reading. At these stages the measure is called a Bill. If the legislature is composed of two Houses, a Bill having passed one House, must go through the several stages of the other House. After it has passed through both

Houses, it requires the assent of the governor. As this assent is very rarely withheld, it has come to be regarded almost as a matter of form. When a Bill has thus passed through all its stages, it is called an Act, and it is part of the law of the country. When a House stops its proceedings, to resume business at another specified time, it is said to adjourn. The House has power to adjourn of its own motion. All the different meetings of a House from day to day, which are ended by adjournments, constitute a session. When the governor dismisses the House without naming any time for it to meet again, thus closing the session, he is said to prorogue the House. All unfinished business then counts for nothing, and Bills which have not passed their final stage, if brought up during another session, must be treated as new Bills. A representative assembly is supposed to carry out the wishes of the people whom it represents: hence if the governor has reason to believe that its sentiments and action are not in harmony with the views of the people, it becomes his duty, even though the full term for which the House was elected has not expired, to make arrangements for the election of a new House. He then dissolves the House: that is, he declares by proclamation that it has ceased to exist, and orders a new election.

Governor Wentworth. On the death of Governor Parr in 1791, Sir John Wentworth became Governor of Nova Scotia, which office he held for sixteen years. He was a man of unbending integrity; but, belonging to the old conservative school, he was much more inclined to uphold the power of the Council and the dignity of the Crown than to govern according to the wishes of the people as expressed by their representatives. He disliked popular assemblies and free discussions, fearing they would tend to revolution. During his rule the interests of country and city frequently came into conflict. The Assembly wished to use the public money on roads and bridges, so as to open up the country for settlement. The members of the Council, residing in Halifax and being independent of the people, cut down the amounts voted by the Assembly, preferring to spend the money on public buildings in Halifax and in large salaries. In these disputes Governor Wentworth supported the Council. William Cottnam Tonge, the leader of the popular party in the Assembly, by his opposition to the Governor's policy, made himself the object of his Excellency's resentment. Tonge was elected Speaker of the House; but Sir John, using a prerogative seldom exercised, refused to accept him, and the House was compelled to elect another Speaker. During Wentworth's term of office the fine stone edifice in Halifax known as "Government House" was built as the official residence of the Lieutenant-Governor of Nova Scotia. On retiring from office, Sir John was allowed a pension of £1000 sterling for life, paid in equal shares by the Governments of Great Britain and Nova Scotia. He died in Halifax in 1820, at the advanced age of eighty-four years. Wentworth was succeeded by Sir George Prevost, who laid the cornerstone of the Parliament building of Nova Scotia, known as the "Province Building." On the promotion of Sir George Prevost to the position of Governor-General, Sir John Cope Sherbrooke became Governor of Nova Scotia.

Royal Visitors. Two princes, sons of George III., visited Quebec and Halifax. Prince William Henry, Duke of Clarence, who held the position of captain in the royal navy, came first. He afterwards, as William IV., occupied the throne of Great Britain. Prince Edward, Duke of Kent, the father of Queen Victoria, came to Quebec in 1791, where for over two years he held command of his Majesty's troops. In 1794 he was removed to Halifax, where he filled the position of commander-in-chief of the British forces in America. Prince Edward was a great favourite with all classes of the community. He was strict in discipline, and he did much to break up the drinking and gambling habits which prevailed in the garrison at the time of his arrival. When off duty he was most affable and courteous. His favourite residence was the "Prince's Lodge," on the shore of Bedford Basin and about six miles from Halifax.

King's College. The founding of King's College at Windsor was an important event in the history of Nova Scotia. It was customary for young men seeking higher education to attend colleges in the United States. The Assembly, fearing they might become disloyal, resolved that the province should have a college of its own, and voted funds for that object. Aid was also obtained from England. The institution was opened in 1790, and a few years later it received a royal charter. Unfortunately, the usefulness of the college was limited by its sectarian rules. Its by-laws required all students to attend the Church of England, and all graduates to subscribe to the articles of that Church, and they forbade members of the University

BEGINNING OF PARLIAMENTARY GOVERNMENT. 205

frequenting Roman Catholic chapels, or the "meeting-houses" of Presbyterians, Baptists, Methodists, or the places of worship of other dissenters.

In the year 1796 about five hundred negroes, known as Maroons, were brought to Halifax from Jamaica, where for many years they had been causing much trouble. *The Maroons.* After remaining in the neighbourhood of Halifax for about four years, supported mainly by the Government of Jamaica, they were removed to Sierra Leone, in Africa.

The Province of New Brunswick grew steadily in wealth and population. Its leading industries — lumbering and shipbuilding — *New Brunswick.* rapidly developed, and both St. John and Miramichi became important centres of trade. In political matters the condition of the province much resembled that of Nova Scotia. Disputes between the two branches of the Legislature began early. The Council rejected a Bill providing for the payment to members of the Assembly of one dollar and a half per day during the session. The Assembly then placed the amount with the appropriations for roads and bridges and other public services. The Council rejected the whole Bill, and for three years no moneys were voted for any purpose. During twenty years Thomas Carleton held the office of Governor.

Meanwhile the current of affairs in the Island of St. John had not been running smoothly. *The Island of St. John.* During the American War, while Governor Patterson was in England, privateers from Massachusetts visited Charlottetown, plundered the town, and carried off the acting Governor and other officers of the Government. General Washington, much displeased with this action, released the prisoners, restored the property taken, and dismissed the officers who had committed the offence.

Serious trouble arose in the island over the non-payment of quit-rents. After much delay, Governor Patterson sold some lands of those in arrears. This would seem to be the proper thing to do; but as the lands sold for a small price, and the Governor was himself in some cases the purchaser, he gave his opponents an opportunity of making charges against him. The proprietors asserted that, owing to the disturbed state of affairs arising out of the American Revolution, they had not been able to carry out their plans of settlement, and petitioned the British Government to interfere in their behalf. The Government directed Governor Patterson to have a Bill passed by the island Legislature providing for the restoration of the lands and for certain modification in quit-rents. He failed to carry out these instructions, and when the island Assembly was about to investigate his irregular conduct, he dissolved the House. As the new House was pursuing the same course, he dissolved it also. Through the votes of the Loyalists who had recently settled in the country, and whose friendship he had won by giving them portions of the confiscated lands, he finally secured an Assembly favourable to himself. But he had given offence to the British Government, and he was soon after dismissed from office. The old proprietors, however, failed to recover their lands.

The inhabitants of the island had long been dissatisfied with its name. There were other places of similar name, and it was sometimes difficult to determine which was meant. The Legislature passed an Act changing the name of the island to New Ireland, but the British Government, according to a fashion it had in those days, disallowed the Act. In 1798, however, the Legislature passed an Act changing the name to Prince Edward Island, in honour of the popular Duke of Kent. This Act received the royal assent, and in the following year the name came into use. At this date, thirty years after their lands were granted, so greatly had the proprietors failed in their engagements, that twenty-three Townships had not a single inhabitant, and twelve others had a population of only about two hundred. In 1803 several hundred colonists, under direction of the Earl of Selkirk, came from Scotland and formed the beginning of important settlements.

The first Legislature of Lower Canada met in the city of Quebec in 1792. The English-speaking population had been considerably increased by the recent arrival of many Loyalists from the United States; but the French people still formed a very large proportion of the population of the country. As might be supposed, a large majority of the Assembly were French, while the Legislative and Executive Councils were chosen chiefly from the English-speaking inhabitants. Thus the conflict of race soon made its appearance in the Legislature, setting the two branches of this body in opposition to each other. The two Councils had very much more power in the management of public affairs than had the Assembly, so that the province was almost wholly under the control of the English minority. Lord Dorchester, while he held the office of Governor-

Lower Canada.

General, was disposed to favour the French, and to allow them a fair share in the government of the country. But under his successors a much less liberal policy was pursued. When the French complained of injustice, and criticised the action of the Government, they were charged by the English with disloyalty. The peace of the country was also disturbed by French agents from the United States, who tried to excite disaffection among the people towards Great Britain, and to awaken the hope that Canada would soon come again under French rule. This led to the making of stringent laws against foreigners and persons suspected of disloyalty.

Lord Dorchester finally left Canada in the summer of 1796. His successor was General Prescott, who held the office of Governor-General for eleven years. During the last eight years of his term he resided in England, and drew his salary of $10,000 a year, while the duties of his office were discharged by a Lieutenant-Governor.

In 1807 Sir James Craig succeeded to the office of Governor-General. The strife between the Governor and Council and the Assembly, already referred to, was greatly increased by his arbitrary manner. The Assembly wanted an elective Legislative Council in place of one appointed by the Crown, the exclusion of judges from the Legislature, and control of all the public funds. These demands at the present day would not be thought extreme or unreasonable; but the Governor and Council saw in them only the elements of disloyalty, sedition, and anarchy. The French, feeling that they were treated as an inferior people, in their opposition to the existing form of government, sometimes spoke severely of their English rulers, thereby incurring the suspicion of disloyalty.

The Assembly, determined on reform, by an almost unanimous vote, excluded judges from the Legislature; but the Council threw out the Bill. Later, when the Assembly brought in the Bill again, Sir James Craig, in the most arbitrary manner, dissolved the House, telling the members that they were wasting time in frivolous debates, and were not working for the good of the people. The disturbing questions were carried to the country; old members were returned, or those of more extreme views took their place. Among the new members was Louis Joseph Papineau, now about twenty years of age, who took a leading part in the rebellion of 1837. When the new Assembly proceeded to pass Bills which were displeasing to the Governor, he again dissolved the House. The newspapers on both sides published severe criticisms of their opponents, and their publishers were imprisoned for libel and violation of privilege. Several members of the Assembly were sent to prison for writing libellous articles against the Government. Acting on the advice of the British Government, Sir James finally assented to the Bill excluding judges from the Assembly.

But withal the country was making progress. Due chiefly to the enterprise of John Molson of Montreal, in 1799 steam navigation was introduced on the St. Lawrence. The *Accommodation*, running at the rate of four miles an hour, was the first boat placed on the route.

In the summer of 1811, owing to ill-health, Sir

James Craig was compelled to resign his position. Though he had little success in the matter of civil government, he was greatly respected, both on account of his ability as a soldier and for the noble qualities of his personal character. He was succeeded by Sir George Prevost, who was transferred from the government of Nova Scotia. Sir George spoke French as his native tongue, which made him popular with the French Canadians.

At this time the duties on goods imported into Upper and Lower Canada were collected in the latter province, forming a common fund, which was divided in the proportion of seven-eighths for Lower Canada and one-eighth for Upper Canada.

The new province of Upper Canada had a most prosperous beginning. This was largely due to its first Governor, Colonel John Graves Simcoe, a British officer who had won distinction in the American war. No more suitable choice could have been made for the work of organising the new province. Governor Simcoe was thoroughly devoted to the duties of his office. He made long and toilsome journeys by land and water through the forest country, forming plans for settlement and for the construction of public roads. Through his wise policy in offering free grants of land, many new settlers came in, so that during the four years of his rule the population of the province was more than doubled. The village of Newark or Niagara was chosen as the seat of government. The first Legislature of the province, comprising an Assembly of sixteen members and a Legislative Council of seven members, met here in 1792.

Among its early measures were the introduction of English law, trial by jury, and an Act for making and repairing public highways. During the next session of the Legislature in the following year, a law was enacted requiring that marriages be celebrated by a clergyman of the Church of England, or, if there was none within eighteen miles of the parties, the ceremony could be legally performed by a justice of the peace. Without effect the Presbyterians petitioned that their clergymen be authorised to celebrate the marriage ceremony. Governor Simcoe opposed the petition, remarking that it was "the product of a wicked head and a disloyal heart." The Act remained in force until 1830.

Governor Simcoe thought it unwise that the capital should be so near the United States frontier. He accordingly removed the seat of Government to York, or Toronto, as the place is now called, where the Legislature met in 1797. Two years earlier, before there was a house in the place, Governor Simcoe made his home in York, living for a short time under a canvas tent. After Simcoe left the province, there was sharp conflict between Assembly and Government. The strife was promoted by the rival newspapers, and the editor of the Assembly's paper was prosecuted for libel against the Government, and thrown into prison.

After Simcoe the office of Lieutenant-Governor was held in succession by General Hunter and Francis Gore. One of the greatest obstacles to the progress of the country at this period was the want of roads and of communication between the scattered settlements. The province was also isolated in great degree from the outside world. A letter was a month in travelling from Montreal to Toronto, and four or five months from Halifax to Toronto.

Shortly after Governor Simcoe left the province, quarrels began between the Governor and Council on the one hand, and the Assembly on the other. The members of the Council managed affairs pretty much as they pleased, and it was charged against them that they enriched themselves and their friends at the expense of the province.

In 1811 Governor Gore obtained leave of absence, and did not return to the province until 1818.

Customs and Social Condition. It is difficult for the people of the present day to picture the conditions under which lived their forefathers of this early time. As there were no roads, the early settlements were along the sea-coast, or by lake or river. The first roads were not always smooth enough for wheels, but were mere paths through the forests, and those who journeyed inland went on foot or on horseback. Sometimes the father, mother, and two or three children were all mounted on one horse. The pioneer settler found no fields ready for tillage, but only a dense unbroken forest. Selecting a suitable site, he built his house of logs rudely squared with his axe. The chinks between the logs he stopped with clay mortar. In clearing his land, he first cut down the trees and burned off the light brushwood. Then came the hard labour of removing the heavy timber. But the men of these early times had a way of lightening toil and at the same time securing social enjoyment. They turned work into play in the "piling frolic" or "logging bee," as it was called

BEGINNING OF PARLIAMENTARY GOVERNMENT. 213

in some parts of the country, at which all the men gathered in a neighbour's "burnt land," rolled the blackened logs into huge heaps, and burned them to ashes. The farmers made their own carts, sleds, harrows, and other wooden implements; while indoors the women carded and spun the wool, and wove the yarn into strong homespun, which they made into clothing for the household. The kitchen had a broad open fireplace with a swinging iron crane, from which, on "pot-hooks and trammels," were suspended the pots and kettles for cooking the family meals. Through the long cold winter the fireplace was supplied with abundance of fuel from the neighbouring forest. In the rear was placed the huge back log, while smaller sticks, resting on andirons, or on long narrow stones instead, were piled up in front. Before the blazing fire on Christmas day and on other festal occasions, the goose or turkey, or perhaps the small pig, suspended by hempen cord from a beam, was kept ever whirling round by some attentive hand, until all sides were alike roasted, crisp and brown.

In these early times there were no friction matches, such as are now used in lighting a fire. At night a hard-wood brand, all aglow, was carefully covered over with ashes to protect it from the air, and in the morning there remained a bed of coals to start the new fire with. Sometimes, however, the brand burned out, and not a spark remained. Fire was then obtained by striking a flint sharply with a bar of steel; or the children were sent to the nearest neighbour's to "borrow" fire.

Ministers of religion travelled long distances to visit their people in the remote and scattered hamlets.

This visit was an event of much importance, and was taken advantage of for the christening of the children of the household, and often, too, for the performing of the marriage ceremony between those about to establish homes of their own.

There was little money in circulation in these early days, and everything was paid for in produce from the farm. The farmer exchanged his wheat, oats, butter, and cheese with the merchant for tea, sugar, molasses, or other articles needed for the household. The stipends of the minister and the schoolmaster were paid in the same way.

A few years later, when the cities had become somewhat populous, and the roads passable for wheels, the farmer carried his fattened pigs and sheep, his butter, cheese, socks, and other home produce to the distant city market. Here he sold his stuff for cash, perhaps all he handled during the whole year.

CHAPTER XX.

THE WAR OF 1812.

AT the beginning of the nineteenth century throughout all the provinces was heard the rough voice of political strife. On the one side the governors and councils believed that they were struggling to resist the tide of anarchy and rebellion; on the other the assemblies were as sure that they were fighting the monster of tyranny and oppression. Order seemed to be the watchword of the one; liberty, of the other. The real question at issue was, Shall the people rule, or shall an oligarchy? State of Affairs.

But now, for a time, disputes between councils and assemblies were silenced by the harsher tumult of war. For several years Canada had been disquieted by rumours of war; but the British Government, when appealed to for aid, had told her that there was no danger. Even after the declaration of war by the United States against Great Britain in June 1812, it was still believed that the difficulty would be settled by diplomacy, and not until three months later did the British Government issue its declaration of war.

Although Canada had given no offence and had done nothing to bring about the war, she had to bear its chief burdens and calamities. The conflict was mainly on Canadian soil, and while it lasted, a period of nearly three years, the people of Canada, almost unaided, were required to repel the invaders from their homes. The country was ill-prepared for war. The total population of the British provinces did not exceed four hundred thousand, whereas that of the United States was eight millions. The regular British troops in the country numbered about four thousand five hundred. Canada had a long border-line to defend, she had little facility for moving forces and supplies, and her treasury was empty. She had, however, the strength that belongs to him "who hath his quarrel just." Her people were fighting for their homes and their hearths. Right nobly did United Empire Loyalists and French Canadians show their patriotism and their valour. The Indians, too, throwing themselves into the struggle, but with less barbarity than had been their wont, by their fidelity and their courage proved themselves worthy of a home on Canadian soil.

It is not easy to find good and sufficient cause for this war. Great Britain did not desire it, for her resources had been seriously taxed by a European war which had been going on for several years. Many people in the United States were opposed to the war, and they said it was unjust. True, in some parts of the country there was great rejoicing over the declaration of war, but in the Northern and New England States much dissatisfaction prevailed. In Boston flags on the vessels in the harbour were hung at half-mast as an expression of displeasure.

Causes of the War

The war was brought about by incidents arising out of the disturbed condition of European affairs. Napoleon I., Emperor of France, had conquered one country after another until he had brought nearly all Europe under his power. Great Britain, standing alone in resisting him, seemed the only obstacle in his way. He sometimes thought of invading her shores; but her insular position, fortified harbours, matchless fleets, and brave warriors presented difficulties which he did not care to cope with. President Madison of the United States, and the Democratic party, which was then in power, favoured Napoleon, and used every means in their power to awaken hostile feeling against Great Britain.

Great Britain was then, as she is now, a great commercial nation, and Napoleon thought if he could destroy her trade, he would weaken her power. Accordingly he published his famous Berlin Decree, forbidding neutral ships to enter British ports. To meet this Great Britain issued similar decrees, known as Orders in Council, by which neutral ships were forbidden to enter the ports of France or of her allies. Any merchant vessels found violating the Orders were seized by the warships sent to blockade the coast. The people of the United States were very angry over these measures, which excluded their ships from most of the harbours of Europe. There was, however, much inconsistency in the way they looked at matters; for while they were enraged at Great Britain, they showed little resentment towards France.

There was also another alleged cause of war. When British vessels entered the ports of the United States it was very common for their sailors, induced by larger pay, to desert. By pretending to be citizens of the United States they defeated legal action taken to compel them to return to their ships. Great Britain then took the matter into her own hands, and authorised her warships to search United States vessels on the high seas for these deserters and take them by force. Such a course at the present day would be regarded as very offensive and good cause of resentment, but at that time it was not contrary to international law. In 1807 a case of this kind occurred which caused a great sensation. The British ship *Leopard* overhauled the United States ship *Chesapeake* off the coast of Virginia. The American captain refusing to allow his ship to be searched, the *Leopard* fired upon him, killing four men and wounding several others. Four deserters were taken from the *Chesapeake* and carried off by the British. Great Britain afterwards apologised for this act, and made compensation to the families of the men who were killed, but she still allowed the practice of search.

By way of retaliation against Great Britain and France, Congress placed an embargo on vessels, forbidding them to leave United States ports. This, which meant refusal to trade with foreign nations, did more harm to the United States than to the offenders. It was specially injurious to the people of the New England States, who owned many trading vessels. Then Congress repealed the Embargo Act and passed the Non-Intercourse Act, forbidding her ships to enter the ports of Great Britain or France. Napoleon now resorted to a trick. He publicly announced that he had revoked the Berlin Decrees, but he secretly instructed his officials to go on as before seizing foreign vessels. The United States Government, supposing that Napoleon was acting in good faith, repealed the Non-Intercourse Act as regarded its application to France. United States vessels thereupon resumed trade at French ports, but after a little, by Napoleon's order, they were seized and made the property of France. France thus gave much more cause of offence than Great Britain, but she had no colonies lying near as convenient objects of attack. The fact is, the war party in the United States thought that Great Britain's strength was taxed to the utmost in her wars with Napoleon, and they expected to make an easy conquest of Canada. Indeed, in the United States there was, no doubt, much misunderstanding as to public feeling in the provinces. Domestic quarrels between assemblies and governors were understood to mean disloyalty to Great Britain. The opinion prevailed that a United States army would be welcomed in Canada as a messenger of liberty. Indeed, many of our neighbours across the border can scarcely yet believe that Canadians feel that they are a free people in the full enjoyment of self-government, or that they are not longing to break the ties which bind them to England. Fascinated by the name and form of a republic, they seem quite unable to understand that the Government at Ottawa is more fully and more readily responsive to the will of the people than is that at Washington.

There was yet another matter which strengthened hostile feeling. The embargo on ships ordered by Congress in 1807 gave so much offence to the people of New England that they talked of withdrawing from the Union. Sir James Craig, who was then Governor-General of Canada, sent an agent named Henry to Boston to gain information in regard to the state of public feeling in that city, thinking that this would help him to judge of the possibility of war. Several years had now passed since this took place. But Henry, not receiving as much for his services as he demanded, went to Washington and sold Craig's letters bearing on the matter to the President, receiving, it is said, $10,000 for the correspondence. No facts of much importance were disclosed, but the publication of the story made a great sensation.

During the war Sir George Prevost held the office of Governor-General and commander-in-chief of the forces. He was not distinguished as a military officer, but he was popular among the French Canadians. He was very successful in raising a militia force of French and English for the defence of the country. Among the French officers deserving of notice was Colonel de Salaberry. This

DE LA SALABERRY

brave officer had been the object of kindly interest on the part of Prince Edward, Duke of Kent, and he had seen much service in various parts of the world. He was now appointed to the command of a regiment of Canadian voltigeurs. In Upper Canada, during the first year of the war, General Sir Isaac Brock, the acting Governor, was in chief command. He was a beautiful character, estimable in private life, and distinguished both as a civil and military officer. Prudent in counsel, brave, energetic, and prompt in action, he was by far the ablest officer in the army. Others deserving of mention were Tecumseh, chief of the Shawnees, and Colonel John Harvey.

MAJOR-GENERAL BROCK

In describing the officers of the United States army, one of their own historians says: "As a class they were old, vain, respectable, and incapable."

Success at the beginning of the war gave our people assurance. Fort Machillimackinac, which commanded the entrance to Lake Michigan, was captured without loss of a man by a small Canadian force. This victory had an important effect in securing the confidence and aid of the Indians. The first hostile movement of the enemy was an invasion of the western peninsula of Upper Canada. General Hull, at the head of two thousand five hundred men, crossing the Detroit River from Michigan, issued a boastful proclamation, stating that he had an army which "would look down all opposition," and offering freedom from British tyranny to all who would accept his protection. General Brock, setting out from York with a force of seven hundred men, regulars and militia, marched against him. On the way he was joined by six hundred Indians under their chief Tecumseh. Without waiting to prove the valour of his men, Hull hastily retreated, and took shelter behind the fortifications of Detroit. On Brock's demand, without striking a blow, he gave up the town, all his military stores, and his entire army. General Hull, his officers, and his regular soldiers, over a thousand men in all, were sent as prisoners of war to Montreal. The militia were allowed to return to their homes. Leaving General Procter in command at Detroit, Brock proceeded to the Niagara frontier.

Machillimackinac and Detroit.

During the war the Niagara district was the scene of many stirring events. The Niagara River, which flows northerly from Lake Erie to Lake Ontario, is about thirty-four miles in

The Niagara Frontier.

length. At the foot of Lake Erie, on the Canadian side, in 1812, was the strongly stockaded Fort Erie. Nearly opposite, in the United States, was Buffalo, a town of five hundred inhabitants. About two miles down the river, on the same side, was the village of

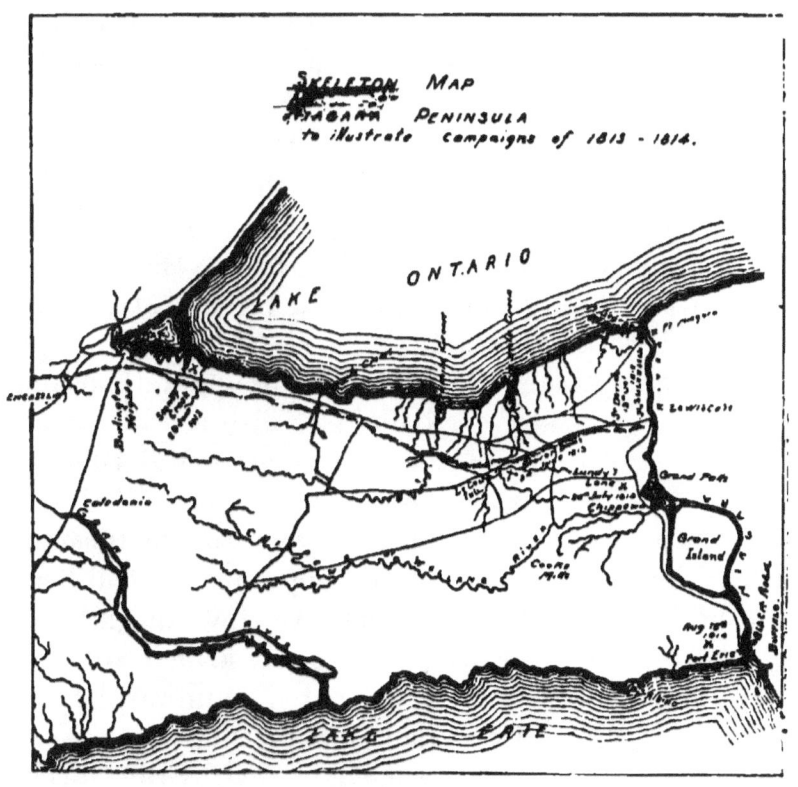

NIAGARA DISTRICT.

Black Rock. Four or five miles farther down, the river is divided by Grand Island, below which, on the Canadian side, where the Chippewa enters the Niagara, was the village of Chippewa. Still farther on, nearly opposite the Falls, was Lundy's Lane. Below the

Falls the river flows through a chasm for about six miles to a point where the highlands abruptly end in rocky cliffs. At this point, ages ago, were Niagara Falls, but slowly the water has worn away the rock, until now the great cataract is removed six miles up the river. Here, on the low plain just under the cliffs, which rise to the height of three hundred and fifty feet, on the Canadian shore, was the village of Queenston. Directly opposite, in the United States, was Lewiston. At the mouth of the river, six miles from Queenston, stretching along the shore of Lake Ontario, was Newark, or Niagara, the first capital of Upper Canada. On the river close by was the strongly fortified Fort George, and across the river, nearly opposite, stood Fort Niagara.

The Enemy along the Niagara. The enemy had collected seven or eight thousand men at Fort Niagara, Lewiston, Buffalo, and other points on the Niagara. Major-General Renssalaer was in command. With the object of making an assault on Queenston, he took up his position at Lewiston, directly opposite. He had here nine hundred regulars and over two thousand militia. The latter, undrilled, half clad, badly armed, without ammunition, and cowardly, presented an unwarlike appearance. While Renssalaer was getting them ready for war, a brief armistice was concluded by the Governor-General of Canada and General Dearborn, chief officer of the United States forces. This came about by reason of the withdrawal of the Orders in Council by Great Britain. As the Orders had been a chief cause of offence to the United States, these officers thought the war might be ended at once. President Madison thought otherwise, and sent instructions to resume hostilities.

The Canadian frontier of the Niagara was defended by about fifteen hundred men. Of these, about three hundred were at Queenston. General Brock was at Fort George with the troops he had brought from Detroit. His position was embarrassing. Subject to the Governor-General as his superior officer, who counselled strictly defensive action, he could only await the enemy's movements, which he supposed were designed against Fort George. But Renssalaer's purpose was to take Queenston, and make it the base of further action in Canada.

The Battle of Queenston, October 1812.

A dark night in October was chosen by the enemy for the capture of Queenston. About one thousand men crossed over, effected a landing, and took possession of the heights overlooking the village. There followed a desperate struggle. General Brock, at Fort George, heard the roaring of the cannon, and rode in all haste to the scene of the conflict. Rallying the forces and inspiring them with his own eager enthusiasm, he led them on to victory. For a time the result was doubtful; but General Sheaffe, arriving with reinforcements from Fort George, turned the scale. Queenston Heights were recaptured, and the enemy were utterly routed. Some of them, in trying to escape, rushed down the steep river-banks, and were killed by falling on the rocks, or were drowned in the attempt to swim across the river. Over nine hundred were taken prisoners. Meanwhile the great body of the United States army stood on the opposite shore, refusing to cross the river. Their courage had fled, and they said that, being militia, they would repel invasion, but that they could not be forced to

P

go out of their own country. The Canadian victory was dearly bought. While in the thickest of the fight, urging on his brave volunteers, Brock fell mortally wounded. His aide-de-camp, the valiant Colonel M'Donnell, was also killed a little later in the battle. The Brock Monument on Queenston Heights marks the hero's burial-place, and perpetuates the loving regard with which his memory is cherished. General Sheaffe succeeded Brock in the government of Upper Canada and in the command of the forces.

Meanwhile General Dearborn, with an army of ten thousand, known as the "Army of the North," was advancing into Canada by way of Lake Champlain. He was met by Canadian militia, who obstructed his progress by felling trees and forming abattis across his line of march. Some skirmishing took place near Odelltown. The enemy forded the river Lacolle in two divisions at different points. Night coming on, the two divisions met in the darkness, and, mistaking friends for foes, they fired upon each other. Finally, Dearborn retired, and went into winter quarters at Plattsburg and Burlington.

The Army of the North.

The first year's campaign gave the Canadians little cause for discouragement or self-distrust. They had more than held their own in the quarrel which had been forced upon them by their big neighbour. Strange to say, in the various engagements on the sea during the year Great Britain was less successful. Several British ships were captured by the Americans.

Summary.

During the second year of the war the Canadians suffered serious reverses on the lakes and in the upper province. They were at great disadvantage from lack of supplies and means of transport. Food was scarce, especially in Upper Canada. Salt pork and hard biscuit for the army were imported from Great Britain. Beef, cattle, and other supplies were brought over from Vermont; for, notwithstanding the war, the farmers across the line

The War continued, 1813.

LAKE COUNTRY AND WESTERN FORTS.

were glad to sell their produce to our people. These supplies were taken up the St. Lawrence from Montreal on flat boats in summer and on sleds in winter. This work was slow and toilsome, and it was attended with danger from the enemy, whose country lay along the south of the river. The industries of Canada were interrupted, and much property was destroyed.

The men were drawn away for the defence of the country, and the women had to work the farms. In many a home there was mourning for lost ones, either killed in the war, or taken prisoners and lodged in jails in the United States.

Great Britain, still engaged in European wars, could send little aid. In the depth of winter, however, a regiment of British soldiers marched on snow-shoes through the forests from Fredericton to Quebec, being nearly a month on the journey. One of the earliest events of the year was the capture of Ogdensburg by Colonel M'Donnell.

Command of the Great Lakes was a matter of the highest importance in the war. During the winter, while our officers were doing little, the enemy were active in building vessels and in drilling their men. Early in the spring Commodore Chauncey of the United States navy, sailing from Sackett's Harbour with fourteen armed vessels and over two thousand men, appeared before York. This place, then the capital of the province, since become the large city of Toronto, was at that time but a small town of a thousand inhabitants. It was defended by about six hundred men under General Sheaffe, the Governor of the province. There was some sharp fighting, but Sheaffe soon gave up the unequal contest and retired with his troops, leaving a subordinate officer to treat with the enemy. As the United States troops were entering the fort, the powder magazine blew up, killing over two hundred of them, including General Pike. Many of the retiring garrison also were killed. The enemy, after pillaging private houses and burning the public

Capture of York.

buildings, seized such military stores as remained, and sailed away for Niagara. General Sheaffe showed such incapacity in the defence of York that he was removed from his command, and Major-General de Rottenburg was appointed in his place.

Chauncey now sailed for Fort George, on the Niagara. General Vincent, the British officer in command, with a thousand men, could scarcely hope to hold the fort against an army of six thousand, supported by a strong fleet. After a severe struggle and heavy loss, he spiked his guns, blew up the fort, and retired to Beaver Dams, sixteen miles distant. Having collected the forces from different points along the Niagara, he made an orderly retreat to Burlington Heights, near where the city of Hamilton now stands. The whole Niagara frontier was thus given up to the enemy. *The Niagara Frontier given up to the Enemy.*

Vincent was closely followed by the United States Generals Winder and Chandler, with an army more than double his own. Learning that his pursuers were carelessly encamped at Stony Creek, six or seven miles distant, he sent Colonel Harvey with seven hundred men to surprise them by a night attack. Stealing along softly at midnight, the Canadians, with fixed bayonets, sprang suddenly upon their foes, and scattered them in utter confusion. Not wishing to expose the smallness of his force, Harvey withdrew before daylight, taking with him over a hundred prisoners, including both generals. We shall meet this gallant officer again as Sir John Harvey, Governor of New Brunswick, and, still later, of Nova Scotia. *Stony Creek.*

A small detachment of Vincent's army under Lieutenant Fitzgibbon was stationed at Beaver Dams. General Dearborn sent a force of six or seven hundred men to take the little party by surprise. A militiaman named Secord, living at Queenston, who was disabled by a wound, by chance heard of the expedition. His heroic wife at once set

Beaver Dams.

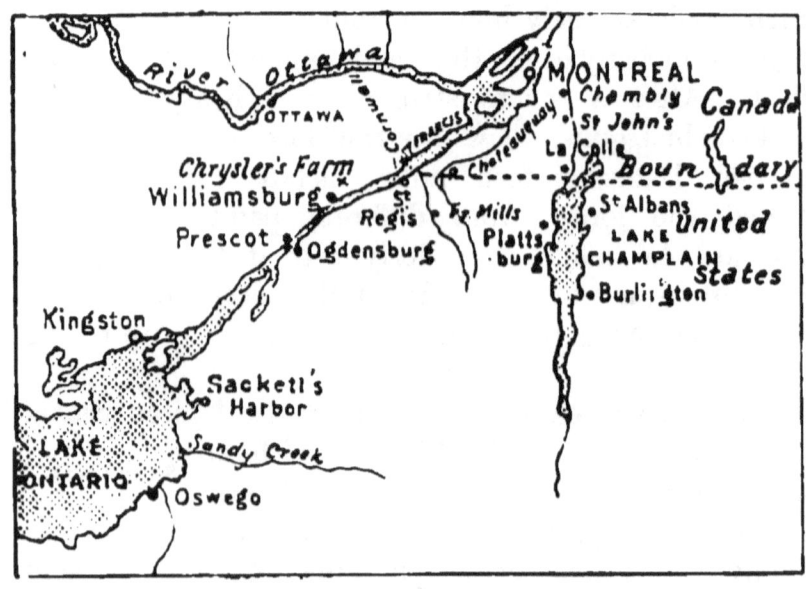

SACKETT'S HARBOUR.

out to give warning to Fitzgibbon. Leaving home before daylight, she cautiously passed the American lines, and, avoiding the highway, travelled a distance of twenty miles through the woods, crossing swollen streams on trunks of fallen trees, to Beaver Dams. Fitzgibbon, forewarned by her, skilfully placed his men in ambush in the forests along a narrow ravine, and took over five hundred of the enemy prisoners.

Meanwhile Sir George Prevost and Sir James Yeo, who had recently arrived in the country, taking advantage of the absence of Chauncey at Fort George, had made an attempt to obtain possession of Sackett's Harbour. *(Sackett's Harbour.)* They sailed from Kingston with a fleet of seven vessels, and about seven hundred and fifty troops, rank and file. The expedition resulted in ridiculous failure. After sturdy fighting, when victory seemed well assured, Prevost ordered his men to re-embark and gave up the siege.

The story of the capture of the *Chesapeake* is almost a household tale. Captain Broke of the British frigate *Shannon* came up *(Capture of the Chesapeake.)* before Boston Harbour and challenged Captain Lawrence of the *Chesapeake* to meet him in the open sea. The two ships were followed from the harbour by a fleet of sail-boats filled with the citizens of Boston, eager to see the battle and take part in the expected triumph. As the *Chesapeake* drew near, there was great excitement among the British tars. "Don't cheer," said Broke, "but go quietly to your quarters."

In fifteen minutes after the first shot was fired, the British flag floated above the stars and stripes on the masts of the *Chesapeake*, while seventy of her men lay dead upon her decks, and her gallant captain was dying of a mortal wound. "Don't give up the ship," were the words addressed to his men by this brave officer as he fell. On Sunday, June 6, the *Shannon* with her prize sailed into Halifax Harbour. Captain Lawrence was buried in Halifax with military honours. Broke, who was severely wounded in the engagement, was rewarded by his Sovereign with the title of Baronet.

In this war, however, Great Britain did not always maintain her prestige as mistress of the sea. One of the most disastrous naval defeats occurred on Lake Erie. Procter, with a small force of troops and Indians, occupied Amherstburg. In the river before the town lay the British Lake Erie fleet of six vessels under command of Captain Barclay. Near by, in warlike attitude, was a United States fleet of nine vessels under Lieutenant Perry. While Barclay had more guns than had Perry, his strength was much inferior as regards number of men as well as of ships. Moreover, food being scarce in Amherstburg, his men were on short allowance, and there was slim prospect of fresh supplies. He was thus forced to risk an engagement, which took place in Put-in-Bay. The battle was gallantly fought on both sides. The United States flagship was named the *Lawrence* in honour of the captain of the *Chesapeake*, and on her blue pennon at the mast-head were inscribed that hero's memorable words— "Don't give up the ship." During the engagement the *Lawrence* was disabled. Perry, seizing her flag, entered an open boat and was rowed amid flying shot and shell to another ship. Barclay fought bravely, but after losing nearly half his men in killed and wounded, and being himself disabled by a wound, he was compelled to surrender the entire fleet.

Defeat of the British on Lake Erie, Sept. 10, 1813.

The loss of Barclay's fleet was a serious matter. Procter, now left without support and the means of obtaining supplies, felt compelled to abandon his position. Having dismantled the forts at Amherstburg and Detroit, with about four hundred troops, and eight hundred Indians under

Moravian Town.

Tecumseh, he retreated across the country and up the valley of the Thames. Closely pursued by General Harrison at the head of three thousand five hundred men, he was forced to give battle near Moravian Town. In the battle he took a position where he would be least exposed, and when he found himself in danger he fled as fast as he was able from the field of battle. His army suffered disastrous defeat. The brave Tecumseh was slain, and his body was treated with great indignity by the victors. Many British soldiers were taken prisoners and sent off to Ohio and Kentucky, where they received very rough treatment. Procter was afterwards tried by court-martial, which sentenced him to be publicly reprimanded, and suspended from rank and pay for six months.

Elated with their successes in the west, the Americans planned the conquest of Lower Canada. For this purpose two large armies entered the province by different routes— one under General Wade Hampton by way of Lake Champlain, the other under Wilkinson by the St. Lawrence. They were to meet at the mouth of the Chateaugay on the south shore of Lake St. Louis, and thence proceed against Montreal. *Battle of Chateaugay.*

Towards the end of September, Hampton, at the head of a well-drilled army of about six thousand men, marching from Lake Champlain, entered Canada near Odelltown. Shortly after he crossed the borders he entered a swampy wood, where he was every now and then fired upon by a foe lying in ambush among the trees. This enemy of unknown strength really comprised only two or three hundred voltigeurs, mostly French Canadians, and a few Indians, under command of the clever Colonel de Salaberry. Sir George Prevost, whose caution was so conspicuous at Sackett's Harbour, had sent this little band to oppose one of the strongest armies that the United States had sent into Canada. Hampton, uncertain as to the strength of the enemy lurking in ambush, abandoned the woods and moved over to the Chateaugay, intending to follow it to its mouth, where he was to meet Wilkinson. De Salaberry took up his position on the borders of a thick wood, at a point on the river which he knew Hampton would pass. Having built a block-house and thrown out abattis for a defence, with his little band he awaited the coming of the enemy. Fortunately, while waiting he was reinforced by Colonel M'Donnell with six hundred French militia. On the following day, October 26, was fought the battle of Chateaugay, in which nine hundred French Canadians, aided by fifty Indians, gained a wonderful victory over an enemy more than six times their number. At one time in the battle, when the voltigeurs, overwhelmed by the enemy, gave way, De Salaberry alone stood firm, and seizing his bugler by the collar, to prevent him from running away, he made him sound the advance. Both by stratagem and bravery M'Donnell performed his part equally well. He distributed his buglers at different points in the forest, and gave them orders to blow with all their might, as if to collect scattered forces for a grand charge. The Indians also helped on the ruse by loud yelling. The enemy, thus led to suppose that a large army was about to advance on them, panic-stricken, fled in confusion. Night coming on, two divisions of United States troops by mistake fought each other. Finally, Hampton, having collected his men, marched back to Plattsburg.

Wilkinson collected his forces, comprising about eight thousand men, at Sackett's Harbour. On the 5th of November, not knowing the ill-fortune of Hampton's army, he began the descent of the St. Lawrence. A British force of about eight hundred men and eight gunboats followed from Kingston, giving him such annoyance that he was compelled to land strong forces to beat off the assailants. As he approached Long Sault Rapids he divided his men, sending a strong division in advance to clear the way, while the other, comprising two thousand five hundred men under General Boyd, was left to guard his rear. Boyd was closely followed by the Canadians under Colonel Morrison. Finally, at the head of Long Sault Rapids, in open field, was fought the battle of Chrystler's Farm, in which the invaders were thoroughly beaten by a force less than one-third their number. At Cornwall, Wilkinson heard of Hampton's defeat. With deep chagrin he burned his boats and went into winter quarters. *Battle of Chrystler's Farm.*

General M'Clure of the United States army, at the head of nearly three thousand men, held the Canadian frontier of Niagara. He treated the people of the district with great severity, pillaging their property, destroying their houses, so as to leave them without shelter at the approach of winter, and sending the principal men across the line as prisoners of war. General Vincent, who occupied Burlington Heights, sent a force of five hundred men under Murray for the purpose of giving the in- *Towns burned.*

habitants some protection. M'Clure retreated to Fort George, and finally he withdrew to Fort Niagara, on the United States side of the river. Before retiring, however, he was guilty of an act of great barbarity. Turning the women and children on the streets on a cold winter's night, he burned the town of Newark. Out of one hundred and fifty houses but one remained after the fire. Indignant at this outrage, the British pursued the enemy across the river, and in retaliation burned the towns of Lewiston, Manchester, Black Rock, and Buffalo. Thus up to within a day or two of Christmas this destruction and cruel warfare continued.

The war was attended with great loss and suffering on both sides. The industries of Canada were interrupted and much property was destroyed. The transport of supplies and war material was attended with great labour and expense. At that time there were no steamers on the lakes and rivers, and there were no canals for overcoming the rapids on the St. Lawrence. Supplies for the West were forwarded on sleds during the winter from Montreal to Kingston, where they were distributed to various points as required. Though the provinces by the sea were removed from the neighbourhood of the war, they were not exempt from its evils. United States privateers, by plundering the settlements on the coast and capturing vessels engaged in trade and fishing, did them much damage. To defend the country, old forts and block-houses were repaired, and cannon were mounted at the entrance of the principal harbours. Halifax was a busy place during the war. A militia force was brought in from the country to defend the

Effects of the War.

capital in case of attack. Halifax Harbour was the headquarters of the British fleet in North America, and ships of war were constantly coming and going. Vessels and other property taken from the enemy were brought here to be sold. Prisoners of war were kept on Melville Island, in the harbour. Increased demand for provisions of all kinds made good markets for the produce of the farmers of the country.

The United States also suffered great damage from the war. The whole Atlantic coast south of New England was under blockade of British ships, and only privateers and other fast sailers entered or left the harbours. The foreign trade of the country was ruined, and domestic trade was seriously interrupted. Express teams were employed to do the work of coasting-vessels. On the highways between the North and the South might be seen hundreds of huge canvas-covered waggons, drawn by long teams of horses or oxen, carrying on exchange of products. The journey from Boston to Augusta, in Georgia, occupied two months. Fabulous prices were demanded for goods. In some parts of the country tea was sold for $4 a pound, flour for $19 a barrel, molasses for $2 a gallon, salt for $5 a bushel. *Effects of the War in the United States.*

Throughout the whole of the year 1814 the war went on. Napoleon, the great disturber of the peace of Europe, was defeated, and confined in the little island of Elba, so that Great Britain was now able to send more help to Canada. *The War in 1814.*

Early in the spring, Wilkinson, with a force of four thousand men, advancing from Plattsburg, renewed his invasion of Lower Canada. Four or five hundred Canadian militia and regulars, taking possession of a large stone mill at Lacolle, opposed his progress. For two hours and a half Wilkinson battered in vain at the thick walls of the mill, when he withdrew across the line and soon after returned to Plattsburg.

Lacolle—Port Dover

The burning of Port Dover, on Lake Erie, by a United States force under Colonel Campbell, awakened deep indignation in Canada. The whole village, including private houses, mills, stores, and other buildings, was wantonly reduced to ashes.

The invasions were not all on one side. Sir Gordon Drummond, the Governor of Upper Canada, and Sir James Yeo, captured Oswego, an important naval depot of the United States on Lake Ontario, and seized large quantities of provisions.

Oswego and Maine.

Later in the summer, expeditions setting out from Nova Scotia, under Sir John Sherbrooke, the Governor of that province, and other officers, took possession of Eastport, Castine, Bangor, and Machias. In fact the whole coast of Maine east of the Penobscot was taken and held by the British until the close of the war.

Once again the chief events of the war centred on the Niagara frontier. The United States forces were collected at Buffalo to the number of five or six thousand men, under General Brown. The British held Fort Niagara, on the United States side, and as it was uncertain where the attack would be made, their troops were scattered at various points. Brown made his first assault on Fort Erie, which he took with little difficulty. He then ad-

Chippewa and Lundy's Lane.

vanced to Chippewa, where he was met by General Riall with about fifteen hundred men. Riall was defeated. He then retired to Lundy's Lane, closely pursued by Brown, who plundered and laid waste the country as he advanced.

General Drummond, who was at Kingston, hearing of the invasion, hastened forward, arriving at Fort Niagara on the morning of July 25. On the same day, taking about eight hundred troops, he moved rapidly to the seat of war. At five o'clock in the evening he met Riall and his troops in full retreat, and turned them back for renewed conflict. On the same evening, July 25, within sound of Niagara Falls, was fought the battle of Lundy's Lane, the most hotly contended of the whole war.

The battle began at six in the evening and continued until near midnight. The United States army numbered about five thousand men. During the first three hours Drummond had about seventeen hundred; but at nine o'clock a reinforcement arrived, making in all about three thousand. The night was intensely dark, and there was much confusion between the contending armies. In some places it was a hand-to-hand struggle. Guns were captured and re-captured, and gunners were bayoneted while loading their pieces. The carnage was fearful. The Americans lost about nine hundred men, and the British nearly as many. General Riall was severely wounded, and afterwards taken prisoner by the enemy. Three United States generals, Brown, Scott, and Porter, were severely wounded. Towards midnight the enemy, worn out in the struggle, retreated from the field, and afterwards took shelter in Fort Erie. The British besieged the fort, but were repulsed with heavy loss. Soon after, the enemy withdrew to the United States side of the river.

Capture of Washington. During the summer the people of the United States began to realise, as they had not done before, the serious nature of the war in which they were engaged. British fleets sailed up and down the Atlantic coast, spreading dismay in every city within reach of their guns. But the event which brought the war nearest home to the United States was the capture of Washington by Admiral Cochrane and General Ross. These officers sailed up the Potomac, landed their forces without opposition, and after a short engagement before Washington took possession of the city. President Madison barely escaped capture. The British added little to their glory by burning the capitol and other public buildings; but they claimed that it was in retaliation for the burning of York, Port Dover, and other places in Canada.

Plattsburg. As Great Britain had sent several thousands of her veteran troops to Canada, Sir George Prevost resolved to use them in an expedition against Plattsburg, on Lake Champlain. The United States forces occupying this place and the warships on Lake Champlain interfered with the sending into Canada of beef and other food supplies from Vermont and New York, a traffic of great importance to our people, but one which the United States Government wished to break up. In September a well-disciplined army, eleven thousand strong, under the command of Sir George himself, aided by a small British fleet, undertook the capture of the place. The undertaking was badly mismanaged, and resulted in complete failure. The fleet, after a sharp conflict lasting over two hours, was utterly beaten. Meanwhile Prevost, with an army which, under proper command, could easily have taken the place, was doing nothing, and he now ordered the troops to retire without striking a blow. His soldiers were greatly disappointed, and his officers broke their swords for very shame and anger, vowing they never would serve again. Sir George was afterwards summoned before a court-martial to answer for his unsoldier-like conduct, but he died before the court met.

A closing scene in this long war was enacted before New Orleans. Early in December a powerful fleet, under Admiral Cochrane, and a strong land-force commanded by Sir Edward Packenham, having for their object the capture of this city, arrived at the mouth of the Mississippi. A battle was fought on January 8, 1815, in which the British were defeated with heavy loss. *New Orleans.*

On the day before Christmas a treaty of peace between Great Britain and the United States was signed at Ghent, a famous fortified city in Belgium. The news did not reach America for several weeks, so that hostilities were continued for some time after the peace was concluded. The territory which had been seized during the war was restored to the original owner; and strangely enough the disputed question of right of search on the High Seas, which was said to be a leading cause of the war, was not even referred to in the treaty. It is difficult to see what either party gained which could justify such expenditure of money *The Treaty of Ghent, Dec. 24, 1814.*

and human life. It is true, however, that the long struggle against a common foe tended to unify the various provinces and develop national sentiment amongst our people. Peace was welcome on both sides of the line.

CHAPTER XXI.

PROGRESS AND AGITATION.

THE war greatly disturbed the regular business of the country. While it gave rise to new occupations, it ruined some old industries. At the return of peace, business resumed its former channels. Thus, many persons who had been occupied in supplying the extra demands of the war period were now left without employment. This was especially the case in Halifax. The withdrawal of the British troops and navy caused depression in business of all kinds, and many persons, unable to obtain means of support, were compelled to leave the city. The farmers in the country also, who during the war found good markets for their produce, seriously felt the change. In Lower Canada failure of the crops intensified the hard times. But these hardships were soon overcome, and the provinces entered upon a course of renewed prosperity.

Hard Times.

The country was full of life. Difficulties were bravely faced, and new strength for the occasion was forthcoming. During the war the provinces had no money to meet the expenses which it involved, and they issued paper money, called "Army Bills," which were mere promises to pay. These bills were now promptly redeemed at their par value. Persons disabled in the war, and the widows and orphans of those who had fallen, were allowed small pensions.

New Settlers. On the return of peace a large number of soldiers, whose services were no longer needed in active warfare, were discharged from the British army. Dull times also in the old country threw many labourers in the factories out of employment. There was abundant room for these people in Canada, and thousands of them came from the British Isles to make for themselves new homes in our forests. The British Government gave them generous aid, including free passage, tools for clearing the land and cultivating the soil, and a year's provisions. These immigrants formed many little settlements in different parts of the country, some of them in the Maritime Provinces, some in the Eastern Townships of Lower Canada, but the larger number in the Upper Province. This colonisation was promoted by a wealthy English corporation called the " Canada Land Company." It purchased a vast quantity of land in Upper Canada, paying the Government over a million and a half dollars. While settlers from the British Isles were made welcome in Canada, people from the United States were at this time regarded with suspicion: they were allowed to remain in the country only as aliens, and were liable to be expelled on short notice. During the twenty-five years following the close of the war the population of the provinces increased from about half a million to a million and a half.

The Cholera, 1833-34. While these new colonists helped greatly to build up the country, they were the means of bringing upon it a terrible calamity. One of the ships entering the St. Lawrence brought with it Asiatic cholera. This fell disease was widely spread, and it swept off many people, old and young, in Quebec, Montreal, St. John, and the cities of Upper Canada.

Among the elements of progress at this period was a striving in the various provinces for higher skill in agriculture. Farmers and others who were interested in their work formed agricultural societies, which tended to secure better stock, farming tools, and methods of tillage. In Nova Scotia this awakening was in large measure due to the letters of "Agricola," published in the *Halifax Acadian Recorder*. The writer was John Young, a Scotchman, who afterwards was a distinguished member of the Assembly. The Earl of Dalhousie, who was then Governor of Nova Scotia, also aided the movement. In New Brunswick the Governor, Sir Howard Douglas, used his influence to secure more attention to the culture of the soil in place of lumbering and shipbuilding. *Agriculture.*

This was an era of marked awakening throughout all the provinces in the matter of education. Colleges and high schools, known as grammar schools, were established, and Government aid was given towards the support of common schools. M'Gill College, in Montreal, was founded in 1823; Upper Canada College, in Toronto, in 1827. One of the earliest promoters of education in Upper Canada was John Strachan, afterwards Bishop Strachan, a native of Scotland. He founded academies at Kingston and Cornwall, and many of his pupils afterwards held high positions in the management of the affairs of the province. Dr. Strachan was himself a pronounced politician of the Conservative type. He was *Education.*

a member of both the Executive and the Legislative Council, and he became the first Anglican bishop of Upper Canada.

In Nova Scotia the religious restrictions of King's College led to the establishment of Pictou Academy, which, under the management of Dr. Thomas McCulloch, a Presbyterian clergyman of Scottish birth, became one of the most noted high schools in the early history of the provinces. In 1820 the Earl of Dalhousie, the Governor of Nova Scotia, founded Dalhousie College, at Halifax, using for the benefit of the college funds derived from duties collected in the district on the coast of Maine seized by Sir John Sherbrooke during the war.

THOMAS M'CULLOCH, D.D.

In 1828, through the influence of Sir Howard Douglas, one of the most intelligent and enterprising governors of New Brunswick, the University of New Brunswick was established in Fredericton.

Prince Edward Island was little behind her sister provinces in early efforts to promote the education of her children. In 1830 a Board of Education was appointed, and shortly after an efficient academy was opened in Charlottetown.

As yet, however, little had been done for the common schools throughout the country. The teachers, or masters, as they were called, were poorly qualified, and there was little or no examination to test their ability. Many of them took up teaching as a last resort, after having failed in almost every other vocation. They took part of their pay in board, staying a few days at each farmhouse, according to the number of children sent to the school. This was called "board-

BISHOP STRACHAN.

ing around." The schoolhouses were rude log structures; the seats were made of long thick slabs with sticks driven into auger holes for legs, and the desks were wide boards sloping from the walls. At the end of the term the teacher went from house to house collecting the balance of his pay, often taking it in farm produce.

Public Roads and Facilities for Trade. Large sums of money were voted by the Provincial Legislatures for making and improving the public roads and bridges. For fifteen years following 1820 there was much activity in Upper and Lower Canada in making canals, and steamboats were placed on the lakes and rivers. The Rideau Canal, constructed along a line of small rivers and lakes, extended from Bytown (Ottawa) to Kingston; the La Chine Canal overcame the obstruction to navigation caused by the La Chine Rapids in the St. Lawrence a short distance above Montreal. Before the construction of this canal, produce was brought down the St. Lawrence in flat boats, which were generally disposed of with the goods. The Welland Canal, opened in 1829, continued the waterway obstructed by the Falls and Rapids of Niagara between Lakes Erie and Ontario.

The Shubenacadie Canal, in Nova Scotia, was begun in 1827. The object of the work was to connect Halifax Harbour with the head-waters of the Bay of Fundy through a chain of lakes and the Shubenacadie River, providing a route to Halifax for the trade of the western part of the province. A large amount of money was expended on this canal, which was finally abandoned without resulting in any practical advantage.

At this time there was little intercourse between the Maritime Provinces and the interior. An overland journey between Halifax and Quebec consumed many days, and traffic, except by sea in summer, was quite impracticable. For the promotion of trade and travel, a large Government subsidy was offered for a steamer to run between these ports. This led to the building of the *Royal William* at Cape Cove, near Quebec, by the Quebec and Halifax Steam Navigation Company. The vessel was launched in 1831, and was named in honour of King William IV., who then occupied the British throne. She made two or three voyages to Halifax, but the breaking out of cholera at Quebec in 1832 brought infection to the ship and ruined her business. In the following summer, laden chiefly with coal, she sailed from Pictou, N.S., for England, and, after a passage of nineteen days, arrived at Gravesend, near London. Thus, in 1833, the *Royal William* had the distinction of being the first steamship to cross the Atlantic Ocean. She was afterwards purchased by the Spanish Government and converted into a war-steamer.

The "Royal William."

In 1820, after thirty-five years' experience as a separate province, the Island of Cape Breton was annexed to Nova Scotia. It was then allowed the privilege of sending two members to the Assembly at Halifax. The people of the island were not easily reconciled to the loss of their independence, as they considered it, and they tried to break up the union. Their efforts, however, were without avail.

Cape Breton.

In 1825 a great calamity befell New Brunswick.

The Miramichi Fire. The eastern portion of the province was laid waste by one of the most memorable fires on record. The season was remarkable for drought and heat, which continued unusually late into the autumn. On the night of October 7, the fire, which had been raging in the neighbouring forests, burst upon Newcastle and other flourishing settlements on the Miramichi River with such suddenness and power as to sweep everything before it. Many people—men, women, and children—were burned to death, and a still larger number were left houseless and destitute at the approach of winter. Generous aid was sent to the sufferers from the other provinces, Great Britain, and the United States.

Political Agitation. The twenty-five years following the close of the American war were stormy times in the provinces. No sooner was the din of war hushed than the old clamour over political grievances was heard afresh. The questions in dispute, while assuming somewhat different forms, were pretty much the same in all the provinces. The grievances complained of were such as at the present time would not be tolerated for a day, but it cost a long and hard struggle to remove them. Existing customs and institutions, though unsatisfactory, are not easily broken up. Briefly stated, the question in dispute was the right of the people to govern themselves. As the agitation went on, there arose two great political parties, known as Conservatives and Reformers or Liberals. The Conservatives, or Tories as their opponents called them, held that the people should submit loyally to the Government placed over them, and branded as rebels those who advocated change. The Liberals believed that the Government should be under the control of the people, and that its policy and its officers should be subject to their wishes as expressed by their representatives. In the meantime the Conservatives held the reins of power.

A leading grievance, and one in which many evils had their origin, was the irresponsible character of the Executive Council. The people's representatives —that is, the Assembly—had no voice in the appointment of this body, and no power to influence its policy or call it to account for its acts. The Council was not chosen with even a show of fairness to the varied interests of the people at large. For the most part the members were residents of the city, and belonged to the Church of England. So closely bound together and mutually helpful were they that the body was in some of the provinces aptly called the "Family Compact." For example, in Nova Scotia, they were, with one exception, residents of Halifax; eight of the twelve were members of the Church of England; five were partners in the same banking establishment; and several were connected by family ties.

The Reformers demanded Responsible Government —that is, that an Executive Council should hold office only so long as its course of action was sustained by a majority of the Assembly. It is easy to see that under the system described the public business would be badly managed. The Council appointed all the subordinate officers of the Government throughout the country, such as judges, sheriffs, and magistrates. It had the control of the Crown lands and a part of the public money. The members of the Council looked well after their own interests, and gave the public offices to their personal friends. They were charged with having obtained for themselves and their friends large tracts of the public lands without paying the full value into the Treasury. The Governor, in his official capacity, sometimes granted Crown lands to himself as a private citizen.

In Upper Canada the agitation for reform was mixed up with a question of religion.

The Clergy Reserves.
The Constitutional Act of 1791 set apart one-seventh of all ungranted lands for the support of a "Protestant clergy." These reserved lands in this province comprised nearly two and a half millions of acres. The term "Protestant clergy" was vague. For many years it was held to mean the clergy of the Church of England; later it was broadened so as to include that branch of the Presbyterian family known as the Established Church of Scotland. The Methodists, Baptists, and many smaller bodies were shut out. Some of those who were thus excluded maintained that the fund should be divided among all denominations; while others, including the Baptists, who were opposed to state aid for the support of religion, held that the fund should be applied to ordinary secular uses. Public feeling over this matter waxed hot, and on it many severe things were said and written. The question was discussed in Assembly and Council, in pulpit and press. Among the leading disputants were, on the one side, the distinguished Dr. Strachan; on the other, Egerton Ryerson, a young Methodist minister, better

known as Dr. Ryerson, the founder of the educational system of Ontario.

In Lower Canada the people of French origin comprised about four-fifths of the population, and they formed a large majority of the Assembly. *Lower Canada.* The English, however, ruled the country, holding nearly all the seats in both Councils and the principal public offices under the Government. It thus came about that, in the political agitation which now disturbed the province, the two races were to a considerable extent arrayed against each other.

The Roman Catholics in the English-speaking provinces had a grievance specially their own. *Catholic Emancipation.* For a century and a half the laws of Great Britain had withheld from Catholics the privilege of the franchise and of sitting in Parliament. It was now beginning to be felt that this restriction, which had come down from a severe age, should be removed. The question of Catholic Emancipation, as it was called, came up first in the Legislature of Prince Edward Island. The Bill, however, was lost by the casting vote of the Speaker. Two years later, in 1827, the barrier was broken down in Nova Scotia. A Roman Catholic, Lawrence Kavanagh, was elected as member of the Assembly for Cape Breton. He could not take his seat on account of the oath of admission, which required him to declare his disbelief in certain doctrines of his religion. A resolution was unanimously adopted by the House in favour of petitioning the King for a change in the oath. Thomas Chandler Haliburton, the clever humourist known as "Sam Slick," supported the resolution in one of the most eloquent speeches ever made in the Nova Scotia Assembly. Having received a favourable reply, the Assembly passed an Act freeing Roman Catholics from all disabilities on account of their religion. The other provinces shortly after adopted measures of the same kind.

At this period of disquietude Prince Edward Island had its full share of troubles. Charles Douglas Smith, appointed Governor in 1813, ruled the island in the most arbitrary manner. He grossly insulted the Assembly, prorogued or dissolved it when it began to discuss grievances, and twice for a period of four years he failed to call the members together. His hard treatment of the farmers almost drove them into rebellion. The Government land-tax, called quit-rent, had been found burdensome,

JUDGE HALIBURTON, "SAM SLICK."

and the holders of land had fallen behind in their payments. The British Government cancelled arrears and reduced the tax. For several succeeding years no demand was made, and the Receiver-General refused to take the money from those who offered to pay. The land-holders were thus led to believe that they would not again be asked to pay the tax. In the early times the lands of those in arrears had been sold to pay the quit-rents, but now the officers of the law demanded payment from the tenants who occupied the lands. Without giving due notice, the Governor sent constables into a district of King's County to demand immediate payment. Many farmers had no money, and they were compelled to give their notes payable in ten days. To raise the money, they carried their grain and other produce fifty or sixty miles, in midwinter, to the Charlottetown market. The market was overstocked, and little money was realised.

The people were indignant, and as there had been no meeting of the Assembly for three years, they scarcely knew where to obtain redress. They applied to the High Sheriff of the island to call public meetings in different counties for the discussion of grievances. At the meetings petitions to the King were prepared, containing serious charges against the Governor, and asking for his removal. John Stewart was chosen as the people's delegate to carry the petitions to England. The Governor was very angry. He punished the Sheriff for calling the meetings by dismissing him from office. Claiming that some charges in the petitions were libellous against the Court of Chancery, of which he was Chancellor, he issued writs for the apprehension of Stewart and other members of the committee who had drawn up the petitions. But Stewart, evading the officers, escaped to Nova Scotia, and hastened on his way to England. His mission was successful. In the following year he returned, accompanied by Colonel Ready, who had been appointed Governor in place of Smith. The new Governor was a great favourite, and for a time matters moved on more smoothly. There was, however, little harmony between the Assembly and the Council. As in the other provinces, the chief subject of dispute was the control of the public money.

CHAPTER XXII.

BRITISH FUR TRADERS IN THE NORTH.

MEANWHILE the great North-West had been occupied as a vast hunting-ground by the fur traders. The Hudson's Bay Company, as already stated, was organised by royal charter in 1670. At this time the territory covered by its charter was claimed by France, and English and French traders regarded each other as intruders. On different occasions the French tried to break up the company's establishment, but though they caused their rivals much damage, they failed to drive them from the field. Notwithstanding great losses from the seizure of its furs and the destruction of its forts, the English company drew enormous profits from its trade. By the Treaty of Utrecht, France gave up all claim to this northern territory. From this date, for half a century, until the end of French rule in Canada, the Hudson's Bay Company was undisturbed by hostile rivals. *English and French Rivalry.*

Shortly after the conquest of Canada by Great Britain a new rival entered the field. Several British merchants of Montreal, mostly Scotchmen, took up the fur trade of the North-West. For a few years each merchant or firm carried on the business independently. The keen rivalry amongst them gave rise to many evils. *The North-West Fur Company of Montreal, 1787.*

Each merchant sought to promote his own interest at whatever cost to his neighbours. Intoxicating liquors were used to entice the Indians, and the trader who gave them the most rum was most successful in securing their trade. Bloody feuds sprang up among the employees in the remote wilderness, life and property were destroyed, and the Indians were demoralised. This ruinous policy was soon abandoned. In 1787 the rival merchants united, forming the North-West Fur Company of Montreal. This company now carried on the fur traffic with marvellous energy and success, and it soon became the most wealthy and influential organisation in Canada. It extended its trade over the whole of the North-West from Montreal to the Arctic Ocean. Scattered through all this vast country, on Lake Superior, Lake Winnipeg, Lake Athabasca, and Great Slave Lake, on the Saskatchewan and on other rivers and lakes, were the company's forts or trading posts. Distributed among these forts was a small army of the company's employees—agents, clerks, and interpreters—to banter and barter with the Indians; and along the streams and lakes were many voyageurs or boatmen, who passed in boat or light canoe to and fro between Montreal and the distant forts, carrying to them the company's merchandise, and bringing back the rich harvest of furs, which were duly shipped to the London market.

The trade was carried on with the Indians without the use of money. The company gave them guns, ammunition, blankets, knives, and many other things, taking their furs in exchange. In fixing prices the beaver was taken as the standard, the value of all other commodities being measured by it.

the Chancellor replied that they had come on important business, and that they must see the "Queen" immediately. When the message was taken to the Princess she came at once, appearing before her early visitors in dressing-gown and slippers. She showed more sadness at the news of her uncle's death than joy over the royal honours which had fallen upon herself.

Some incidents in the early history of her reign reveal interesting features in the character of the youthful Queen. We are told that she was quite overcome with a deep sense of her responsibility, and that she could not realise her right to the exalted position to which she had been elevated. "I can scarcely believe, mamma," she said to her mother, "that I am really Queen of England. Is it indeed true?" "Yes," replied the Duchess, "you are really Queen. Do you not hear your subjects on the streets cheering and shouting 'God save the Queen'?" Then the Queen is said to have asked to be left alone, and in the seclusion of her private room she spent the first hours of her reign in meditation and prayer for herself and her people.

Queen Victoria had been brought up in retirement, and she was quite a stranger to her subjects when she ascended the throne. But she soon won their admiration by her unassuming manner and the quiet dignity with which she bore her royal honours. Among those who in her presence were required to subscribe the oath of allegiance were her two uncles, brothers of the late King. As the aged Duke of Sussex, now quite infirm, was stooping to kiss her hand, the Queen rose from her chair, and kissing him said, "Do not kneel, dear uncle; if I am Queen, I am your niece."

CHAPTER XXV

REBELLION

Lower Canada, 1837. The young Queen with all her virtues could not send tranquillity to her Canadian subjects. British statesmen had secured responsible government for their people at home, but they thought it scarcely suited to the colonies. And so Canadians were left with unredressed grievances until agitation developed into rebellion. For five years the Assembly of Lower Canada had refused to vote a Civil List, leaving the judges and other public officers without their salaries. This state of affairs could not continue. The British Government instructed the Governor-General to take money from the treasury without the authority of the Assembly and pay all arrears of the Civil List. The large sum of $700,000 was thus drawn from the public treasury. This caused great excitement throughout the province. The Reformers, or "Patriots" as they called themselves, held meetings in various parts of the country, at which Louis Papineau, in violent and seditious language, appealed to the passions and prejudices of the people, urging them to strike for independence or annexation to the United States. Papineau's ablest associate was Dr. Wolfred Nelson, a man of Loyalist descent, who, as surgeon, had served in the War of

1812. Nelson was now about fifty-five years of age. Scholarly and possessed of considerable wealth, he had great influence over the English-speaking people.

The Governor-General, Lord Gosford, issued a proclamation, warning the people against sedition. Copies of this document were posted on the churches and in other public places. The excited people tore them down, shouting "Long live Papineau!"

The first outbreak was a riot in the streets of Montreal. The rebels, who called them- selves "Sons of Liberty," were dispersed without loss of life. Risings followed in different parts of the province. In some places the loyal inhabitants, alarmed at the threatening attitude of their rebellious neighbours, left their homes and fled to Montreal. A band of rebels under Dr. Nelson posted themselves in a stone mill at St. Denis, on the Richelieu, where for a time they successfully resisted the troops sent to dislodge them. Another rebel force at St. Charles was dispersed with considerable loss. Warrants having been issued for the apprehension of the leaders of the rebellion, Papineau fled to the United States. Nelson, seeking the same refuge, was caught hiding in the woods, and with several other rebels was thrown into prison. Later in the autumn, a force under Sir John Colborne marched against a body of insurgents collected at St. Eustache, on the Ottawa. Most of the rebels fled at the approach of the soldiers. About four hundred took refuge in a church, which was soon battered down by shot and shell and set on fire, while most of those who thus sought shelter were killed, taken prisoners, or perished in the flames.

Rebellion in Lower Canada.

Lord Gosford was recalled by the British Government, and the Earl of Durham, an able statesman of the Liberal party in England, was sent in his place. In addition to his office of Governor-General, the Earl was invested with special authority as High Commissioner to look into the character of the government in the various provinces. Already, on account of the disturbances, the British Parliament had set aside the legislature of Lower Canada, and Lord Gosford had appointed a special Council in its place.

<small>The Earl of Durham, 1838.</small>

The Earl of Durham arrived in Canada towards the end of May 1838. He was accompanied by able assistants, chief of whom was his secretary, Charles Buller. His position was a difficult one, as a country in a state of rebellion could not be governed by ordinary forms of law. In dealing with the rebels he adopted a bold policy, which, while it was merciful and humane, set all law at defiance. Except a few of the chief leaders, he pardoned all who had taken part in the rebellion. A most fitting occasion for this act of clemency was afforded by the Coronation day of Queen Victoria, June 18th. The leaders he disposed of without even the form of trial. Papineau, Cartier, and some others who had fled to the United States he proclaimed outlaws, and forbade to return to Canada under pain of death. Eight other chief offenders, among whom was Dr. Wolfred Nelson, who had been captured, he banished to Bermuda, imposing the same extreme penalty if they should return.

Lord Durham's mode of dealing with the leaders in the rebellion was severely criticised by his opponents in England, and even his political friends failed to stand by him. The Government which had sent him to Canada disallowed his action. It was asserted that he had no power to make a penal colony of Bermuda, or to send these men into exile. Nor was it a capital offence, according to British law, for an exile to return to his country without leave. While this is quite true, it should have been remembered that any trial of the rebels in the courts of Lower Canada would have been a farce, for no jury selected by legal process would have found them guilty. A trial by court-martial would have sent them to the gallows.

The noble Earl was proud-spirited, and he was deeply indignant over the censure which had been meted out to him. Accordingly, after a short stay of five months, without permission from the Home Government, he left his post and returned to England. His mission appeared like a failure, and it was so as regarded its effect on his personal renown. He had been for some time in bad health; he went home greatly disheartened, and he died a few months after his return. It has, however, been well said that if his mission ruined Lord Durham, it saved Canada. During his short stay in the country he had carefully studied its condition and wants. His report to the British Government, the main features of which were afterwards adopted, is regarded as one of the ablest state papers on colonial policy which has ever been written.

In the autumn of 1838 some of the rebels who had fled to the United States returned, accompanied by adventurers from that country. Under the leadership of Robert Nelson, Wolfred Nelson's brother, they sought to carry out their wild schemes of rebellion. They boldly proclaimed the independence of Canada, pledging themselves by an oath to support republican government. In some parts of the country loyal people were compelled to flee from their homes to save their lives, while their property was wantonly destroyed. Sir John Colborne, who was now acting in place of the Governor-General, by vigorous measures soon put down the rebellion. Twelve of the leaders, having been tried by court-martial, were executed at Montreal.

<small>Renewed Insurrection, 1838.</small>

Meanwhile the "Patriots" in Upper Canada had been playing their part at rebellion. Many of the Reformers in this province were seeking, by lawful agitation and other proper means, to secure better government, and they refused to join in any movement which involved civil war. If Sir Francis Bond Head had been more prudent, and had carried out his instructions from home, there probably would have been no resort to arms. But when he actively opposed the Reformers in the election, helping to secure their defeat, MacKenzie, Rolph, and other excitable leaders rushed into active rebellion. They issued a manifesto, urging the people to free themselves from British authority and assert their independence. Baldwin, Bidwell, and others refused to join them in their course. Sir Francis Bond Head had warning from various sources that MacKenzie was plotting insurrection, but he used no means to thwart his plans. He sent all the troops that were in the province to Montreal, and took no steps to supply

<small>Upper Canada.</small>

their place by a loyal volunteer force. Without hindrance men were arming and drilling in various parts of the province for the overthrow of the Government.

At a secret meeting held in Toronto, MacKenzie, Rolph, Morrison, and others formed their plans. The insurgents, to the number of eight or nine hundred, were collected at Montgomery's Tavern, about four miles from Toronto. Their plan was to march into Toronto at night, seize four thousand stand of arms, which were stored in the City Hall, and take the city by surprise. If the rebels had acted promptly, they might have succeeded in their purpose. By waiting for reinforcements they missed their opportunity. The plot became known. The people of Toronto were aroused from their midnight slumbers by alarm bells. The loyal citizens rushed to the City Hall and prepared for defence. Tidings of the rebellion soon spread throughout the country. Colonel M'Nab, who was at Hamilton, hastened by steamer to Toronto, bringing a small force with him; and loyal farmers armed, some with old guns, others with pitchforks, rushed in for the defence of the city.

Failure of the Plot.

Within a few days an engagement took place near the city. The rebels were defeated with heavy loss. They fled in confusion, many of them throwing away their guns and hastening to their homes. The rebel leaders, finding themselves deserted by a large part of their followers, made haste to provide for their own safety. Dr. Rolph, who, trying to stand well with both sides, played a double part, with several other leaders fled to the United States.

Insurrections in other parts of the province were put down with equal promptness. MacKenzie was proclaimed an outlaw, and a reward of $5000 was offered for his head. Through the aid of friends he escaped across the border.

It was soon shown that the rebellion had no solid support in Upper Canada. Indeed it would now have been at an end, but for the sympathy and direct aid it received from the United States. As on several other occasions, the Government of that country, in times of peace with Great Britain, allowed hostile expeditions against Canada to be fitted out on its border territory. Mob forces were organised at Buffalo, Cleveland, Detroit, and other cities for invading our country.

Aid to the Rebels from the United States.

The most Quixotic organisation of all was one which had its seat on Navy Island, in the Niagara River, about two miles above the Falls. In December 1837 this island was taken possession of by MacKenzie and his followers, consisting partly of Canadian rebels and partly of a rabble gathered from the neighbouring cities of the United States. This was the "Patriot Army"! Its flag bore the motto, "Liberty and Equality," and two stars, one for each of the Canadas. MacKenzie, as chief ruler, issued a flaming proclamation, declaring Canada a republic, and promising free grants of land and other bounties to all his followers when his government was established. To crown all, he offered a reward of $2500 for the head of the Lieutenant-Governor of Upper Canada.

Navy Island.

A United States steamer, named the *Caroline*, was

employed to carry men and supplies to the island. Colonel M'Nab guarded the Canadian shores. A small force, sent by him, captured the *Caroline* at night, as she lay moored on the American shore. Unable, on account of the current, to bring her to the Canadian side, they set her on fire and let her drift over the Falls. The seizure of the vessel was a violation of international law, and gave much offence to the Government of the United States. The agitation over it, however, was quieted by an apology from Great Britain. Navy Island was shortly after abandoned by MacKenzie and his followers.

In the early part of the following year the "Patriots" and some of their American friends came over from the United States, expecting that the people would flock to their standard. The two chief points of attack were Windsor and Prescott. The invaders took possession of Windsor, and were marching against Sandwich. They gained little support, and soon found it wise to seek safety in the United States. Four of their number, who were taken prisoners, were shot without trial.

At Prescott about two hundred posted themselves in a windmill, a large circular building having thick stone walls. After three days' siege, when about fifty of their number had been killed, they surrendered.

The rebellion was now over, and it remained to deal with the misguided men who had so sadly disturbed the peace of the country, and who were now crowding the jails. One hundred and eighty of them were sentenced to be hanged. Some of these suffered this extreme penalty; some were banished to Van Diemen's Land; while others, on account of their youth, were pardoned.

<small>The End of the Rebellion.</small>

Papineau and MacKenzie.

After a few years of exile, those who had been outlawed or exiled were pardoned and allowed to return to Canada. Even Papineau and MacKenzie were permitted to come back and enjoy the full privilege of loyal citizens.

MacKenzie had during his exile experienced hard fortune. For some offence against law in the United States he was for many months confined in prison. During this period his mother, now in the ninetieth year of her age, lay on her deathbed. To enable him to visit her his friends got up a lawsuit, and summoned him as a witness. The trial was held in the house which the old lady occupied. Both MacKenzie and Papineau, after their return to Canada, held seats in the Assembly of the United Provinces.

CHAPTER XXVI.

RESPONSIBLE GOVERNMENT.

THOUGH the Earl of Durham remained but six months in Canada, he carefully studied the condition and wants of the provinces, and the able report which he submitted to the British Government is a lasting memorial of his service to the country. Among the important things recommended in this report were the following :– <small>The Earl of Durham's Report.</small>

(1.) A federal union of all the provinces under one general Parliament and Government, and providing each with a separate Legislature for local matters. But as this measure did not seem to be at that time practicable, he advised a union of Upper and Lower Canada under one Legislature and Government.

(2.) Less interference in provincial affairs by the Government of Great Britain, giving to the provinces full control of all matters of purely local concern.

(3.) An Intercolonial Railway connecting the various provinces.

(4.) Such change in the manner of appointing the Executive Council as would bring that body into harmony with the Assembly.

At the present time, when all these recommendations have been carried into effect, we recognise the far-sighted wisdom of the eminent statesman who proposed them.

The British Government saw the wisdom of uniting Upper and Lower Canada into one province. The Hon. Charles Poulett Thompson was appointed Governor-General, and was charged with the delicate duty of helping on the union of such diverse elements as were then found in these provinces. He came to Canada in 1839, where he soon proved his eminent fitness for the work entrusted to him. There was much opposition to the scheme in both provinces, and it was not desirable to force it on an unwilling people. The French inhabitants of Lower Canada feared it would bring them too much under the control of the English; and the members of the "Family Compact" in Upper Canada strongly opposed the measure, because they foresaw that it would speedily overthrow their power. The matter was adroitly managed.

Union of Upper and Lower Canada, 1841.

Lower Canada had no representative Assembly. On the recommendation of the Governor-General, the Special Council of this province adopted the Union Bill. There was need for skilful management in the Upper Province. The party most opposed to union was loud in its professions of loyalty to the mother-country. By presenting the scheme as an object strongly desired by the British Government, Mr. Thompson appealed to sentiments which they could not easily disregard, and the Union Bill was carried without difficulty.

In accordance with the desire of the two provinces thus expressed, the Imperial Parliament passed the Act of Union, which, by royal proclamation, came into effect on February 10, 1841. Governor Thompson's success in Canada gave great satisfaction to the British Government, and he was raised to the peerage as Baron Sydenham of Kent and Toronto.

The Union Act gave Canada a Legislature of two Houses, in which each of the old provinces had equal representation. The House of Assembly was composed of eighty-four members elected by the people. The Legislative Council was to comprise at least twenty members, appointed for life by the Crown. The Executive Council, sometimes called the Ministry, and also the Cabinet, consisted of eight members. Earl Russell, the Colonial Secretary, instructed the Governor-General that the members of this Council were to hold office only as long as their policy had the approval of the Assembly. There was a peculiar feature in the relations of the Council to the Assembly involving a sort of double responsibility. It was provided that the Ministry must be sustained not only by a majority of the whole House, but also by a majority of the members from each province, taken separately. There was another provision, which was evidently intended to meet a possible emergency, but which did not give general satisfaction: the Governor-General had power to retain or dismiss a Ministry in opposition to the wishes of the Assembly, when, in his judgment, the honour of the Crown or the interests of the Empire made it necessary. This power was liable to abuse.

The New Constitution.

On condition of making due provision for the

salaries of public officers and the expenses of carrying on the Government, the Assembly was given full control over all the revenues. While most of the principles for which the Reformers had contended were secured, there still remained an Upper House appointed by the Crown.

Important Business—Death of Sydenham. The election of members of the Assembly took place in the winter of 1841, resulting in the return of a nearly equal number of each political party. Lord Sydenham chose his Executive Council partly from each side. Very soon, however, the Reformers, becoming dissatisfied, retired, and left the Government wholly to the Conservatives. The Legislature met in Kingston in June. Much of the business done was of the highest service to the country. The Municipal Act gave power to counties, cities, and towns to elect councillors or aldermen for the care of roads, bridges, public buildings, and other local matters. Acts were passed relating to education, canals, and other public works, and to trade. While affairs were thus rapidly assuming orderly shape, a sad calamity befell the country. Lord Sydenham, while out riding, fell from his horse, receiving injuries of which he died.

The First Reform Ministry. Sir Charles Bagot succeeded Lord Sydenham. Though a Conservative, he faithfully carried out the principles laid down for the Government of Canada. He formed a new Ministry, composed entirely of Reformers, under the leadership of Baldwin and Lafontaine. Francis Hincks, who later on became prominent in the public affairs of Canada, was a member of the Cabinet. The strife among party politicians at this time was often embarrassing to the Governor-General; but Sir Charles managed matters with great prudence and fairness. On account of failing health he soon resigned his office, and died shortly after at Kingston in May 1843.

Sir Charles Metcalfe was the next Governor-General. He was sent to Canada by a Tory Government of Great Britain, and he was himself a Tory of the old school. *The Administration of Lord Metcalfe, 1843.* He had great contempt for responsible government. In his opinion the members of the Executive Council, in selecting persons for public offices, sought to strengthen their own position by rewarding their supporters rather than to promote the interests of the country. As for himself, according to his way of thinking, he was quite impartial, and had no motive to do what was not for the public good. He was probably quite conscientious, and his private character was such as to secure the respect of even those who were opposed to his political opinions. Carrying out his principles, the Governor-General, without consulting his Ministry, appointed Conservatives to certain offices. Baldwin, Lafontaine, and their colleagues, considering this a violation of the Constitution, placed their resignation in his hands. Although the Reformers had a majority in the Assembly, the Governor called on Mr. Draper, a Conservative, to form a new Government. At the same time he dissolved the Assembly and ordered a new election, in which he himself took an active part. In the new House the Draper Ministry was sustained by a small majority.

Meanwhile the seat of Government had been removed from Kingston to Montreal. The Legislature held its first session in this city in 1844.

The Conservative Government of Great Britain approved of the policy of the Governor-General, and rewarded him by raising him to the peerage with the title of Baron Metcalfe of Fern Hill. He did not long enjoy his honours. A deadly disease had fastened on him, and he returned to England, where he died in 1846.

Rebellion Losses. The Loyalists of Upper Canada had, for some time, been asking indemnity from the public funds for losses sustained by them during the rebellion. Under the Draper Government the Legislature voted a large sum for this purpose. A similar claim was then made by those who had suffered loss in Lower Canada. But the amount appropriated was so small that it failed to give satisfaction. The question was a difficult one. Some who had taken part in the rebellion were asking to have their losses made up. In the meantime no further action was taken by the Legislature, but the matter remained unsettled.

Lord Elgin, 1847. In 1847 a Liberal Government, with Lord John Russell at its head, came into power in England. Lord Elgin, a man of scholarly attainments, liberal views, and fine administrative ability, was sent out as Governor-General of Canada. He had married the daughter of the Earl of Durham, and he was ambitious of carrying into effect those principles of government which his father-in-law had recommended. Moreover, he was instructed by despatches from Earl Grey, the Colonial Secretary, to govern the country according to the advice of his Ministry. These despatches finally settled the long-vexed question of Responsible Government in Canada.

When Lord Elgin arrived in the Provinces the Draper Ministry, holding on by the frailest thread, was still clinging to power. A general election was pending, and the friends of the Government were using every means to prevent its overthrow. Among other influences brought to bear on the electors of Upper Canada was the assertion that if the Reformers came into power the rebels of Lower Canada would be rewarded out of the public treasury. Notwithstanding the vigorous canvass against the Reformers, the election resulted in giving them a large majority. On the meeting of Parliament early in 1877, the Draper Ministry resigned and the Baldwin-Lafontaine Government was reinstated.

Among the members of the Assembly elected at this time were Louis Papineau and Wolfred Nelson.

During the year in which Lord Elgin came to Canada, a large number of immigrants arrived at Quebec. With hundreds of thousands of their fellow-countrymen they had been driven from their homes by famine in Ireland, caused by failure of the potato crop. Densely crowded in ill-ventilated ships, many of them were seized on the passage with deadly fever. On arriving at Quebec they had little means with which to provide for their wants. Every possible effort was made, both by the Government and by private charity, to care for them, yet large numbers died from pestilence and exposure. *Immigration and Pestilence.*

One of the earliest measures of the Baldwin-Lafontaine Government was a Bill to provide for the

U

payment of rebellion losses in Lower Canada. The Conservatives opposed the Bill, asserting that the Government intended to pay all who had suffered loss, rebels as well as loyalists. This charge was denied, but none the less the country was soon greatly agitated over the action of the Government. Montreal, Toronto, and other cities of the West were wild with excitement over the matter. "No compensation to rebels" became a party cry. Many of the old Loyalists, who had taunted the Reformers with lack of fidelity to the British Crown, now openly talked of annexation to the United States. Meanwhile the Bill which was calling up such a storm passed both Houses.

Rebellion Losses.

Lord Elgin was urged by the opponents of the Bill to withhold his assent. But whatever may have been his private opinion in regard to its merits, he felt bound to follow the advice of his responsible Ministry. Accordingly, coming down to the Parliament House, he in due form gave his assent to the Bill. On leaving the building he was saluted with hisses and groans, and his carriage was pelted with sticks, stones, and rotten eggs by the excited multitude that thronged the streets. In the evening, while the House was in session, a mob collected around the building, broke the windows, and bursting open the doors rushed into the Assembly room. The members fled in confusion. One of the rioters, seating himself in the Speaker's chair, with mock dignity proclaimed—"Gentlemen, the French Parliament is dissolved." The mob proceeded to tear up the seats, break the chandeliers, and destroy all movable property within

Parliament House burned.

their reach. They then set the building on fire, standing guard to see that the flames were not extinguished. In the morning Parliament House was a mass of ruins, and a valuable library and many public documents which could not be replaced were reduced to ashes.

Let us now return and pick up the broken thread of our story in the Maritime Provinces. The Reformers marked the course of events in Canada with great interest, and they contended that Earl Russell's despatches to Governor Thompson applied to all the provinces. Sir Colin Campbell, the Governor of Nova Scotia, refused to be influenced by these despatches. With the view of forcing the Executive Council to resign, the Assembly, by a majority of thirty to twelve, passed a "vote of want of confidence" in this body. But Sir Colin told the Reformers that he was quite satisfied with his Council. Sir Colin was highly respected for many excellent personal qualities, but this treatment of the people's representatives gave great offence. The Assembly, by a large majority, adopted a memorial to the Queen, asking for his recall. Political meetings were held throughout the province to discuss the questions of the day, and many severe things were said by both parties.

Nova Scotia.

Shortly after his arrival in Canada the Governor-General, the Hon. Poulett Thompson, visited Halifax. He held interviews with the leaders of both parties, and although he was guarded in his expressions, he must have seen that Howe and his party were contending for the very principles which he himself was instructed to carry

Coalition Government.

out. Shortly after his visit, Sir Colin Campbell was recalled, and Lord Falkland was sent in his place. The new Governor belonged to the Liberal party in England, on account of which the Reformers in Nova Scotia expected great things from him. For the same reason the Conservatives regarded him with suspicion. As in Canada under Lord Sydenham, it was thought advisable in Nova Scotia to form an Executive Council composed of leading men selected from both parties. Accordingly Mr. Howe and some of his colleagues accepted positions made vacant for them in this body. But it was soon found that this Coalition Government was composed of two distinct and hostile parties which would not work in harmony with each other.

JAMES W. JOHNSTON.

The leader of the Conservative party at this time

was the Hon. James W. Johnston. A statesman of singularly acute mind and of high-toned moral principle, Mr. Johnston for the third of a century shared with Mr. Howe the affections of the people of Nova Scotia. Throughout his long public career he had the unwavering confidence of his party and the respect of his political opponents. Scarcely in anything except in patriotism did he and Mr. Howe agree.

Besides disagreeing on the great question of responsible government, they were at variance on a question of higher education which then agitated the province. Mr. Howe advocated the endowment by the Government of one provincial college. Mr. Johnston was in favour of giving public aid to various denominational colleges. Howe's attitude on this question gave offence to many of his old supporters throughout the country.

Lord Falkland, following the advice of the Conservative party in his Council, dissolved the Assembly. In the new Assembly Mr. Johnston's party had a small majority. Lord Falkland, whose policy was similar to that which Sir Charles Metcalfe was at the same time pursuing in Canada, without consulting Howe and his friends, appointed another Conservative to the Executive Council. The Reformers at once sent in their resignation.

The Coalition broken up, 1844.

Lord Falkland and Mr. Howe soon became open enemies to each other. Mr. Howe ridiculed the Governor in the public papers, and the Governor, in his despatches to the Colonial Secretary, said that Howe was a troublesome man with whom he could hold no further intercourse. The cause of Reform, however, was rapidly gaining strength, and Lord Falkland, finding that he was waging an unequal warfare, resigned his office and returned to England.

Sir John Harvey, who had already held the position of Governor in three provinces, succeeded Lord Falkland. He invited Mr. Howe and his friends to take their old place in the Council; but feeling that Liberals and Conservatives could not work well together, they declined the invitation.

Responsible Government, 1848.

Hitherto the election of members of Assembly took place at different times in the various counties, and voting was continued on successive days at the various polling-places in each county. A crowd of idlers went from place to place, often causing much disturbance. A new Assembly was elected in 1847, when for the first time in Nova Scotia the votes were all cast on a single day. When the House met in the following January, the Reformers were found to have a majority of seven. Meanwhile Sir John Harvey had received despatches from the Colonial Secretary, stating that the Executive Council must stand or fall according to the will of a majority of the people's representatives. Mr. Johnston and his colleagues resigned, and a Liberal Government was formed, of which the Hon. James B. Uniacke was Premier, and Joseph Howe, Herbert Huntington, Michael Tobin, and Hugh Bell were prominent members. From this time forward in Nova Scotia the Ministry could remain in power only so long as it had the confidence of a majority of the Assembly.

The struggle for responsible government was carried on in New Brunswick along the same lines, though not with as much acrimony, as in Nova Scotia. As in the last-named province, the privileges contended for were gained at intervals, one by one, and sometimes defeat followed victory. It happened, too, that bad use of what had been won sometimes brought discredit on the cause. Thus, when an overflowing treasury was placed under the control of the Assembly, reckless expenditure by that body during succeeding years not only exhausted the surplus funds, but burdened the province with a heavy debt. Public money was voted in a loose sort of way. Each member had his pet scheme, and in order to secure help from others to carry his measure, he voted for theirs. This was the very result which Tory governors and councils had predicted. Its effect was to retard the progress of popular government. It seemed to show that the people's representatives could not be trusted with the management of public affairs. As a check on careless expenditure the Colonial Secretary advised that all money bills should be introduced by the Government. This wise principle was adopted a few years later.

New Brunswick.

The indiscretions of the Reformers strengthened the Conservative party. A Bill providing that the Executive Council must have the confidence of the people's representatives was defeated in the Assembly by the casting vote of the Speaker. Sir John Harvey, unlike most of the Governors of his time, was in favour of reform, and under his moderate rule Tory principles were shorn of many of their objectionable features. In 1841 Sir John was succeeded by Sir

William Colebrooke, when affairs took a different turn. A general election in 1842 gave increased strength to the Conservative party in the Assembly. Resolutions were passed by both branches of the Legislature, favouring the doctrine of the Governor-General, Sir Charles Metcalfe, who claimed the right of the Governor to appoint Crown officers without consulting his Executive Council. Two years later, however, this article of the Conservative creed received so rude a shock that it never regained its old-time force. On the death of the Hon. William Odell, who had held the office of Provincial Secretary for twenty-six years, Sir William Colebrooke appointed his own son-in-law to the position. This was too much to suit even the stanchest Tory. Indeed, the matter caused so much dis-

CHARLES FISHER.

satisfaction that the Governor's son-in-law was compelled to resign. Shortly after, the Reform leaders, Lemuel A. Wilmot and Charles Fisher, urged the adoption of responsible government. But the state of feeling in the Assembly was not sufficiently developed for such a forward movement. Accordingly the Conservatives, under the leadership of Hon. Robert Hazen, held the reins of power, though with weakening grasp, a little longer.

Meanwhile the boundary line between New Brunswick and Maine, which had caused such serious dispute, was settled by the Ashburton Treaty. *The Ashburton Treaty, 1842.* The boundary had been fixed in 1783 and laid down upon a map, the existence of which was at this time unknown. The true boundary line as thus shown followed the water-shed of the St. John River, giving the basin of the Aroostook and of the other tributaries to Great Britain. After various fruitless efforts to secure a settlement of the difficulty, two Commissioners were appointed, Lord Ashburton by Great Britain and Daniel Webster by the United States, to determine the boundary line. The "Disputed Territory" comprised about twelve thousand square miles. The Commissioners gave five thousand square miles to New Brunswick and seven thousand to Maine, a settlement which has since been found unduly favourable to the last-named country. At the same time the Commissioners fixed the boundary between British America and the United States from New Brunswick westerly to the Rocky Mountains.

Earl Grey's instructions in his despatches of 1847, that the Governor must be guided in his public acts by the advice of his Executive Council, and that this

Responsible Government in New Brunswick, 1848.

Council must hold office only so long as it had the confidence of the Assembly, was intended to apply to New Brunswick as well as to Nova Scotia and Canada. Accordingly, in 1848, on the motion of Charles Fisher, these principles were adopted by a large majority of the Assembly. In this vote the leading Conservatives united with the Reformers. The two most prominent Reformers, Wilmot and Fisher, accepted seats in the Council with their old-time opponents who had now accepted their principles. Thus 1848 was noted as the first year in the era of responsible government in British America.

Prince Edward Island.

Under the rule of Colonel Ready and his successor, Sir Aretas Young, Prince Edward Island made much progress in population, education, and general thrift. During the administration of the last-named Governor, in 1833, an important change was made in the duration of the Assembly, requiring the election of a new House every four years in place of once in seven years.

In 1836 the popular Sir John Harvey became Governor of the island, a position which he held for only one year, when he was transferred to New Brunswick. His successor was Sir Charles Fitzroy, who arrived in the island a few days after Queen Victoria ascended the throne. At the time the country was greatly agitated. For some years the absent landlords had not asked the tenant-farmers for the yearly rents, but they were now demanding all arrears. Failing to pay, many farmers were ejected from the lands which they had long occupied. Exasperated by such treatment, they resisted the officers of the law who were sent to discharge the disagreeable duty of eviction.

A large part of the lands owned by the absent proprietors was still in its natural state, held for advance in price. Small settlements, scattered here and there, were thus, to their great disadvantage, separated by vast tracts of forest. The Legislature of the island imposed a tax on these lands. The proprietors appealed to the British Government to disallow the Act. But the Government, influenced by a report from the Earl of Durham, who was then Governor-General of Canada, refused to interfere.

In 1839, agitation for reform in the government of the island led to the appointment of an Executive Council and a Legislative Council, in place of a single Council with a double function. *Executive Council.*

Sir Henry Hunt, who succeeded Sir Charles Fitzroy as Governor, lacked discretion, and sometimes allowed personal feelings to influence his public acts. A motion in the Assembly for an addition to his salary was opposed by the Hon. Joseph Pope, Speaker of the House and member of the Executive Council. Without consulting the other members, the Governor dismissed Pope from the Council. This action did not meet with the approval of the British Government, and Sir Henry was required to reinstate the offender, and confer with his Council as to the proper mode of dealing with him. Mr. Pope, however, relieved the Council of responsibility in the matter by resigning his seat. He soon found opportunity to show his resentment. The Governor's friends sent a petition to the Queen, asking that his term of office, which was drawing to a close, might be extended. This led to a counter petition, and the appointment of Joseph Pope and Edward Palmer as delegates to England to secure the recall of the Governor. The opposing force prevailed, and Sir Donald Campbell was appointed as Sir Henry's successor.

As in the other provinces, a responsible executive was secured in the island only by decided measures. The matter had been agitated for some time, when in 1849 the Legislature proposed to the British Government that it would provide for the Civil List on condition that responsible government was granted, quit-rents abolished, and the Crown lands given to the island authorities. In reply, the Colonial Secretary, Earl Grey, offered everything asked for but responsible government. For this he thought the island was not yet prepared. This answer was received in the island with murmurings of discontent. The Assembly which met in 1850 passed a few necessary bills, and then refused to go on with the public business until the Government was so remodelled as to bring the Executive under the control of the people's representatives.

Responsible Government. 1851.

Meanwhile the popular Governor — Sir Donald Campbell - died, and was succeeded by Sir Alexander Bannerman. On meeting the Assembly in the following year, the Governor announced that responsible government had been granted, on condition that the Legislature would provide pensions for certain retiring officers of the existing Government, who had received their appointment for life.

RESPONSIBLE GOVERNMENT.

These terms were readily accepted. The Honourable George Coles, who had been the most prominent figure in the reform movement, became the leader of the new Government which now came into power, and his principal colleagues were Charles Young and Joseph Pope. In the same year quit-rents were abolished, and a uniform letter-postage of twopence for any part of the island, and of threepence for letters going to the other provinces, was adopted.

The population of the island at this time was about 65,000.

Many important changes have taken place in our civil affairs since the establishment of responsible government. It is safe to say, however, that the principles then laid down have been in no way disturbed. On the contrary, they have rather been given freer play and wider application.

THE HON. GEORGE COLES.

CHAPTER XXVII.

OLD QUESTIONS SETTLED AND NEW SCHEMES PROPOSED

Seat of Government. We left the Province of Canada in the midst of the storm caused by the "Rebellion Losses Act." When the heat of passion had cooled down a little, the riot at Montreal, with the burning of the Parliament Building, was felt to be a disgrace for which no good citizens cared to be held responsible. The people of Montreal were punished by the removal of the seat of Government from their city. For the next fifteen years, until Ottawa was made the capital, the Legislature met alternately, for four consecutive years, in Toronto and Quebec. Lord Elgin was so much disturbed over the riot, of which, in the discharge of the duties of his office, he had been the occasion, that he sent in his resignation. His action, however, was fully sustained by the Imperial Government, and he continued to hold the position of Governor-General with great acceptance for many years.

Progress in Canada. The Canadian people had gained much through hard struggle, but they were not yet satisfied. Each new achievement only served to awaken further striving. There were still some remaining evils, legacies of the past, to be removed, while foundations of new institutions were to be laid and strengthened.

Education. The education of the youth of the country was regarded as one of the first and highest concerns of the Government. Dr. Egerton Ryerson had already, by the Draper Ministry, been appointed Superintendent of Education. This distinguished clergyman, who had for many years taken an active part in the political affairs of the country, now, by close observation in Europe and in the United States, made himself acquainted with the most improved educational systems in the world. During the long period of thirty years he devoted his energies to the development of the common and high school system of Upper Canada. The high

REV. EGERTON RYERSON, D.D.

appreciation in which Dr. Ryerson's services were held by the country was shown at the close of his public career by the action of the Legislature of Ontario in granting him his full salary as a retiring pension.

Commerce. The trade of the provinces had hitherto been hampered by a high tariff on foreign goods, imposed by the Imperial Parliament for the purpose of giving an advantage to the British manufacturer. These trade restrictions were now, in 1849, removed, and the provinces were allowed to arrange their own tariff independently of the Home authorities. General intercourse throughout the provinces and with the United States was promoted by telegraph lines and by increased postal facilities. In 1851 the Post Office, which had hitherto been under the control of Great Britain, was handed over to the Provincial Governments. This resulted in the establishing of more postal routes and offices throughout the country, and in the reduction of rates. The use of postage-stamps also added much to the public convenience.

Railways. Improvement in means of travel and conveying goods also received attention. We have seen in a preceding chapter how the obstructions to navigation caused by falls and rapids in the Niagara and St. Lawrence Rivers were overcome by canals, thus giving a water-route between remote inland settlements and the great centres of trade. For several months in the year, however, rivers, lakes, and canals were closed, and the country was shut out from the great world by a barrier of ice.

The era of railways had now dawned. The first line built in the country was a short one, opened in 1839 between La Prairie and St. John's, in Lower Canada. After an interval of several years, in 1851, the Northern Railway, in Upper Canada, was begun. This was followed by the Great Western, from Niagara Falls to Windsor, and by the Grand Trunk, from the Great Lakes in the West to the tidal waters of the St. Lawrence. A little later, to secure access to the open sea in winter, a branch of the Grand Trunk was built to Portland, in Maine. Other lines were built in different parts of the country, some of which failed to prove a financial gain to the shareholders, yet indirectly were useful in developing the resources of the country.

Several perplexing questions now agitated the public mind. The Clergy Reserves was an Upper Canada question which for many years had been a source of bitter contention. *The Clergy Reserves.* It will be remembered that one-seventh of the public lands of the province was set apart in 1791 for the support of the Protestant Clergy, and that the Anglican Church alone was allowed to enjoy the benefit of this liberal appropriation. Dissatisfaction over such disposal of the funds was one of the leading causes of the rebellion in Upper Canada. In 1840, before the union of the Canadas, a settlement was made which, it was hoped, would set the matter at rest. The lion's share of the spoil was given to the Anglican Church, a much smaller slice was allotted to the Presbyterians of the Church of Scotland, while the remaining fragments were distributed in an ungenerous sort of way among other religious bodies. But the matter would not stay settled in this fashion, and as time passed dissatisfaction in Upper Canada strengthened, until it forced the Legislature to reopen the question. The matter was a difficult one to deal with. In the first place, the Legislature of Canada could take no action on it without permission from the Parliament of Great Britain. Besides, the members from Lower Canada were opposed to any change.

But Lower Canada had a "burning question" of its own. The modified Feudal System introduced in the early times into French Canada, as described in a foregoing chapter, had outlived whatever usefulness it may have had at first, and it was now in great disfavour. Under the modern conditions of society this system of holding lands was troublesome and oppressive, as well as a hindrance to the progress of the country. It will be remembered that when the censitaire or tenant sold his lands he had to pay one-twelfth of the receipts to the Seignior. As lands were now much more valuable and transfers were more frequent than in the olden time, this condition had become very burdensome. Besides, there was little inducement for the censitaire to make improvements when what he expended would not be wholly for his own benefit. The annual rents, too, had become excessive, and the poor habitant was often made the victim of dishonest greed. Different remedies for getting rid of the evil were proposed, of which the most radical consisted in cancelling the claims of the Seignior without any compensation.

Seigniorial Tenure.

The Baldwin-Lafontaine Government did not find

OLD QUESTIONS AND NEW SCHEMES.

it an easy matter to solve these knotty questions. Its supporters were not agreed among themselves, the measures which were popular in the West being offensive in the East. The extreme Reformers, known as "Clear Grits," led by George Brown, editor of the *Toronto Globe*, insisted on the "secularising of the Clergy Reserves"—that is, taking them from the religious bodies and using them for common public purposes. As the Government did not seem disposed to adopt such a measure, it lost the support of this party, and being left in a minority, was compelled to resign.

The Reformers divided.

HON. GEORGE BROWN.

A new Ministry was formed, of which the English leader was Francis Hincks. Mr. Hincks was a native of Ireland, but he had in early life removed to

Toronto, where he edited a paper. He was a man of eminent ability, and for many years took a prominent part in public affairs. The French leader was Augustus Morin, a brilliant and patriotic statesman. Dr. Rolph, a noted leader of the Rebellion in Upper Canada, was a member of the Government, and among its supporters in the House were the old-time rebels, Louis Papineau and William Lyon MacKenzie. One of the most distinguished members of the Assembly was George Brown of the *Toronto Globe*. Mr. Brown was an honest, energetic, and highly gifted Scotchman who had made Canada his home. In his paper and on the floor of the House he was a sturdy advocate of the two great reform measures before the public. He was a Ministerialist, that is on the Government side; yet he was sometimes so extreme in his views that he could not easily be kept in line, and while he was a powerful opponent, he was an uncertain supporter. On the Opposition side of the House was a young lawyer who was rapidly rising to the first position in his party, and who during the succeeding forty years exerted a powerful influence in moulding the institutions of the country. This was John A. Macdonald, better known in later times as Sir John. Mr. Macdonald was born in Scotland, and when about five years of age came with his parents to Canada.

The Hincks-Morin Government, 1851.

The building of railways was the leading public enterprise of the time. The Grand Trunk line had a strong patron in Mr. Hincks. It received large subsidies from the public funds, and was aided by the credit of the province in borrowing money.

During the reign of the Hincks Ministry an Act

OLD QUESTIONS AND NEW SCHEMES. 325

was passed by which, on the security of the Government, municipalities were enabled to borrow money for making roads and bridges and for other public purposes. The easy terms on which money could be obtained led to some unwise expenditures, and to the incurring of debts which afterwards proved burdensome.

The year 1852 is memorable for a disastrous fire in Montreal, which left ten thousand persons homeless.

The Reciprocity Treaty, 1854. The Reciprocity Treaty, arranged by Lord Elgin and Mr. Hincks for the regulation of trade and other matters between the British Provinces and the United States, was one of the principal measures of the time. It provided for exchange, free of duty, of the natural products of the farm, the forest, the mines, and the

SIR JOHN A. MACDONALD.

sea. It also provided that the subjects of the United States should have equal privilege with British subjects in the coast fisheries of the provinces and in the navigation of the St. Lawrence River and the Canadian canals. Canadians also were given the privilege of navigating Lake Michigan. The treaty was to remain in force for ten years, after which it would terminate on twelve months' notice given by either party.

Another measure adopted under the Hincks-Morin rule increased the membership of the Assembly from eighty-four to one hundred and thirty, giving each division sixty-five members.

In the autumn of 1854 Lord Elgin was succeeded as Governor-General by Sir Edmund Walker Head. Mr. Hincks's power was now near its end. George Brown and his party, becoming impatient of the delay in dealing with the Clergy Reserves and other matters which they thought demanded immediate action, withdrew their support from the Government. After a general election the Ministry had a small majority in Lower Canada, but it had suffered sad reverses in the West. It was defeated by the combined vote of the Conservatives and extreme Reformers, led by Mr. Brown.

The M'Nab-Morin Government, 1854.

No one of the three parties was strong enough to resist the united opposition of the other two. The Governor-General called on Sir Allan M'Nab, the leader of the Conservatives, to form a Ministry. This he succeeded in doing by a coalition with the late Ministerialist party, which he had just helped to drive out of power. In the new Government the members of the late Government from Lower Canada were given their former places, while those from the

OLD QUESTIONS AND NEW SCHEMES. 327

West were replaced by Conservatives. In this Coalition Government John A. Macdonald was Attorney-General.

It fell to the M'Nab-Morin Ministry to settle the two great questions which had long disturbed the country. The Parliament of Great Britain had already given Canada the power to deal with the Clergy Reserves. The Act of Settlement which was now adopted by the Legislature provided that the clergy who were then receiving allowances should have their stipend secured to them for life, and that the remainder of the fund after such allowances were paid should be divided among the various municipalities for general public use. *Settlement of Burning Questions.*

The land question of Lower Canada was settled by compromise. The Seigniors were required to abate a portion of their claims, while the amount paid them was made up partly by the censitaires and partly by a grant from the public treasury. As a large amount from the provincial funds was thus applied for the benefit of Lower Canada, a corresponding amount was given to the municipalities of Upper Canada, and also to various townships in Lower Canada, where the old manner of holding lands had not existed. In all about $10,000,000 of the public funds were used.

There still remained another grievance, a vestige of the old-time Tory rule, for the removal of which the Reformers had long struggled in vain. This was the Legislative Council appointed by the Crown. An Act was now passed designed to bring about, in the easiest possible manner, the desired change. The Act did not disturb the members of the Council who had been appointed under the old system, but provided that as vacancies occurred new members should be elected for the term of eight years.

Meanwhile some important changes were made in the Ministry. Colonel Taché succeeded Morin as leader for Lower Canada. Another brilliant French-Canadian, George E. Cartier, who had for many years taken an active part in political affairs, and who had a conspicuous part still to play, was added to the Ministry. In his youth he had followed Papineau, fought in the ranks of the rebels under Dr. Nelson, and saved himself from the stern hand of the law by escaping across the border into the United States. Sir Allan McNab, now enfeebled by the infirmities of age and by disease, retired from the Cabinet. Finally John A. Macdonald,

The Macdonald-Cartier Ministry. 1857.

SIR GEORGE E. CARTIER.

OLD QUESTIONS AND NEW SCHEMES. 329

who for some time had held the first place in the esteem of the Conservative party, and who had been its virtual head, took the position of Premier, while Cartier became leader for Lower Canada. On the side of the Opposition were such distinguished chiefs as George Brown, Oliver Mowat, and D'Arcy Magee.

The machinery of government in the united province had never run smoothly. The two Canadas were too unlike each other to work together very harmoniously. There was almost constant friction from one cause or another, and as the years went by matters grew worse. At the time of union Lower Canada had the larger population, but she was now about three hundred thousand behind. On the ground of its greater population, wealth, and contributions to the public treasury, Upper Canada had for some time been pressing its right to larger representation in the Legislature. George Brown became the unyielding advocate of this claim, and there followed him a large party whose battle-cry was "Representation by population," or "Rep by Pop," as it was commonly called. The Macdonald-Cartier Government, deserted by many of its old followers in the West, held its position through the support of Lower Canada. Estrangement was growing up between the West and the East. The cry of "French domination" from the one quarter was met by "Danger to our laws, our customs, and our religion" from the other. *[margin: Representation by Population.]*

As the frequent change in the seat of Government between Quebec and Toronto was expensive and inconvenient, it was felt desirable to select some place as a fixed capital. Several cities were ambitious of being chosen, but it *[margin: Ottawa the Seat of Government, 1858.]*

was difficult to agree on any one of them. The matter was finally left to the Queen, and the competing cities were asked to furnish statements of the advantages they had to offer. Her Majesty's choice fell upon Ottawa. When the decision was announced in the Legislature there was a strong outburst of adverse feeling from the friends of the various rival cities, and a resolution of disapproval was carried by a majority of fourteen. In a vote on another question taken immediately after, the Government was sustained by a majority of eleven. It was thus shown that the former vote was not intended to express lack of confidence in the Government. For some reason, however, not easy to explain, the Ministry placed their resignation in the hands of the Governor-General. His Excellency called on George Brown to form a new Government. Mr. Brown's Cabinet included several strong men, of whom may be named John Sandfield Macdonald, Oliver Mowat, and A. A. Dorion. The reign of the new Ministry was brief. On their names being announced in the Assembly, a vote of want of confidence was carried by a majority of forty. Mr. Brown and his colleagues, claiming that the Assembly did not fairly represent the opinions of the country, asked for a dissolution; but his Excellency refused to follow the advice of his new Ministers, and after a reign of two days they were forced to resign. Mr. Brown and his colleagues considered that the Governor-General, in refusing an appeal to the people, had not shown them proper courtesy, and they left the Council-board holding towards him no very friendly feeling.

The Conservative leaders were recalled. George

Cartier took the first place in the Ministry, which was known as the Cartier-Macdonald Government. A new question now came up.

The "Double Shuffle."

A rule under responsible government requires that Ministers of the Crown, on accepting office, shall return to their constituents for re-election. The rule was not followed on this occasion. A clause in an Act of the Legislature provided that a Minister who had resigned his office might, within a month, accept another without re-election. As the law did not allow the Ministers to take their old offices in this way, they exchanged portfolios on entering the Cabinet, and afterwards exchanged again, resuming their former places. The Opposition regarded this course as an evasion of law, and gave it the name of the "Double Shuffle."

A great railway bridge over the St. Lawrence, near Montreal, was to be opened in the summer of 1860. The work was regarded as a wonderful feat of engineering skill, and its completion was thought worthy of signal distinction.

Visit of the Prince of Wales, 1860.

Accordingly the Legislature of Canada decided to ask Queen Victoria to honour the event with her presence. The Speaker of the Assembly, Hon. Henry Smith, was sent to England to bear the invitation. Her Majesty, being unable to take so long a journey, sent her eldest son, the Prince of Wales, then about nineteen years of age, as her representative. The Prince visited the various provinces, receiving in all a royal welcome. By driving the last rivet he gave the finishing stroke to the Victoria Bridge, and on coming to Ottawa he took the place of honour in laying the corner-stone of the new Parliament Buildings which now grace the capital of the Dominion.

Death of the Prince Consort, 1861.

The year 1861 is memorable for the death of the Queen's husband, Prince Albert. Though a German by birth, the Prince thoroughly identified himself with the British people, and showed the deepest interest in everything which concerned the prosperity of the Empire. He gave his powerful influence in aid of many schemes of national progress, and he is regarded as the originator of international exhibitions, the first of which was held in London in 1851.

War in the United States, 1861.

A war cloud appeared on the western horizon. The Southern States had broken off from the Union and set up an independent government. This action gave rise to a great war between the North and the South, which lasted four years. An event of the first year of the war threatened to involve Great Britain and the United States in hostilities and to make of Canada a bloody battlefield. Two Southern commissioners, Mason and Slidell, who had taken passage for Europe in the British steamer *Trent*, were seized by the officers of a United States warship and carried off as prisoners. This violation of international law aroused strong feeling of indignation in Great Britain. The British Government demanded the immediate release of the prisoners, and at the same time made preparation for war in case the demand was refused. Happily the affair was settled by the prompt surrender of Mason and Slidell to British officers appointed to receive them.

The civil war in the United States made brisk times in the provinces. Horses and farm produce of all kinds brought high prices in that country, and

Southern cruisers drove Northern merchant vessels from the seas, leaving to our vessels the larger portion of the carrying trade.

Lord Monck succeeded Sir Edmund Walker Head as Governor-General. Frequent change of advisers during his term of office gave him good opportunity to become acquainted with Canadian statesmen. The Cartier-Macdonald Ministry, defeated on a Militia Bill, which involved a large expenditure of money, was succeeded by a Liberal Ministry led by John Sandfield Macdonald. By reconstructing his Government, changing old colleagues for new ones, this Premier struggled on for about two years, when he laid down the reins of power. Lord Monck now had difficulty in finding any one who felt able to take control. One and another declined. Finally a Conservative Ministry was formed by Sir E. P. Taché and John A. Macdonald. D'Arcy McGee, who had formerly been a Liberal, was also a member of the new Government.

Defeat of the Cartier-Macdonald Government, 1862.

This Ministry, too, was soon in deep waters, and was considering the alternative of resigning or advising a dissolution of the House. There had already within three years been two general elections, and a fresh appeal to the people did not promise much relief from the embarrassment.

During the past two years four different Ministries, two Conservative and two Liberal, had by hook or by crook tried to govern the country. Each party, in order to keep itself in power for any length of time, was forced to depend either on Upper Canada alone, or on Lower Canada alone, for

The Situation.

its support; or by some compromise of principle it had to form coalitions with old opponents. A large majority of Upper Canadians were arrayed against a similar majority of Lower Canadians.

A committee of the leading members of both parties had been appointed to consider measures of relief from existing embarrassments. The committee reported in favour of separate governments for local affairs in the two Canadas, and a federal government for matters of common interest. It was proposed also, if possible, to bring the Maritime Provinces into the federal union. This report met with general approval.

A Surprise.

In the spirit of patriotism, laying aside all party questions and personal feeling, the leading members of the Opposition, with George Brown at their head, offered to aid the Conservative Government in carrying out a scheme of federation.

The announcement of this proposal from the Opposition, coupled with the name of the unyielding George Brown, was greeted with a loud and hearty burst of applause. As a guarantee of their good faith, and with the view of giving all possible aid to the scheme, three of the foremost Liberals, George Brown, Oliver Mowat, and William MacDougall, entered the Cabinet with the Conservatives.

CHAPTER XXVIII.

THE MARITIME PROVINCES UNDER RESPONSIBLE GOVERNMENT.

WE shall in this chapter trace the leading events in the history of the Maritime Provinces from the introduction of responsible government to the movement for Confederation. At this time the two great political parties, Liberals and Conservatives, were distinguished not so much by difference of principle as by their attachment to their leaders. Both parties were agreed in accepting responsible government as a fixed fact. From time to time one side or the other raised some new question as a rallying cry. *[General Features.]*

In Nova Scotia for eight years the Liberals held the reins of power. The most prominent men of the party were Joseph Howe, William Young, James B. Uniacke, and Michael Tobin. James W. Johnston was the leader of the Opposition.

In New Brunswick the condition of things was somewhat different. It will be remembered that on the introduction of responsible government a Coalition Ministry was formed, the two leading Liberals, Wilmot and Fisher, to the great disgust of their followers, uniting with their old opponents. Several years passed before the Liberals recovered sufficiently from the loss to form a strong Opposition.

In Prince Edward Island the new order of things began, as already stated, three years later than in the other provinces. The two parties were so evenly balanced that business was often obstructed and Government and Opposition changed places. The most prominent leaders in public affairs were George Coles, Charles Young, and Edward Palmer.

The Maritime Provinces were included as parties in the Reciprocity Treaty of 1854 with the United States, spoken of in the preceding chapter. In Nova Scotia, however, there was little enthusiasm over the matter. Strong objections were urged in the Legislature against treaty-making of this sort, in which the province had no representation.

At this time the railway fever was in the air and spread from land to land. While the Province of Canada was building its great roads, the Grand Trunk and the Great Western, New Brunswick and Nova Scotia were astir in a similar movement. The first scheme proposed was an Intercolonial Railway between Quebec and Halifax. It had been spoken of long before, and Lord Durham had urged the importance of such a work in his famous report. But the scheme received little attention. The people in the West took more interest in connecting the remote parts of their own great country. After some delay, however, the Governments of Canada, New Brunswick, and Nova Scotia agreed to build the road, if Great Britain would by a guarantee aid them in obtaining money on favourable terms. Failing to obtain this assistance, they abandoned the idea of an

Railways.

Intercolonial Railway, and each province began building such local railways as seemed best to serve its own purposes.

The first railway built in New Brunswick was between Shediac, on Northumberland Strait, and St. John. The plan included an extension westerly to connect St. John with the railways of the United States.

The first railways in Nova Scotia connected Windsor and Truro with Halifax. These roads were built and owned by the Government. The scheme provided for extensions from Truro to Pictou and the New Brunswick frontier.

Early in 1857 the Liberal Government was overthrown. Its defeat was due chiefly to dissensions between Hon. Joseph Howe and the Roman Catholics, who had been in the main, up to this date, supporters of the Liberal party, but who now went over in a body to the Opposition. The Hon. J. W. Johnston, the Conservative leader, was called to the helm. The second place in the Ministry was held by Dr. Charles Tupper, a man of great ability and force of character, known in later years as Sir Charles Tupper. *Conservative Government in Nova Scotia, 1857.*

One of the first matters taken in hand by the new Government was the breaking up of a monopoly in coal-mining which had been established in the province. Certain minerals, as coal and gold, are reserved as rights of the Crown. Thus a person has no claim to any minerals of this kind which he may find on his land. He must get leave of the Government to work the mines, and he *The Mines and Minerals.*

Y

is required to pay a royalty on all the minerals which he obtains. As explained in a former chapter, these minerals are not the King's private property; they belong to the people, and the royalty is paid into the public treasury. Kings, however, have not always clearly understood this matter. Thus George IV. gave the minerals of Nova Scotia to his brother the Duke of York. In 1825 the Duke transferred his right to a company, known as the General Mining Association, on condition that the company should pay him a share of the profits. For many years the Government of Nova Scotia disputed the claims of the company, holding that the King had no power to give the minerals away.

SIR CHARLES TUPPER.

The Government now undertook to settle the question of ownership. Mr. Johnston, the leader of the Government, and Mr. Adams G. Archibald, one of the ablest leaders of the Liberal party, were sent to England to arrange terms of settlement. A compromise was effected. The company gave up all claims to the minerals of the province, except within certain limits around the mines already opened.

The year 1858 is memorable for the laying of the first telegraphic cable along the bed of the Atlantic Ocean between Europe and America. *The Atlantic Cable.* It was with great delight that those interested in the world's progress learned that the work was successfully completed, and that beneath the wide ocean friendly greetings had been exchanged between the Queen of Great Britain and the President of the United States. But the good news was followed quickly by tidings of disaster. Before any other messages were sent the cable parted in mid-ocean.

On the meeting of the Legislature in 1860, after a general election, the majority was found on the side of the Opposition. The leader of the Government, however, stated *The Liberals again in Power, 1860.* that certain members of the Opposition at the time of their election held offices which excluded them from the Legislature, and he moved that the House proceed to investigate the charges which he had made. It should be here stated that persons holding offices of emolument under the Government, such as sheriffs, registrars, postmasters, and custom-house officers, are thereby disqualified for sitting as members of the Legislature, and they must resign such offices before they can be legally elected. The object of the law is to secure the freedom of the members of the

Legislature from all influences that might lead them to sacrifice the public good for selfish interest.

The Opposition objected to the motion proposed by the leader of the Government. The question could be decided only by a vote of the House, and counting the doubtful members the Opposition had the majority, and thus outvoted the Government. Mr. Johnston and his colleagues asked the Governor to dissolve the House and have a new election; but their advice being rejected, they placed their resignation in his hands. The most prominent members of the new Government were Joseph Howe, William Young, and A. G. Archibald.

The Liberal Government, under the leadership of Mr. Howe, was kept in power by a slim majority for

SIR J. WILLIAM DAWSON.

four years. At the next general election this majority was shifted to the other side, bringing Mr. Johnston and Dr. Tupper again to the head of affairs. Shortly after, Mr. Johnston having been appointed Judge of the Supreme Court, Dr. Tupper became Premier. The principal matters dealt with by the new Government related to the public schools and confederation of the provinces.

REV. ALEXANDER FORRESTER, D.D.

Free Schools 1864

For nearly a quarter of a century a Free School system had been talked of throughout the province as a thing to be desired. It had been urged by Governors and recommended by educational committees of the Assembly, but without effect. Taxation was not popular among the people, and the law-makers feared to incur their displeasure. Meanwhile, however, potent forces

were at work which eventually so far overcame opposition as to render the measure practicable.

In 1850 John William Dawson, since well known as the principal of McGill University, and also as the distinguished scientist, Sir William Dawson, was appointed Superintendent of Education. Though holding the office but a short time, he, by means of lectures, reports, and teachers' institutes, awakened the public mind to a greater interest in general education and to a stronger desire for free schools. The movement was carried forward by Rev. Alexander Forrester, D.D., a most energetic worker and enthusiastic educationist, who in 1855 was appointed Superintendent of Education, and Principal of the Normal School, which was opened in the autumn of that year.

The Free School Bill, passed in 1864, though introduced by Dr. Tupper as a Government measure, was not dealt with by the Legislature in a party spirit. Adams G. Archibald, William Annand, and other leading men of the Opposition gave it hearty support. The Act provided for the separation of the offices of Principal of the Normal School and Superintendent of Education. Theodore H. Rand, D.C.L., was appointed to the latter office, and upon him devolved the duty of bringing the Free School law into practical operation — a task of no small magnitude. Owing to the obnoxious feature of taxation, the new system at first met with strong opposition. Many sections refused to appoint trustees, or to organise schools under the law, and for a year or two there was much confusion. Gradually, however, opposition disappeared, and the Free School system came to be looked upon as a necessary part of the machinery required for the wellbeing of society.

Prince Edward Island established free schools in 1852, and, four years later, a normal school for the training of teachers. The two political parties in the island were sometimes so evenly balanced that neither party could secure a working majority. Another difficulty in carrying on public business arose from lack of harmony between the Assembly and the Legislative Council. Important measures passed in one House were rejected by the other. As a remedy for this trouble five new members were added to the Council. One feature of responsible government was not very popular in the island. The people objected to their representatives holding offices of emolument in the Government, such as that of Attorney-General or Provincial Secretary. Hence, members of the Cabinet holding portfolios, on returning to their constituents, often failed to secure re-election. They did not, however, on this account always retire from the Cabinet, as the principles of responsible government demanded. *Prince Edward Island.*

By far the greatest evil with which the people of the island had to contend was the system of absentee proprietorship of the land. This gigantic wrong, recklessly imposed on the colony in its infancy, had now, by the growth of a century, gained so firm a foothold that little short of a rebellion could shake it off. It sapped the life-blood of the country. The farmers had good crops, but much of the money they realised must be sent abroad to pay the rents, and still they were sadly in arrears. Sometimes they were driven to insurrec- *Landlords and Tenants.*

tion by the hard hand of the bailiff sent to enforce the claims of the absent landlord.

Various methods of removing the evil were tried, but with little success. In some few cases the Government purchased the lands and sold them again on easy terms to the farmers. But this plan could not be followed to any great extent. The proprietors were not willing to sell at reasonable prices, and the Government had little money to use for this object. In vain had the British Government been appealed to for some remedy. Finally, at the suggestion of the proprietors, the Colonial Secretary proposed that the matter should be left to three Commissioners, one appointed by the British Government, one by the Island Government, and one by the proprietors. This plan was adopted. The Commissioners consisted of John Hamilton Grey of New Brunswick to represent the Crown, Joseph Howe of Nova Scotia to represent the tenants, and John W. Ritchie of Nova Scotia to represent the proprietors.

In the summer of 1861 the Commissioners sent in their report. They recommended that the proprietors should sell the lands on certain specified terms, and that the Island Government should purchase the lands, and afterwards sell them to the farmers on such easy conditions as could be met without embarrassment. They proposed also that the Government of Great Britain should, by guarantee, aid the Island Government in borrowing $500,000 for the purchase of the lands. The Legislature of the island at once accepted the award. But the proprietors refused to sell their lands on the conditions named, nor would the Imperial Government aid the island in borrowing the money. The scheme accordingly fell through.

CHAPTER XXIX.

BRITISH COLUMBIA.

MEANWHILE there had arisen in the far West a great maritime province. We have seen how the enterprising fur traders of the North- *Oregon.* West were the pioneers who led the way to this land facing the setting sun, and asserted the right of England in its soil. But for their persistent hold the British flag would not to-day wave over its hills and harbours, and the Dominion of Canada would not span the Continent. For many years the whole territory from California to Alaska was known by the general name of Oregon. Great Britain claimed the northern portion, and the United States the southern portion. The Ashburton Treaty, as already stated, had fixed on the forty-ninth parallel as the separating line between the territory of the two nations from the Lake of the Woods to the Rocky Mountains. Farther west the boundary was not determined. The Hudson's Bay Company, however, occupied the coast country as far south as the mouth of the Columbia River. Over a vast region lying north of this the company held a monopoly of the fur trade, secured by royal charter for twenty-one years, dating from 1838. The name New Caledonia was given to the portion of country occupied by the

Hudson's Bay Company, the name Oregon being then restricted to a part of the territory owned by the United States.

Disputes arose regarding the international boundary on the western side of the Continent. The British claimed that the line should continue along the forty-ninth parallel from the Rocky Mountains to the Columbia River, and that it should then follow the river southerly to its mouth. This would give both nations free access to the interior. On the other hand some of the Americans began to assert claims to the whole country on the west of the Rocky Mountains. By way of showing how much in earnest they were over the matter, they raised the cry, " Fifty-four-Forty or Fight." By this they meant, come peace, come war, they would have the country to north latitude 54 40', the recognised southern limit of Alaska, which was then owned by Russia.

Boundary Disputes.

Meanwhile colonists of both nations were settling on the coast, especially in that portion of the territory which was of doubtful ownership. It therefore became necessary to determine the boundary, that the colonists might know to which Government they owed allegiance.

For many years the Hudson's Bay Company's chief trading post on the Pacific coast was Fort Vancouver, on the Columbia River, ninety miles from its mouth. In view of the uncertainty as to the location of the boundary, the company decided to select as its headquarters a new situation farther north. A place on the south of Vancouver Island was chosen for this purpose, and in 1843 buildings for the use of the company were erected, and fortified by a stockade. This place was at first called Fort

Fort Victoria.

Camosin, but the name was soon after changed to Fort Victoria. The choice was wisely made. Here, to-day, beautiful for situation, on the margin of the land, with the picturesque harbour at its feet and the snow-clad Olympian heights on the horizon, stands Victoria, the capital of British Columbia.

In 1846 the boundary was agreed on by the Governments of Great Britain and the United States. But to the surprise of her subjects in British Columbia, Great Britain gave up the territory on the Columbia River south of the forty-ninth parallel. It was agreed that the line should follow this parallel to the sea, and that it should then be continued southerly through the middle of the channel which separates Vancouver Island from the Continent, and through the middle of the Strait of Fuca to the Pacific Ocean. *The Boundary settled, 1846.*

There now began a movement for colonising Vancouver Island. In 1849 the British Government gave the Hudson's Bay Company authority to bring in colonists and sell them lands on such terms as might be considered favourable to the opening up of the country for settlement. The company was not vested with any right of Government. The island was made a Crown colony; that is, it was placed under the government of officers appointed by the Crown. Richard Blanshard was sent from England as the first Governor, arriving on the island in 1850. He seems not to have found his position either profitable or agreeable. He had no salary, and though he had been promised a thousand acres of land on the island, he learned on his arrival that he was merely to have the use of the land while he remained in the *Colonisation of Vancouver.*

country. At the end of two years he resigned his office and returned to England.

James Douglas, the Hudson's Bay Company's chief agent at Victoria, was the next Governor. During the first few years he was assisted by a Council of three members. In 1856 a representative Legislature was elected. An important event in this period of the island's history was the discovery of coal in 1850 near the site of the present city of Nanaimo.

The company's colonising schemes made little progress. The few colonists who had been settled on the island were dissatisfied, and complained that their interests counted for little when they were in conflict with those of the company. Some of them left the country for the Californian gold mines, then a great centre of attraction. A change in the management of affairs was considered necessary. Accordingly, in 1858 the British Government withdrew the company's charter and took the colony under its own direct control.

But now suddenly the whole aspect of affairs both on island and mainland was changed. The moving force was the discovery of gold on the Fraser River. The gold fever was epidemic and overpowering. News of the discovery soon spread far and wide, and there followed a rush of eager seekers for the precious metal to the rugged wilderness of British Columbia. They came from the neighbouring lands of Washington, Oregon, and California, from the Eastern Provinces, and from beyond the ocean. The crews of vessels arriving on the coast deserted, and hastened

Discovery of Gold, 1858.

to the gold diggings. To the quiet-going inhabitant of the province the whole world seemed unbalanced. It was a mixed crowd, rude and lawless, that was now taking possession of the land. A strong ruling force was needed to establish order and maintain peace.

The mainland was formed into a Crown colony under the name of British Columbia. A place called Queensborough, on the Fraser River, was chosen as the seat of Government, its name being changed to New Westminster. Governor Douglas had shown such superior qualifications for the difficult task of ruling the country that he was made Governor of both colonies. At the same time, he was required to give up all connection with fur-trading companies.

British Columbia a Crown Colony, 1858.

In place of being an Indian hunting-ground, British Columbia soon began to wear some of the aspects of civilisation. Steamers went to and fro on its rivers and lakes, waggon roads were made at vast expense through the rugged mountain districts, and villages sprang up here and there at various places. The country was found to possess other resources than furs and gold, which might make it a land of desire to the colonist. The timber of its forests and the fish in its rivers and coast waters were recognised as sources of exhaustless wealth.

While these stirring events were taking place, the boundary question came up again. In 1857 Commissioners were appointed by Great Britain and the United States for the purpose of locating the line which had

The Boundary Question again.

been agreed on. They set up iron posts through the territory at intervals of one mile to mark the position of the forty-ninth parallel. But when they came to the Gulf of Georgia they could not agree. The treaty stated that the line should run through the middle of the channel which separates Vancouver Island from the Continent. There were found to be three channels between the island and the mainland. The British officer claimed that Rosario Strait, the most easterly channel, was the one through which the line should pass; the United States officer insisted that Haro Channel, the most westerly, was the one intended by the treaty. The chief object of the dispute was the ownership of the small island of San Juan, which lies between these channels.

San Juan

The Island of San Juan had long been occupied by the Hudson's Bay Company, but within a few years a number of citizens of the United States had taken up their residence on the island. The neighbouring state of Washington now set up a claim to it as a part of its territory. An officer was sent over from this state to collect taxes from British subjects. When payment was refused he seized their property. A company of armed men was then placed on the island, for the purpose, it was said, of protecting the interests of the United States citizens. Matters now wore a serious aspect, and it was only through the prudence of Governor Douglas that hostilities were averted. It was finally agreed that each nation should occupy the island with a small force until the difficulty was settled.

Governor Douglas, or Sir James Douglas as he now became, closed his official career in 1864. He was succeeded in Vancouver by Arthur Kennedy, and in British Columbia by Frederick Seymour. In 1866 the two colonies were united as one province under the name of British Columbia, with Victoria as the seat of Government.

British Columbia and Vancouver united, 1866.

CHAPTER XXX.

CONFEDERATION.

MEANWHILE the Maritime Provinces were also discussing the subject of union. In this quarter, however, the movement did not originate in any pressing political necessity. In the provinces by the sea the machinery of government was running smoothly enough, but union promised certain advantages of a financial nature which made it worth seeking. Nor did there seem any great obstacle in the way. These provinces were very like each other in their physical features, their institutions, and their interests; their inhabitants were one people. Why should they at unnecessary cost maintain separate governments, or why should they by restrictive tariffs isolate themselves from each other?

Union Movement in the Maritime Provinces, 1864.

The movement in its origin did not contemplate anything wider than union of the Maritime Provinces. The bringing of all the provinces under one government was scarcely thought practicable. For several years this question of union had been agitated, Nova Scotia taking the lead in the matter. On their visit to England to settle the mining interests of the province, Johnston and Archibald had discussed the subject with the Colonial Secretary, and had learned that the project was favoured by the British Government. In 1864 the Governments of Nova Scotia, New Brunswick, and Prince Edward Island appointed delegates to meet at Charlottetown to arrange terms of union for the three provinces. It was proposed to adopt a legislative union, that is one in which the provinces would be united under a single Legislature and Government for both local and general affairs.

With great satisfaction the Canadians learned of the movement in the Maritime Provinces. The Coalition Government, which had been recently organised for the special purpose of bringing about some political change, secured permission to send representatives to the Conference, and a deputation of seven members came down the St. Lawrence, and found cordial welcome among the delegates at Charlottetown.

<small>The Charlottetown Convention, September 1, 1864.</small>

The minor union of the Maritime Provinces was scarcely thought of in the Convention, being quite overshadowed by the grander idea of a confederation of all the provinces. No determinate action was taken at Charlottetown in the arrangement of terms. Efforts were made, however, to impress the public mind in favour of the scheme. The delegates visited Nova Scotia and New Brunswick, where they set forth its advantages in glowing colours. Before leaving Charlottetown they arranged to meet later in the season at Quebec for the purpose of drawing up a basis of Confederation.

Accordingly, in the autumn of the same year, another Convention was held in the old Parliament House of Quebec. All the provinces, including

Newfoundland, were represented. For eighteen days the delegates sat with closed doors, and no whisper of their doings reached the curious public ear. Everything was to be kept secret until the proposed scheme should be laid before the Legislatures of the different provinces; but long before the Legislatures met, the Quebec scheme was public property.

The Quebec Convention, October 1864.

The union resolutions, as agreed on by the Convention, were submitted to the Canadian Parliament, which, in the following February, met for the last time in the city of Quebec. It was strongly urged, and very properly too, that in a matter of such importance the people should be consulted before final action was taken; but the advocates of the people's rights were in the minority.

Reception of the Scheme, 1865.

In the Maritime Provinces matters did not go so smoothly. A reaction had set in, and there was a storm of opposition. Newfoundland and Prince Edward Island refused to have anything to do with Confederation. In New Brunswick, before the union resolutions were submitted to the Legislature, a general election took place. Not a single member of the Quebec delegation was returned. A new Ministry, under the leadership of Albert J. Smith and George L. Hatheway, thoroughly opposed to the scheme, came into power.

In Nova Scotia there were murmurings of dissatisfaction, but the people had no opportunity of expressing their views at the polls. On the meeting of the Legislature, Dr. Tupper, the leader of the Government, stated that, on account of the opposition in

New Brunswick, the subject of union would not be brought before the House that session.

In the course of a few weeks, however, a great change was wrought in the public sentiment of New Brunswick. Governor Gordon and a majority of the Legislative Council had from the first been in favour of union, and the Imperial Government urged it as a measure of prime concern both to the provinces and to the Empire. In his speech from the throne on the opening of the Legislature, Governor Gordon, in opposition to the views of his advisers, recommended the measure. Such a course on the part of a Governor under responsible government was unusual, and it can be justified only under extraordinary circumstances. The Ministry, regarding the procedure as unconstitutional, resigned office, and a union Ministry, with Samuel L. Tilley as Premier, was called upon to take its place. The new Administration, appealing to the people through a general election, was sustained.

An Unexpected Change.

This action of New Brunswick changed the whole aspect of affairs. The Legislature of Nova Scotia was still in session. The Government, contrary to previous announcement, introduced resolutions in favour of Confederation. There was strong opposition. Many who did not object to the principle of union disliked the terms of the Quebec Scheme. To meet these views the Government brought in a measure providing for a new basis to be drawn up by the British Government, aided by delegates from the various provinces. This was opposed by a strong party, who took the ground that in a matter of such great concern the voice of the people should be heard through a general election. The measure was carried, however, by a large majority.

Canada and New Brunswick gave their assent to a revision of the Quebec Scheme, and each province appointed delegates to meet with the members of the British Government for the purpose of carrying out this object.

The scene was now changed to the Colonial Office in London. Sixteen delegates, representing Canada, New Brunswick, and Nova Scotia, met here for the perfecting of a scheme of Confederation. But the Opposition in Nova Scotia, though defeated in the Legislature, was not disposed to yield. Joseph Howe, who at this time was not a member of the Legislature, had hitherto been a silent though interested onlooker. He now

SIR S. L. TILLEY.

Union accomplished

joined the ranks of the anti-Confederates, giving them courage and strength. He and two others were sent to London as the "People's Delegates" to thwart the union scheme. But Mr. Howe worked at great disadvantage in the contest. He was waging war against himself; for no one had in former days advocated union more forcibly than Joseph Howe. His former utterances were now effectively turned against his present attitude. The strongest argument he could use, and one never fully answered, was the fact that the people of Nova Scotia had not been consulted on the question. The "People's Delegates," however, could not stay the movement. The terms of Confederation were finally agreed on, and in February 1867 the Constitution of the Dominion of Canada, as thus prepared, was ratified by the British Parliament in what is known as the British North America Act. The British Government at the same time became pledged to guarantee for Canada a loan of $15,000,000 for the construction of the Intercolonial Railway. Finally, by royal proclamation, on July 1, 1867, the four provinces were declared united into one state under the name of the Dominion of Canada.

The British North America Act forms the Constitution or basis on which the various provinces of British North America are united under a common Government. The powers of the Dominion Parliament and of the Provincial Legislatures are defined and limited by this Act, and can be changed only by the British Parliament. Cases of doubt or dispute as to the powers of Parliament or Legislature are determined by the courts, as

The Canadian Constitution.

interpreters of the Constitution. The highest court of appeal is the Judicial Committee of the Imperial Privy Council in London.

The provisions of the Act, though in some respects different from the Quebec Scheme, embody the same general principles. The legislative union between Upper and Lower Canada was dissolved. The name of Upper Canada was changed to Ontario, that of Lower Canada to Quebec, and the whole territory of the united provinces was designated the Dominion of Canada. Provision was made for the admission of the other provinces and the North-West at any time when such action should be desired. The Union is of a federal character; that is, each province is given its own separate Government and Legislature for the management of its local affairs, while for the whole Dominion there is provided a Central Government having control over matters of common interest to all the provinces. In this regard the Constitution is like that of the United States. It differs, however, from the Constitution of the American Republic in securing greater strength to the Central Government. In the Canadian Constitution any power not expressly given to the province belongs to the Dominion, whereas the converse of this is true in the United States. The Ministry both in the Dominion and in the provinces is responsible to the elective branch of the Legislature, and is dependent for existence on its vote. The Ministers must also hold seats in the Legislature, so that failing to secure their election by the people they must retire from the Cabinet. In this regard our Government is modelled after that of Great Britain.

In general, the Dominion Parliament and Government have control over such matters of common interest as tariff, currency, coinage, banking, mails, criminal law, defence, navigation, fisheries, and the higher courts of law. The powers of the Provincial Governments relate to such matters as education, Crown lands, minerals, and municipal affairs. The Acts of the Provincial Legislatures are subject to review by the Dominion Government, though it is not permissible for the Central Government to interfere in matters which are of purely local concern.

The Governor-General, who represents the Sovereign and is appointed by the Crown, is the highest officer in the Dominion Government. He receives a salary of $50,000 from the Dominion Treasury. He is the commander-in-chief of the military and naval forces of the Dominion, including the militia. He also has power to commute the sentence of a court of justice. The Governor-General in Council appoints the members of the Senate, the Lieutenant-Governors of the various provinces, the judges of courts of law, postmasters, custom-house officers, and various other officers.

The Dominion Parliament comprises two Houses or Chambers, called the Senate and the House of Commons. No measure can become law until it has been adopted by both Houses and has received the assent of the Governor-General. While the Governor-General has the nominal right to veto a Bill which has passed both Houses of Parliament, he has never exercised the power.

The Senators are appointed for life by the Governor-General in Council. A Senator must be over thirty years of age, possess property worth $4000, and reside in his own province. Originally there were in all seventy-two Senators. The number has since been increased to eighty-one.

The members of the House of Commons are elected by the people for the term of five years. The number of members for each province is readjusted after each decennial census—the number for Quebec remaining at sixty-five, and those for the other provinces bearing the same proportion to their population as sixty-five to the population of Quebec.

The revenue of the Dominion is derived mainly from duties on imports and excise duties. The provinces receive annually from the Dominion Government a sum equal to eighty cents per head on their population, and also a fixed sum for legislative expenses. The provincial revenues are supplemented by royalties on minerals, by the sale of Crown lands, and from other sources.

The United States and Great Britain.
The civil war in the United States, already referred to, taxed to the utmost the resources and energies of the Northern States, but ultimately, in 1865, the armies of the South were vanquished and the Confederacy was crushed. During the war several events occurred which embittered the people and Government of the United States against Great Britain and Canada. Among the various causes of offence was the determined attitude of Great Britain in demanding the giving up of Mason and Slidell, Southern envoys, captured on board a British steamer by a United States man-of-war. This feeling of resentment was increased by the sympathy with the Southern Confederacy shown by

certain British and Canadian newspapers. The impression was created that our people would be pleased to see the Union broken up.

Another thing which made the United States angry with Great Britain was the damage done to their commerce by privateers built in England for the Confederate Government. By far the most noted of these privateers was the <u>Alabama</u>, built at Birkenhead, on the Mersey. While this craft was on the stocks, the United States Minister in England, learning the purpose for which she was intended, asked the British Government to stop her from going to sea. The agents of the Confederate States, learning that action was about to be taken in response to this appeal, sent the *Alabama* off hastily on her career of destruction. She made sad havoc of the commerce of the Northern States, and her name soon became a terror to their merchantmen.

There was yet one other cause of affront to our American neighbours. Southern men who came to Canada during the war were received with much parade of welcome, and some of them abused the hospitality shown them by making raids across the border and retreating to Canada for protection. A band of them, setting out from our shores, captured and plundered two American vessels on the Great Lakes. Again, some of them, crossing over into Vermont, robbed a bank in the town of <u>St. Albans</u>, killing a man in the affray, and then escaped to Canada with booty amounting to $223,000. The United States Government asked for their extradition. The robbers were arrested by Canadian authorities, and a part of the stolen money, amounting to $90,000, was taken from them. The judge before whom they were brought, finding some technical point in their favour, ordered them to be set at liberty. At the same time their plunder was given back to them. This money the Canadian Government had afterwards to refund to the parties from whom it was taken.

At the same time, there were some strong reasons which should have convinced our neighbours that Great Britain was disposed to act a friendly part towards them. Cotton manufacture is one of Great Britain's leading industries. She was accustomed to obtain her raw cotton from the Southern States, which were then the great cotton producers of the world. But in order to cripple the rebellious States the American Government placed them under blockade, so that vessels found trading with them were liable to seizure. At this time France wanted Great Britain to unite with her in recognising the Southern Confederacy. Such recognition would have given the Southern States great advantage, and might have turned the scale in their favour. But Great Britain refused to take this course. The people and Government of the United States, however, were very ill-humoured towards Great Britain, and they treasured up their resentment for a day of reckoning.

In the spring of 1865 General Grant, at the head of the United States forces, took possession of Richmond, the capital of the Confederate States, and compelled General Lee to surrender with all his army. The resources of the South had now become completely exhausted. Yet one sad event marked the close of the war, and threw its shadow over the victorious North. On the 14th of April, five days after the surrender of

Richmond, Abraham Lincoln, the President of the United States, while sitting in his box in a Washington theatre, was shot dead by a Southern sympathiser.

The ten years for which the Reciprocity Treaty had been entered into now expired, and the United States Government gave notice for its discontinuance. Under the treaty international trade had greatly increased, reaching the annual value of seventy millions of dollars. Its termination was, for a few years, severely felt in Canada. The markets of the United States were practically closed to certain of our products. In the end, however, this did us little harm. Our people learned a lesson of self-reliance. Trade soon found other channels, and Canada set about manufacturing many kinds of goods which she had previously imported from abroad. *Termination of the Reciprocity Treaty, 1866.*

The United States at this time gave shelter and countenance to a bitter enemy of Canada. This enemy was an organisation known as the Fenian Brotherhood, composed chiefly of Irishmen. The professed aim of the Fenians was the overthrow of British rule in Ireland. It is difficult to discover any connection between this object and marauding expeditions against the provinces. It gratified the members of the organisation, however, to show their hatred for anything that was British, and it suited their leaders to keep up a show of action in order to draw larger contributions from their deluded supporters. Several bands of armed men were thus collected at different points along the American frontier, prepared for any raids which promised booty with little risk. The United States Government could *The Fenian Invasion.*

easily have checked the movement, but it seemed not to know what was going on.

In the spring of 1866 the Fenians seized the Island of Campobello, in the Bay of Fundy, intending to make it their headquarters for an attack on New Brunswick; but finding troops and volunteers ready to meet them, they soon dispersed.

In June about fourteen hundred Fenians, under "General" O'Neil, crossed the Niagara River and took possession of Fort Erie. From this place they marched in the direction of the Welland Canal. Several regiments of Canadian volunteers hastened from Toronto and Hamilton to repel the invaders. An engagement took place near Ridgeway, in which seven volunteers were killed and several were wounded. The Fenians, meeting a different reception from what they had expected, soon retreated to Fort Erie, from which, under cover of night, they returned to the United States, leaving several of their comrades behind as prisoners.

Bands of Fenians gathered at various points on the American side of the St. Lawrence, but they were deterred from crossing the river by the presence of Canadian troops on the opposite side. About two thousand, however, came over from St. Albans, in Vermont, and began to plunder the country. They were promptly met by Canadian forces and compelled to make a hasty retreat. Finally, through the remonstrances of the British Minister at Washington, the United States Government was induced to interfere and put an end to these marauding expeditions.

The Fenians probably expected some aid from the

Irish people in Canada. If so, they were sadly disappointed. None of our people were more loyal or more ready to repel the invaders. Archbishop Connolly of Halifax and Thomas d'Arcy McGee voiced the feeling of their countrymen by denouncing in the strongest terms these foolish and wicked attempts to disturb the peace of our country.

CHAPTER XXXI.

THE DOMINION ORGANIZED AND EXTENDED.

JULY 1, 1867, was the natal day of the new Dominion.

The New Ministry. Lord Monck, having been sworn in as Governor-General, called upon the Hon. John A. Macdonald to form a Ministry. The Governor-General also, by command of the Queen, conferred upon the Premier the honour of knighthood. In choosing his colleagues, Sir John had special regard to a fair representation of all the provinces of the Dominion. He also sought to ignore party distinctions, choosing the Ministry from both Liberals and Conservatives. He and his followers claimed that old issues were buried, and that, as both the old parties had united on Confederation, there was now really but one party. Assuming their right of succession and heirship to these parties, they took to themselves the name *Liberal-Conservative*.

The Opposition. There were many who refused to accept this doctrine of one party. It was no surprise to his friends that George Brown declined to march under the Liberal-Conservative banner, or to recognise Sir John A. Macdonald as his leader. He had united with his old-time opponent for the purpose of securing Confederation, but he had retired from the Coalition Government before the union was effected.

A stalwart opponent of compromise was Alexander MacKenzie. Although the name of this remarkable man is now mentioned for the first time in our story, he had for several years held high rank in the Liberal party. Mr. MacKenzie was a Scotchman of humble birth. His educational advantages were meagre, his school-days being confined to the winter months of his boyhood. In summer, for a pittance, he herded cows and sheep for the neighbouring farmers. At thirteen years of age he finally left school. Like his distinguished fellow-countryman Hugh Miller, he started out in life as a stone-cutter. In 1842, when about twenty years of age, he came to

HON. ALEXANDER MACKENZIE.

Canada, making his home first at Kingston and later at Sarnia. In 1861 he was first elected to Parliament as member for Lambton, which county he represented till near the close of his life, over thirty years later.

Another strong man who, though trained for the law at the feet of Sir John, yet refused to accept his politics, was Oliver Mowat.

The First Parliament. In the summer of 1867 the elections both for the Dominion Parliament and for the Provincial Legislatures came off in the various provinces. Sir John's Ministry was well sustained by majorities from all the provinces except Nova Scotia, from which he could claim but a single supporter, Dr. Tupper.

The Dominion Parliament met for the first time in November of the same year. At Christmas it took a long vacation, not meeting again until March 20, 1868. The two principal matters under consideration at this session were the Intercolonial Railway and the acquisition of the North-West Territory and Rupert's Land. Several members of this Parliament held seats also in one or other of the Provincial Legislatures; but a law has since been enacted which prevents a man from holding a seat at the same time in a local Legislature and in the Parliament of the Dominion.

D'Arcy McGee. Among the notable events of the session was the tragic death of Thomas d'Arcy McGee. In his younger days McGee was a rebel against British rule in Ireland. Discovered as a partner in some conspiracy, he, in order to escape the vengeance of the law, fled from Ireland disguised as a priest. He lived some time in the United States and then removed to Canada. He had now outgrown his disloyalty and had become a patriotic British subject. By his denunciation of the invasion of Canada by the Fenians he incurred the bitter hatred of the "brotherhood," and made himself the object of their revenge. On the evening of April 6, during a discussion on Nova Scotia affairs in the Commons, he made a powerful appeal for conciliatory measures towards this province. This was the last speech of the brilliant orator. The House sat till two o'clock in the morning. On its adjournment McGee went to his lodgings. As he was inserting his latch-key in the door, he was shot by a Fenian miscreant who had been lying in wait, and he fell dead across the threshold.

Nova Scotia was the wayward child in the Dominion family. She would break loose from these bonds which were thrown around her without her consent. In the strife old party lines were obliterated, and old party names were forgotten. Those who, as Liberals and Conservatives, had opposed each other on the great political questions of former days were surprised to find themselves standing side by side under the same banner. General Sir Fenwick Williams, who had gained renown in the recent war carried on by Great Britain and her allies against Russia, and who was the first native Governor of the province, tried to quiet the agitation. But even the hero of Kars could not pacify those who were bent on repeal. The new Government of the province, led by Hon. William Annand, set itself in good earnest to take Nova Scotia out of the Union. In this movement it had ample support from the people, for, with two excep-

<small>Agitation for Repeal in Nova Scotia.</small>

tions, the whole Assembly was at its back. The Legislature petitioned the Queen, asking that the province be set free from Confederation. Delegates, comprising William Annand, Joseph Howe, and others, proceeded to England to add the weight of their presence to the memorial of the Assembly; but their efforts were unavailing. Mr. Howe soon saw the hopelessness of the cause and gave up the struggle: or, as he phrased it, he "only laboured to make the best of a bad bargain." Acting on the advice of the Colonial Secretary, Sir John A. Macdonald sought to pacify the angry province. In this endeavour he chose to treat with Mr. Howe. On the offer of better financial terms for his province, Mr. Howe abandoned the agitators for repeal, and accepted office in the Dominion Cabinet. Many of the party followed the example of their chief: while others, indignant over his desertion of them and their cause, pursued him with unmeasured censure. Mr. Howe appealed to his constituents in Nova Scotia for approval of his course, and was triumphantly elected. The Government of Nova Scotia accepted the added subsidy, the price of Howe's conciliation, but with no less fervour sounded for itself the notes of war. It should be added that since the arrangement for "better terms" the province has always returned to the Dominion Parliament a large majority of members opposed to the repeal of the Union.

Acquisition of the North-West. The thought of the fathers of Confederation was a broad one, including within its scope the whole of British North America. The measure for the acquisition of the North-West Territories, adopted during the first session of the Dominion Parliament, was an important step towards the carrying out of this conception. The annexation of these territories was not a new idea with Canadian statesmen. Ten years earlier the Government of the Province of Canada had asserted claims to the country, and had sent Chief-Justice Draper to urge these claims before a committee of the British House of Commons.

The Hudson's Bay Company, whose charter was now about to expire, was desirous of retaining its hold of a country which had for two hundred years been to its shareholders so rich a harvest-field. The company had always discouraged the settlement of the Territory, representing it as a remote land, difficult of access, frozen and barren, suited only to the production of fur-bearing animals. Explorers and travellers, however, who had visited the country, told of the wonderful fertility of its prairies. The winter, they admitted, was severe, but they claimed that the climate was by no means ill-adapted to agriculture. They reported that during the long hot days of summer vegetation was rapid, and that the grains and vegetables of temperate climates were matured without difficulty. Red River Settlement gave proof of great agricultural capabilities, and needed only facility of intercourse with the outside world to make it attractive to enterprising colonists.

One of the most strenuous advocates for the annexation of the Territory was the Hon. William M'Dougall, a member of the Dominion Cabinet. He urged, both from Imperial and Canadian standpoints, the importance of the measure, contending that the fur traders' monopoly should be broken up, and that the fertile lands which had been so long a close preserve should be thrown open for settlement. The Bill authorising the purchase of the Territory passed with little opposition. In 1868 a delegation, consisting of Mr. M‘Dougall and Sir George E. Cartier, proceeded to England to arrange for carrying the measure into effect. Terms having been agreed on with the Hudson's Bay Company, the Imperial Parliament passed an Act providing for the transfer of the North-West Territories to the Dominion Government.

According to the terms agreed on, the Hudson's Bay Company was allowed to retain its trading posts, with adjacent lands to the extent of fifty thousand acres in all, and also one-twentieth of all the lands which should be laid out for settlement in the fertile belt lying south of the North Saskatchewan. All its other property, rights, and privileges the company ceded to the Dominion Government for a cash payment of £300,000 sterling.

During its session of 1869, Parliament passed an Act providing for the temporary government of the North-West Territory by a Governor and Council. In the autumn of 1869, before the payment of the money or the formal transfer of the Territory, surveyors were sent into the country by the Dominion Government to lay out townships, lots, and roads. Many of the inhabitants of Red River Settlement looked upon their action with suspicion. Having no title by deed or grant to the lands which they occupied, they became alarmed lest they should be dispossessed. Little pains were taken to explain to them the object of the survey, and no assurance was given them that they should not be disturbed.

Some of the people were dissatisfied with the form of government provided for them; and some ambitious and ill-advised persons in the settlement used their influence to encourage suspicion and disaffection. Among these the most prominent were John Bruce, Louis Riel, and Ambrose Lepine. Affairs began to wear a threatening aspect.

The Honourable William M'Dougall, having been appointed Lieutenant-Governor of the North-West Territories, set out for Red River Settlement. His route was by way of St. Paul, in Minnesota. Meanwhile Red River Settlement had become the scene of an organised rebellion, under the guidance of Riel and Lepine. The insurgents took possession of Fort Garry, the Hudson's Bay Company's headquarters, which occupied a site within the present city of Winnipeg. They seized arms, ammunition, and valuable stores belonging to the company. Louis Riel was the ruling spirit, and he soon became absolute dictator, assuming the title of President.

Rebellion in Red River Settlement

Although forbidden by the rebels to enter the Territory, Governor M'Dougall crossed the boundary-line, and halted at a fort belonging to the Hudson's Bay Company. Armed horsemen, sent by Riel, appeared before the fort and ordered him to leave the country immediately. The Governor obeyed the order, retired to Minnesota, and soon after returned to Ottawa.

Intoxicated with his newly gained power, Riel through the winter acted with a high hand, confiscating property, seizing the agents of the Dominion Government, plundering the Hudson's Bay Company's stores, banishing persons whom he distrusted, and imprisoning those who disputed his authority. Among those imprisoned were Major Bolton and Dr. Schultz, the latter a prominent citizen of the settlement, who afterwards became Lieutenant-Governor of Manitoba, and was knighted by the Queen. Dr. Schultz escaped from prison, and, raising a small force, compelled Riel to set the others at liberty. But afterwards, fearing Riel's threatened vengeance, he escaped from the country. It was midwinter, and deep snow covered the ground. The only route of travel was by way of St. Paul, in Minnesota, but it was closely guarded by Riel's men. Dr. Schultz resolved to journey on foot through the vast wilderness to the settlements in the United States at the head of Lake Superior. Accompanied by an English half-breed, he set out on snowshoes, travelling by way of Winnipeg River, Lake of the Woods, and Rainy Lake, to Duluth, occupying about two months in the journey.

Riel sentenced Bolton to be shot for treason against his Government, but after much entreaty urged by influential friends he spared his life. A victim through whose sacrifice he hoped to establish his authority was found in Thomas Scott. Fearless and outspoken, Scott had given offence to the dictator. He was tried by a so-called court-martial and sentenced to be shot. Scott was not allowed to be present or to make defence at the trial. Every effort was made by clergymen and others to save his life, but Riel would listen to no entreaty. On the morning after the trial, blindfolded, Scott was led out of his cell to the place of execution, where he fell pierced by three bullets. His death aroused the deepest indignation throughout the Dominion, especially in Ontario, where he had formerly resided. No immediate action could be taken to quell the insurrection, as the country was then inaccessible in winter.

In May 1870 the Dominion Parliament passed an Act forming Red River Settlement into a province under the name of Manitoba, with a representative Assembly and a responsible Government. *The Province of Manitoba organised.* The Legislature provided by the Act comprised a House of Assembly and a Legislative Council, but after a few years the Council was abolished.

The area of the province, as then formed, was about fourteen thousand square miles. The population was about twelve thousand, the majority of which were Métis or half-breeds. The remaining portion of the North-West Territory was placed for the time under the authority of the Governor of Manitoba. The whole territory acquired from the Hudson's Bay Company was formally annexed to the Dominion by royal proclamation on June 23, 1870. As yet, however, Riel's power was supreme in Red River Settlement.

The Honourable Adams G. Archibald was now appointed Lieutenant-Governor of Manitoba and the North-West. To restore order *The Rebellion ended.* an armed force of about twelve hundred men, regular troops and Canadian volunteers, was sent in advance of the Governor and his party. The officer in command was General Sir Garnet Wolseley, who afterwards gained military renown in Asiatic and African wars. The expedition proceeded by way of the Great Lakes to Fort William, on Thunder Bay. The United States Government refused to allow the troops to pass through the St. Clair Canal, and they were accordingly compelled to march around the rapids on the Canadian side. From Fort William they proceeded through a rugged wilderness, a distance of nearly five hundred miles. Along the water stretches of lake and stream they went in boats. When they came to a portage, with immense labour they dragged their boats across the land.

Over three months were spent in the toilsome march.

On the arrival of the forces at Fort Garry, Riel and Lepine fled hurriedly, taking refuge among their friends near the Assiniboine. General Wolseley had gained a bloodless victory. The rebellion was at an end, and as there was nothing for him to do, he soon set out on the return journey. Many of the volunteers received lands and remained in the country.

Early in September Governor Archibald organized

SIR ADAMS G. ARCHIBALD.

his Government at Winnipeg, the Fort Garry of the Hudson's Bay Company. Thus the new Province of Manitoba, Minerva-like, with full-grown powers at birth, took her place beside her elder sisters.

While these events were taking place the Fenians had again been causing trouble along the United States border. They crossed the lines at different points, but they were promptly driven back. *Riel and Governor Archibald.* During the summer of 1871 a band of these ruffians, led by one O'Donoghue, crossing over from Minnesota, appeared on the borders of Manitoba. Governor Archibald was in difficulty. He had small means of defence. He invited Riel and Lepine to bring their Métis to aid him in repelling the invaders. With the utmost readiness they responded to the call, and the Fenians, seeing little prospect of success, retreated to the United States. Governor Archibald's action in accepting aid from these fugitives from justice was much criticised. It must, however, be supposed that he adopted it, not with any feeling of satisfaction, but that he chose it rather than the serious alternative of facing a combined attack of Fenians and Métis.

While Nova Scotia was seeking to break loose from Confederation, her sister province on the shores of the Pacific was knocking for admission. *British Columbia enters the Union.* The people of this province were strongly in favour of Confederation. They had at this time no representative assembly, but in 1867 the Council adopted union resolutions, asking Governor Seymour to confer with the Dominion Government on the matter. The Governor, not being favourable to the movement, took no action. His opposition served but to arouse the people to more decided effort. A vigorous agitation began not only for Confederation, but for a representative assembly and a responsible ministry. The people memorialized the Dominion Government, and also sent a delegate to England to bring their wishes before the Colonial Secretary.

On the death of Governor Seymour in 1869, the Hon. Anthony Musgrave, the Governor of Newfoundland, was transferred to British Columbia. Governor Musgrave was an enthusiastic supporter of Confederation. The matter was now urged forward. Union resolutions were passed by the Council, and delegates were sent to Ottawa, where they found the utmost facility for carrying out their mission. Satisfactory terms of union were readily agreed on.

A leading condition in the compact was the construction by the Dominion Government of a transcontinental railway to connect the sea-board of British Columbia with the railway system of Canada. It was agreed that this railway should be begun within two years and be completed within ten years from the date of union. The terms of union were adopted by a special Council convened by Governor Musgrave, and were afterwards confirmed by Imperial legislation. Thus, in 1871, British Columbia became a province of the Dominion with a local representative Assembly and a responsible Government similar to that of the other provinces.

Meanwhile there had been a change in the representative of royalty in the Dominion. In the autumn of 1868 Lord Monck was succeeded by Sir John Young, afterwards raised to the peerage with the title of Lord Lisgar.

DOMINION ORGANIZED AND EXTENDED. 379

Several matters affecting the relations of Great Britain and Canada with the United States required to be adjusted. The chief of these were the Alabama claims—that is the claims of the United States against Great Britain for damage to the commerce of the Northern States by Confederate cruisers fitted out in Great Britain—the claims of Canada against the United States for damage caused by Fenian raids, the boundary between Vancouver Island and the State of Washington, the use of Canadian coast waters by United States fishermen, and the navigation of the St. Lawrence River and Canadian canals by the citizens of the United States. For the purpose of settling these questions, a Joint High Commission composed of five commissioners of each nation met in the city of Washington in 1871. Sir John A. Macdonald was one of the five appointed to represent Great Britain. *The Washington Treaty.*

The Alabama claims were referred to arbitration. The arbitrators, who met at Geneva, in Switzerland, in the following year, awarded to the United States $15,500,000 damages, which amount was promptly paid by Great Britain.

The question of compensation to Canada for damages caused by Fenian raids was not brought before the Commission. The British Government had, through some oversight, neglected to give proper notice that such claims would be made, and the United States Commissioners, accordingly, refused to consider the matter. The British Government, however, made amends for its neglect by giving a guarantee which enabled our Government to borrow money on favourable terms for the construction of public works.

The boundary question was referred to the Emperor of Germany, who decided that the line should pass through Haro Strait. This decision gave the Island of San Juan to the United States.

In the matter of coast fisheries it was agreed that there should be an exchange of privilege between the United States and Canada, the fishermen on each side of the line to have free use of the coast waters on the other side. But as the fisheries of British America were the more valuable, it was agreed that the United States should pay to Canada such sum of money as represented the difference in value. This amount was to be fixed by a special Commission to be appointed for the purpose.

It was further agreed that citizens of the United States should be permitted to use the Canadian canals and the River St. Lawrence on the same terms as were allowed to British subjects, and that Canadians should have similar privileges in Lake Michigan and St. Clair Canal.

New Brunswick Schools. The Education Act of New Brunswick, passed in 1871, is one of the most important measures adopted in that province since Confederation. For this Act, which has been so effective in extending school privileges to every child in the province, improving the quality of the instruction given, and awakening public interest in educational matters, the province is largely indebted to the Hon. George E. King, at that time Premier in the Government. Scarcely less credit is due to Theodore H. Rand, D.C.L., to whom, as Chief Superintendent of Education, fell the task of carrying the new law into effect. Dr. Rand brought to the work much executive ability and a ripe experience acquired through the discharge of similar duties in Nova Scotia. He was thus instrumental in establishing such influences as have, through the help of other workers in the same field, brought the common schools of Nova Scotia and New Brunswick into the front rank.

The New Brunswick School Law became a matter of general interest to the Dominion. The Act required that all schools deriving support from the public funds should be free from religious instruction of a sectarian character. The Roman Catholics of the province protested against this provision, and claimed a share of the public money for the support

THEODORE H. RAND, D.C.L.

of separate schools in which the peculiar doctrines of their religion might be taught. This claim they based on a clause in the British North America Act, which provides that local Legislatures shall not deprive any religious body of school privileges established by law at the time of union. They petitioned the Governor-General, asking him to disallow the Act. Failing here, they brought their grievance before the Dominion Parliament. Still without redress, they appealed to the Judicial Committee of the Privy Council in England, but this court also declined to interfere. The different authorities to whom the question was submitted regarded it as a matter assigned by the Constitution to the local Legislature and Government, and that any interference on the part of the Central Government would be destructive to provincial rights, and would endanger the peace and stability of the Dominion.

<small>Prince Edward Island enters the Union, 1873.</small> Prince Edward Island, which, in 1867, had so decidedly turned her back on Confederation, now asked for admission to the Union. The request was readily granted, and on July 1, Dominion Day, 1873, her name was added to the roll of Dominion provinces. Prince Edward Island obtained liberal terms. It was allowed a representation of four members in the Senate and six in the House of Commons. The Dominion Government aided the island in ridding itself of the system of tenantry and non-resident landlords which had so long vexed both Government and people. Three years after the Union the local Legislature passed an Act requiring the proprietors to sell their lands at a valuation price fixed by three appraisers. One of the

appraisers was appointed by the Governor-General, one by the Lieutenant-Governor, and one by the proprietor.

In the summer of 1873 two distinguished Canadian statesmen, Sir George E. Cartier and Hon. Joseph Howe, were removed by death. The former died in London. His remains were brought to Montreal and buried with imposing ceremonies at the expense of the Dominion Government. Mr. Howe died at Government House, Halifax. As a reward for a self-sacrificing life in the service of his country, he had a few weeks previously been appointed Lieutenant-Governor of Nova Scotia. His evening-time of rest and dignity was short.

Death of Cartier and Howe.

The Province of Ontario claims some notice at this stage of our story. At once after the Union this province entered upon that career of prosperity which, continuing down to the present time, has given it an enviable position among the countries of the world. Inhabited by an industrious and enterprising people, and possessing varied and boundless resources, it has been a land of peace and plenty. At first there was little party politics to create division in the management of local affairs. The Government claimed to be a coalition. Its leader, John Sandfield Macdonald, once a prominent Liberal, had now become tolerant of the men whom he formerly opposed. His administration of the affairs of the province was successful. The public revenue was more than enough to meet the necessities of the country, and the generous surplus was applied to the development of the province and to the founding of such important institutions as the Agricultural College,

Ontario.

institutes for the blind and the deaf and dumb, and to the subsidising of railways. The leading Liberals, however, were not satisfied with his policy. Some matters relating to the use of the public funds, which they thought should have been submitted to the Legislature, were determined by the Government after the old Tory fashion. They thought, too, that he was using his influence to keep Sir John A. Macdonald and his Government at Ottawa in power.

The general election which took place in the winter of 1871 was keenly contested, and the John Sandfield Macdonald Government was defeated. In the new Cabinet, formed shortly after, Edward Blake was Premier and Alexander MacKenzie was Provincial Treasurer. Under the dual system of representation at the time allowable, both of these gentlemen were also members of the Dominion House of Commons. In 1872 this system was discontinued, and called upon to make choice, they resigned their position in the Ministry and Legislature of Ontario. At the same time the Hon. Oliver Mowat (now Sir Oliver), who had withdrawn from political life for a seat on the bench, was persuaded to resign the judgeship and accept the position of Premier of the province, a position which he continued to hold for nearly a quarter of a century.

In 1876 it was thought advisable to place the educational interests of the province under the direct supervision of a member of the Cabinet. Dr. Ryerson, who had been Superintendent of Education since 1844, retired on full salary, and the Hon. Adam Crooks became Minister of Education.

CHAPTER XXXII.

THE MACKENZIE ADMINISTRATION.

IN the summer of 1872 the Earl of Dufferin succeeded Lord Lisgar as Governor-General. Distinguished alike for his eloquence, grace of manner, and diplomatic skill, he was one of the most popular Governors that ever represented royalty in Canada. *The Pacific Railway Scandal.*

The five years' term of the first Dominion Parliament having expired, a general election took place in the autumn of 1872. The new Parliament met in the following March. While the Ministry was well sustained, its majority was smaller than in the former House. As authorised by Parliament, the Government had recently entered into a contract with a Company for the construction of the railway promised to British Columbia. The president of the company was Sir Hugh Allan, a man of wealth and influence, and the owner of a fleet of ocean steamers.

For a few days the business of the House went on quietly, but early in April, Mr. Huntington, member for Shefford, made the startling charge that the Government had given the contract to this company in consideration of large sums of money received from Sir Hugh to aid in carrying the elections. A committee of five of its members was appointed by the House to investigate the charge, and pending the action of this committee the House adjourned. On the reassembling of Parliament on August 13 to receive the report, it was found that, owing to lack of power to place witnesses under oath, the committee had made no investigation. As it had been understood that the meeting would be purely formal for the reception of the committee's report, and that the House would be immediately prorogued, many of the members from remote parts of the Dominion were not present. Of those in attendance, however, the members of the Opposition far outnumbered the Ministerialists. This boded ill to the Government. The members of the Opposition petitioned the Governor-General that Parliament should not be prorogued, but should be allowed to investigate the charges made by Mr. Huntington. His Excellency declined to adopt this course, giving reasons why he could not comply with their wishes. Still the Opposition sought to keep the House in session and force an investigation. When the Speaker took the chair, Mr. MacKenzie rose and submitted a resolution to this effect. He was interrupted, however, by the Usher of the Black Rod, who appeared at the door of the House and summoned the members to the Senate chamber, there to be prorogued by the Governor-General. The Ministerialists followed the Speaker to the Senate chamber, but the members of the Opposition refused to obey the summons.

On the following day the Governor-General appointed a Royal Commission, consisting of three judges, to investigate the charges. On October 23, Parliament was convened to receive the report of the Commission. The report simply recited the

THE MACKENZIE ADMINISTRATION. 387

facts elicited, giving no judicial opinion as to their bearing on the charges preferred. Mr. MacKenzie, the leader of the Opposition, moved a resolution involving censure of the Government. For several days, amid much excitement, the question was discussed. Sir John A. Macdonald made a long and able defence of himself and his colleagues. But while the larger number of the Conservative members remained loyal to their chief, it became evident that many of them would support Mr. MacKenzie's resolution. To avoid an adverse vote, Sir John placed the resignation of the Ministry in the hands of the Governor-General.

A new Government was at once formed under Mr. MacKenzie as Premier. Among the more prominent members of the Cabinet were Edward Blake and A. A. Dorion. Within a few weeks the House was dissolved for the purpose of testing the country on the question which had led to the change of Government. *A New Government.*

Parliament met again in the following March (1874). The Ministry was sustained by a large majority; indeed, its supporters comprised nearly three-fourths of the House of Commons. Among those who presented themselves to take the oath required of members was the outlawed Louis Riel, who had been elected by the constituency of Provencher, in Manitoba. He was made to understand that his past offences were not fully condoned, and by a formal vote was expelled from the House. Finding that he was liable to arrest for the murder of Scott, he hastily left Ottawa.

Mr. MacKenzie was a man of sterling integrity. He

adopted no measure simply to secure popularity, and he promised nothing which he did not mean to perform. He was, however, not skilled in the political tactics required in a successful party leader, and while it may be said of him that he commanded the respect of his opponents, he failed to secure the enthusiastic loyalty of his followers. One of the strongest features of his administration was his decided stand for Canada's right to the free and full management of her own affairs. He was a firm believer in the supreme authority of the Ministry so long as it had behind it the majority of the people's representatives.

At this period the Governor-General's instructions from the British Government authorised him to reject the advice of his Ministers whenever he saw sufficient cause for so doing. This doctrine was not in accord with Mr. MacKenzie's sentiments, and so effectively did he urge his views on the attention of the British Government that the objectionable clause was struck out of the Governor's commission.

An attempt made in 1874, to secure a new reciprocity treaty between Canada and the United States, afforded an opportunity for urging our right to a voice in the transaction of international business in which we are deeply concerned. Here, too, Mr. MacKenzie was successful. The Hon. George Brown was appointed as the colleague of Sir Edward Thornton, the British Minister at Washington, to act with the agents of the United States Government in framing a treaty. The draft treaty thus prepared, being rejected by the United States Senate, never came into force.

The most difficult matter with which the Government had to deal, and probably the one in which it was least successful, was the Pacific Railway. Sir Hugh Allan's Company had given up its contract. Four years had passed since British Columbia entered the Union, and little had been done towards the construction of the promised road, which was to be completed within ten years. A murmur of dissatisfaction was rising from the Pacific province, and its Government was protesting against the violation of the terms of Union. It seemed impossible to carry out the contract, and the Dominion Government sent an agent to British Columbia for the purpose of making some new arrangement. The mission was a failure. The Premier of the province proceeded to England with complaints to the British Government. A compromise proposed by the Colonial Secretary was adopted by the Canadian House of Commons, but it was rejected by the Senate.

The Pacific Railway.

Meanwhile dissatisfaction increased in British Columbia, and secession from the Union began to be agitated. At this juncture the Government luckily decided to avail itself of the good offices of the Governor-General to allay the rising storm. In the summer of 1876 the Earl of Dufferin visited British Columbia, proceeding by way of San Francisco. By his genial manner and persuasive words he won the confidence of people and Government, and he placed before them such facts as gave them assurance that his Ministry would deal in good faith with the province.

New measures were now carried through Parliament for the construction of the Pacific Railway. It was resolved at first to open up a mixed rail and water route for use in summer between Eastern

Canada and the North-West. The Great Lakes and the numerous water stretches of lake and river west of Lake Superior were thus to form portions of the highway. Sections of railway were to connect these waters, and a branch road was to be constructed from Winnipeg to Pembina to connect with the railways of the United States. It was resolved not to give the railway to a company, but to build and own it as a Government work. No time was set for its completion.

Important Measures. Among other important measures of the five years' rule of the MacKenzie Government were a new Election Law, the establishment of a Court of Appeal at Ottawa, the Canada Temperance Act, the settlement of the fishery claims against the United States, and the organization of the North-West Territories under a distinct Government.

The Election Law of 1874 provided that, with the exception of some remote districts, the election of members of Parliament should be held on the same day throughout the Dominion. It also introduced the system of voting by ballot. Some regarded the old method of open voting the more manly and worthy of a free people; but the ballot was adopted as a means of preventing bribery and a protection against undue influence over the electors.

The Canada Temperance Act, usually known as the "Scott Act," took its name from its chief promoter, Senator Scott. The law gives any municipality the power by vote of its inhabitants to prohibit the sale of intoxicating liquor within its limits.

It will be remembered that the Washington Treaty of 1871, in arranging for an exchange of fishing privileges, provided that, as the Canadian fisheries were the more valuable, the United States should pay to Canada such sum of money as would represent the difference. Half of the term had passed, during which United States fishermen had free access to Canadian waters, and the amount to be paid had not been agreed on. A commission, consisting of Sir Alexander Galt, representing Canada, Judge Kellogg, representing the United States, and Mr. de la Fosse, the Belgian Minister at Washington, met in Halifax to determine this amount. After careful investigation the commission awarded to Canada the sum of $5,500,000, which was duly paid by the Government of the United States.

Meanwhile the Province of Quebec had furnished an interesting question in state-craft. The MacKenzie Government appointed the Honourable Luc Letellier St. Just Lieutenant-Governor of this province. *Governor Letellier de St. Just.* The Governor and his Ministry, being on opposite sides in politics, failed to work together harmoniously. The Governor complained that his Ministers did not treat him with due courtesy. They published proclamations over his name without consulting him, and they introduced into the Legislature Bills which they had not submitted to him for inspection. The strife grew to such proportions that, although the Ministers had the support of a majority of the Assembly, the Governor dismissed them, and called on Mr. Joly, the leader of the Opposition, to form a new Government. At the same time he dissolved the House and ordered a new election, thereby appealing to the people to judge between himself and his Ministers. This was a bold and hazardous course. If the popular vote had sustained the rejected Ministry, the only thing left for the Governor would have been resignation. A majority of one for the new Ministry saved him from this embarrassment.

Governor Letellier's action was discussed in the House of Commons, and Sir John A. Macdonald moved a resolution of censure against him. The matter was dealt with chiefly as a question of party politics, and the resolution was voted down by the Liberal majority. Subsequently, when Sir John was Premier, a Conservative majority passed a resolution of censure, and the Governor of Quebec was removed from office.

The Liberal-Conservative party was almost disorganized by the "Pacific Railway Scandal." For a time it seemed as if Sir John A. Macdonald's political triumphs were numbered. But though his following in Parliament was numerically weak, it included several men of commanding ability, who never lost their hold on the electorate of the Dominion. Circumstances over which neither party had control favoured the Opposition. The years which followed Mr. MacKenzie's accession to power were not prosperous. The trade of the Dominion was greatly depressed, and the public revenue year after year showed large deficits. When times are dull the people are apt to blame the Government. The Conservative leaders took advantage of the situation. They proposed a remedy for the hard times, appealing to the patriotic sentiment of the people by naming it the "National Policy." The new scheme involved an increase of duty on certain classes of imports, for the avowed

The National Policy.

purpose of encouraging home production. "Canada for Canadians" was the watchword of the party.

For two years the Opposition leaders urged their policy on the House, and from the platform and through the press they sought to impress the public in its favour. Mr. MacKenzie and his followers, while admitting that the proposed tariff changes might be advantageous to a few persons, maintained that the tariff as a whole would not benefit the country at large, but that the money which enriched the manufacturers would come from the pockets of the people. Nevertheless, at the general election in 1878, through the "National Policy," which promised a new era of prosperity, the Liberal-Conservative leaders again secured the reins of power.

On the 20th of June 1877, a large part of the city of St. John was reduced to ashes. The fire swept over a district of about two hundred acres in extent, burning about sixteen hundred buildings, including private houses, churches, and other public buildings. *Fire in St. John, N.B.*

Meanwhile important changes were taking place in the North-West. The Indian tribes of the Territory—Ojibways, Crees, Assiniboines, Blackfeet, and others—claiming rights in the land, were treated in a generous manner. The Dominion Government set apart extensive reserved lands for their use, besides agreeing to give them yearly presents and make provision for the education of their children. *The North-West.*

The Métis, or half-breeds, formed an important element among the inhabitants of the country. Every year also large numbers were added to the population by immigration. New settlers came from the older provinces, especially from Ontario, and also from various countries in Europe. A change in the Government was demanded.

In 1876 the Territory was separated into two divisions. The easterly division, under the name of Keewatin, was placed under the jurisdiction of the Governor of Manitoba. The westerly and more important division, retaining the name North-West Territory, was organized under a Government of its own. The Government as at first formed consisted of a Lieutenant-Governor and a Council of six members appointed by him. This body was endowed with both executive and legislative powers. Provision was made for the enlargement of the Council from time to time as the population increased, by the addition of members chosen by the inhabitants of electoral districts. The Honourable David Laird, of Prince Edward Island, was the first Lieutenant-Governor under the new organization. The Council held its first meeting at Livingston, but Battleford, on the Saskatchewan, was shortly after made the seat of Government.

CHAPTER XXXIII.

THE DOMINION CONSOLIDATED.

IN the general election which took place in the autumn of 1878, as already stated, the Liberal-Conservatives with their "National Policy" won the day. *A New Regime.* In the new Cabinet, Sir John A. Macdonald was Premier, and among his colleagues were several strong men, as Sir Leonard Tilley, Sir Charles Tupper, Sir Hector L. Langevin, and others scarcely less noted.

Shortly after the new Government was formed, Lord Dufferin, who had been Governor-General for six years, retired. He was succeeded by the Marquis of Lorne. Descended from an old and honourable line of Scottish nobles, of the Clan Campbell, of distinguished ability, and closely connected with the Queen as the husband of the Princess Louise, Lord Lorne was welcomed with much enthusiasm by the Canadian people.

During its first session the new Parliament revised the tariff, imposing higher duties on certain classes of imports, and adding to the list of articles imported free of duty. In this way it aimed to secure a larger revenue, and at the same time, according to the principles of the "National Policy," protect home industries.

By Act of Parliament in 1880, the Government was authorized to appoint an agent, called Canadian High Commissioner, to represent the Dominion in England. The first Commissioner, was Sir Alexander Galt.

The question of the proper boundary-line between Ontario and Manitoba caused some agitation in these provinces as well as in the Dominion Parliament. A large territory was claimed by both provinces. Arbitrators appointed to investigate the matter reported in favour of Ontario. The Dominion Government declined to regard this as a final decision, and the question was referred to the Judicial Committee of the Privy Council of Great Britain. This court ratified the finding of the arbitrators, and in 1883 the territory was annexed to Ontario.

Boundary between Ontario and Manitoba

The Canadian Pacific Railway was one of the most important matters that engaged the attention of the Government. Under the late Administration the road had made slow progress. The Macdonald Ministry did not favour the policy of carrying it on as a Government work. It accordingly entered into a contract with a strong company, of which (Sir) George Stephen and (Sir) Donald Smith were leading members, authorizing the company to construct and own the road. The Government agreed to give the company the portions of the railway already constructed, together with a subsidy of $25,000,000, and 25,000,000 acres of land along the line of railway. The road was to be completed within ten years, dating from 1881. With such marvellous energy was the work carried forward that the whole line of railway, from its point of con-

The Canadian Pacific Railway.

nection with the railway system of Ontario to the Pacific Ocean, was completed and open for traffic in the summer of 1886—that is, in about half of the time specified in the contract.

The Canadian Pacific Railway is one of the greatest and the best-equipped railways in the world. The company has built various branch lines and made connections with other roads, so that it now controls about nine thousand miles of railway. Through the Canadian Pacific and the Intercolonial, a continuous line of railway crosses the entire Continent from Halifax to Vancouver. The Company has also established lines of first-class steamers on the Pacific Ocean, which run from Vancouver, in British Columbia, to Japan, China, and Australia.

The Canadian Pacific Railway was a vast undertaking. It is Sir John A. Macdonald's grandest monument. Foresight, self-reliance, and energy were essential characteristics of the statesman who could afford to propose such an enterprise. The importance of this railway can scarcely be over-estimated, for it has done more to develop national feeling and to consolidate the Dominion than perhaps any other agency. Without it British Columbia would be shut off by the great Rocky Mountain wall from the other portions of the Dominion; Manitoba and the North-West would be separated by the wilderness on the north of Lake Superior from Eastern Canada. In a similar manner the Intercolonial Railway is the vital bond of union between the provinces in the east.

Meanwhile the Marquis of Lorne had bidden adieu to Canada. He was succeeded in the office of Governor-General by the Marquis of Lansdowne.

Many of the Métis, or half-breeds, who were concerned in the Red River Rebellion, were but ill reconciled to Canadian rule. On the organization of Manitoba large numbers of these people removed farther west to the country of the Saskatchewan. With much suspicion and murmurings of dissatisfaction, they saw the Government surveyors laying out lands for settlement, and

Rebellion in the North-West, 1884.

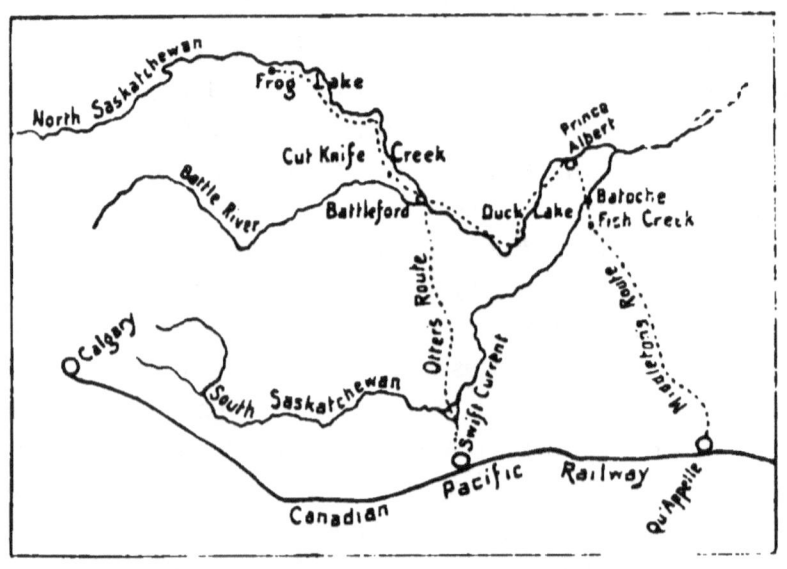

MAP OF THE SCENE OF THE NORTH-WEST REBELLION.

immigrants taking possession of territory to which they thought they had first claims. Having no legal title to the lands which they occupied, and fearing that they might be dispossessed, they petitioned the Dominion Government to give them free grants of their farms, as had been done for their people in Manitoba. Moreover, since the opening of the country for settlement, the buffalo, once a source of wealth for half-breeds and Indians, had become nearly extinct. The railway was not yet completed, and agriculture was not well established in the country. Under these conditions the Métis of the North-West found the struggle for life increasingly severe.

Failing to receive from Ottawa any reply to their petition, or assurance that their interests would be cared for, the Métis became more mistrustful of the future. In their anxiety they sent for Louis Riel, their old leader, in whom they still trusted, who, yet an outlaw, was living in Montana. Regardless of personal danger, Riel came at once at their call. He held public meetings, the effect of which was to arouse in them deeper sense of wrong and stronger suspicion of the evil intentions of the Government. Under Riel's direction they sent a petition to Ottawa, setting forth in strong terms their demands. Riel also gained the sympathy of the Indians by telling them that they were the rightful owners of the country, and that the Government should have bought it from them rather than from the Hudson's Bay Company. While thus instigating rebellion, he had the effrontery to inform the Government that the half-breeds were wholly under his influence, and that for the sum of $35,000 he would restore order in the country.

Affairs in the North-West wore a threatening aspect, and not without cause did the English inhabitants of the country begin to be alarmed. The Government at Ottawa, however, was unmoved. Apparently unconscious of any wrongs to be redressed or any dangers to be guarded against, it gave no heed to petitions, and took no precautions against insurrection. Meanwhile the spirit of rebellion was rapidly gaining strength. The Métis, under the guidance of Louis Riel and Gabriel Dumont, entered upon a course of plunder and violence. They set up an independent Government with Riel at its head. They seized arms, ammunition, and other property belonging to the Dominion Government, the Hudson's Bay Company, and private individuals. Any one who questioned Riel's authority was arrested and thrown into prison. The first serious outbreak occurred towards the end of March 1885, when the insurgents attacked a company of volunteers and mounted police at Duck Lake near Fort Carleton, killing twelve of their number. Some of the Indians were incited to deeds of violence. On Good Friday, with the atrocity of untamed savages, a band of Indians, ruled by a chief known as Big Bear, attacked a settlement at Frog Lake, killing nine persons, among whom were two Catholic priests. At the same time the wives of two or three of the murdered men were carried off by the Indians.

The rebellion was now an undoubted fact, and one which might prove serious enough. A rebellion of the half-breeds alone might not be a very difficult matter to deal with; but if the Indians of the North-West, numbering many thousands, whose loyalty in such a crisis was very doubtful, started on the war-path, the task of restoring peace could not be easily measured. The seat of the rebellion was distant and difficult of access. The country occupied by the insurgents lay two hundred miles or more from the Pacific Railway, and portions of the road were not completed. The difficulties were increased by the season of the year. Troops could reach the country only by long marches through snow and slush. The call for men by the Government, however, met with enthusiastic response. Hundreds of volunteers in the east, from Halifax to Winnipeg, were soon on the move for the scene of the rebellion. General Middleton was chief commander of the expedition.

The forces, collected at Winnipeg, were divided into two bodies. The larger division, under Middleton, including about one thousand men, was to proceed against Riel and Dumont, who with the main body of the insurgents were intrenched at Batoche, on the South Saskatchewan. The men of this division were sent by rail from Winnipeg to Qu'Appelle, from which to Batoche, two hundred and thirty miles distant, they had to march through the melting snow. The other division, under Colonel Otter, was intended for the relief of Battleford, on the North Saskatchewan, to which six hundred defenceless people, two-thirds of whom were women and children, from various parts of the country had fled for safety.

Colonel Otter's troops went by rail to Swift Current, five hundred miles west of Winnipeg. From this place they marched in all haste across the prairie one hundred and eighty miles to Battleford. Their arrival on April 23 was hailed with delight by the anxious people who had sought refuge in the fort. After strengthening the defences, Colonel Otter resolved to advance against the Indians under the chief Poundmaker, who were pillaging the country far and wide. It was a tedious march of thirty or forty miles from Battleford to Poundmaker's camp near Cut Knife Creek. The expedition proved unfortunate. For six hours Colonel Otter and his men fought the Indians, and, after sustaining considerable loss in killed and wounded, a retreat upon Battleford was found necessary.

General Middleton had a toilsome march of eleven days before he reached the enemy's encampment. His first encounter with them was at Fish Creek, where he met an advanced division of the rebels under Dumont. The fighting lasted several hours, and resulted in a loss to Middleton of ten killed and forty wounded. The rebels fought under cover of the banks of a deep ravine and suffered little loss. After waiting here a fortnight for the arrival of a steamer which was bringing supplies from Swift Current, Middleton advanced to Batoche, a few miles distant. Here also the insurgents were well protected by ravines and rifle-pits. But after three days' fighting, the troops with fixed bayonets made a gallant charge against the enemy and routed them at all points. The victory was complete, and practically ended the rebellion. In the charge five volunteers were killed and twenty-two were wounded. Riel was captured two or three days after by a scouting party, and brought to General Middleton. Dumont escaped to Montana.

The Indians throughout a large part of the country were in a state of unrest and were ready for revolt. Vigorous measures were taken to hold them in check. At Calgary, Major-General Strange, a retired British officer, collected a force of over a thousand men and rendered effective service in pacifying the tribes of the far West. Poundmaker and his braves soon surrendered. Big Bear, having over sixty white prisoners, retreated towards the North. Most of the captives were soon rescued, and the chief, reduced by famine, was finally compelled to give himself up.

The volunteers, who had, with so much enthusiasm, entered upon the campaign, and had, with such heroic spirit, followed it up to a successful issue, now returned to their homes in the East. It remained for the civil authorities to deal with those who had acted as leaders in the foolish revolt. After careful trial Louis Riel and some of the Indian chiefs paid with their lives the penalty of their rash deeds of treason and murder. It is estimated that the rebellion cost the Dominion $5,000,000.

The year 1887 was noted as the fiftieth anniversary of the accession of Queen Victoria to the throne. The Jubilee year was celebrated throughout all portions of the Dominion of Canada with much enthusiasm. In no part of the British Empire was there felt more loving regard for the person of her Majesty or more true loyalty to her throne. *The Queen's Jubilee.*

In the following year, 1888, Lord Lansdowne was succeeded by Lord Stanley of Preston as Her Majesty's representative in Canada.

During the French period large tracts of land in Canada were granted to the Jesuits at different times by the King of France. When by the fortunes of war the country fell to Great Britain, these lands, known as the Jesuits' Estates, comprising over half a million acres, were confiscated to the Crown. Shortly after the conquest of Canada the Jesuit Order was suppressed by the Pope, and for several years in the early part of the present century there were no Jesuits in Canada. In 1831 the lands which formerly be- *The Jesuits' Estates Act.*

longed to the Order were granted by the British Government to the Province of Quebec for educational purposes, and thus they came under the direct control of the Legislature of that province. The Roman Catholic Church, however, claimed that the conquest of the country did not alienate title to property, and that the Crown had therefore no right to seize the Jesuits' Estates. The Church authorities in Quebec further claimed that the Jesuits simply held their lands in trust for religious and educational purposes, and that on the suppression of the Order the property passed to them as representatives of the Roman Catholic Church.

Subsequently the Jesuits, having been restored by the Pope, established themselves again in Canada. They now urged their right to the estates which, as they insisted, had been unjustly taken from their Order. Thus there were three claimants to the property—the province, the ordinary Church authorities, and the Jesuits. When the Government placed any of the lands in the market, the hierarchy forbade the sale. This protest weakened the title, and the lands could be sold only at great sacrifice. In 1888 the Mercier Ministry of Quebec, then in power, under authority of the Jesuits' Estates Act, passed by the Legislature of the province, made a compromise with the Jesuits and Church authorities, giving them $400,000 in discharge of all claims. Of this, the sum of $160,000 was given to the Jesuits, $140,000 to Laval University, and the remainder to various schemes of the Roman Catholic Church. The Legislature also voted $60,000 to the Protestants of the province for educational purposes. Against this compromise there arose a storm of opposition among the Protestants throughout the Dominion, and an application for disallowance of the Jesuits' Estates Act was made to the Governor-General in Council. The Dominion Government, however, declined to interfere. In the following year, 1889, the question was brought up in the House of Commons, and a resolution was moved, asking the Governor-General to disallow the Act. The resolution, being in direct opposition to the course advised by the Ministry, was in effect a motion of want of confidence. On the taking of the vote after full discussion, the Ministry was sustained by a large majority.

The two distinguished statesmen who had in turn guided the public affairs of the Dominion were not far removed from each other in their death. Sir John A. Macdonald died in June 1891, in the seventy-seventh year of his age; the Hon. Alexander MacKenzie died in the following April, having little more than fulfilled his threescore years and ten. For nearly half a century Sir John had been prominent in political affairs, and the record of his life since the Union is in large measure the history of the Dominion during that period. He was strong in the attachment and loyalty of his followers, whom he held together and guided almost whither he would by the magnetic force of his personality. *Death of Canada's Premiers.*

Mr. MacKenzie was a great and good man, who, from a humble beginning, rose, as we have seen, to the high position of Premier. He was not ambitious of preferment, or fond of personal distinction. Though for five years he held the highest position in the gift of his country, the place was not of his seeking. Three times he declined the honour of knighthood. About a year after the defeat of his Government he resigned the position of leader of the Opposition, and the Hon. Edward Blake was chosen in his place.

CHAPTER XXXIV.

RECENT EVENTS.

PARLIAMENT was in session when Sir John A. Macdonald died. It adjourned for a week, during which he was buried with state ceremonies, at the public expense. The loss of their leader was keenly felt by the Liberal-Conservatives. There were able men in the Cabinet, but no one seemed to possess that pre-eminence of gifts and influence which entitled him to take the place of the great statesman who had passed away. The choice finally fell upon Sir John Abbot. *Premier Abbot.*

During its session of 1891 the Dominion Parliament was much agitated over serious charges against the management of affairs in the office of the Minister of Public Works. It was asserted that certain contractors had received from the Minister's office secret information which enabled them to secure important contracts, and that Mr. Thomas M'Greevy, member for the city of Quebec, had obtained from the successful contractors large sums of money for the purpose of influencing the elections in the Province of Quebec. These charges were so fully sustained that Sir Hector Langevin, Minister of Public Works, was forced to retire from the Cabinet, and Mr. M'Greevy was expelled from the House of Commons. *M'Greevy and Mercier.*

Closely following the scandal connected with the Office of Public Works came a disclosure of grave irregularities on the part of the Mercier Government of Quebec in the use of subsidies granted from the public funds for the construction of railways in that province. Lieutenant-Governor Angers dismissed Mr. Mercier and his colleagues, called on Mr. de Boucherville to form a Ministry, and dissolved the Assembly. The people fully endorsed the action of the Lieutenant-Governor by electing an overwhelming majority of supporters of the new Government.

In the autumn of 1892 Sir John Abbot, through failing health, was compelled to resign the Premiership. He was succeeded by Sir John Thompson, a comparatively new man in Dominion politics, who had rapidly risen to first rank among Canadian statesmen. Mr. Thompson began his public career in the Legislature of Nova Scotia, holding for a few years the portfolio of Attorney-General in the Provincial Government. In 1882 he was appointed a judge of the Supreme Court of Nova Scotia. In 1885 he resigned his seat on the bench, was returned to Parliament, and became a member of the Cabinet as Minister of Justice.

Sir John Thompson Premier.

A marked feature of the year 1893, in which Canada shared, was the World's Fair in Chicago, organised for the purpose of celebrating the four hundredth anniversary of the discovery of America by Columbus, and hence called the Columbian Exhibition. In its vast extent and varied character it surpassed all former exhibitions of any country. Through the comparison of her exhibits with those gathered from other lands, Canada took

The Columbian Exhibition.

high rank among the civilised countries of the world. The products of her fields, her forests, her fisheries, her factories, and her mines, showed the wealth and variety of her resources as well as the enterprise of

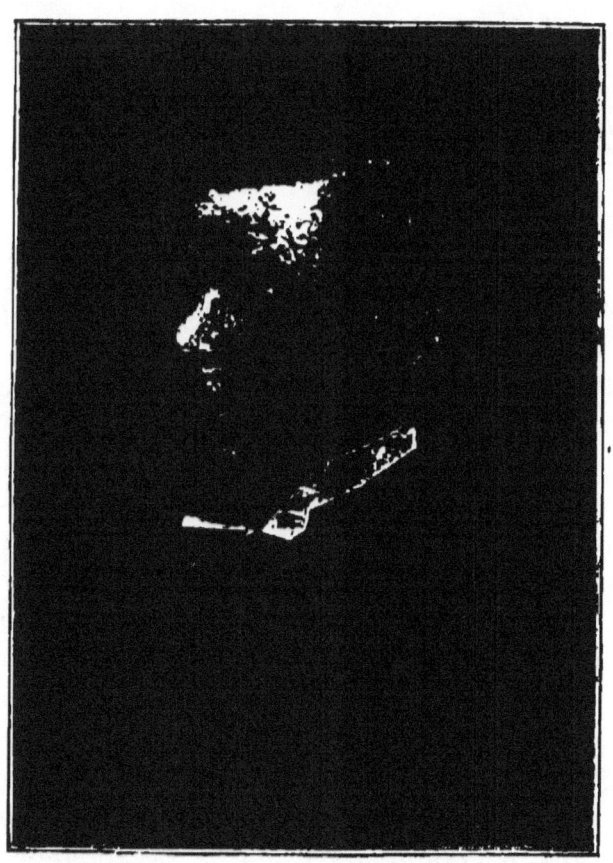

RIGHT HON. SIR JOHN THOMPSON.

her people. In the matter of public education, too, as regards system, method, text-books, and appliances, she had a standing not inferior to that of any country in the world. The awards, including prizes, medals, and certificates of merit, given to us on various exhibits, numbered about two thousand. On dairy products, while the United States gained but fifty-four awards, Canada secured six hundred and nineteen, of which three hundred and eighty-eight went to the Province of Ontario.

The Bering Sea Arbitration, 1893.

A large territory called Alaska, situated on the north-west of the Dominion of Canada, belongs to the United States. The west coast of this territory is washed by an arm of the Pacific Ocean called Bering Sea, which at certain seasons of the year is thronged with fur-bearing seals. According to international law a nation has territorial rights in its coast waters within three miles of the land, and also in the waters of small bays. The Government of the United States asserted for itself similar rights and jurisdiction in the whole of Bering Sea, and hence the ownership of all animals in its waters. Again, this Government claimed the seals that resort to Bering Sea, because they have their home and breeding-grounds on the Pribyloff Islands, which lie off the coast of Alaska. The case was similar, so it was asserted, to that of a farmer's sheep or cattle which might stray from his pasture and be found on the highway or the open plains; they would belong to him all the same, and his neighbour would have no right to appropriate them. Canadians regarded this claim as absurd. They maintained that Bering Sea, outside the three-mile limit, is open and free alike to all nations, and that the seals found in its waters are as much common property as are the codfish three miles from the coast of Newfoundland. But insisting on its exclusive rights, for the one reason or the other, the United States Government seized Canadian vessels found hunting seals in Bering Sea, and confiscated the furs they had on board.

The nations of the world have usually settled disputes of this kind, and even differences of a less serious nature, by war. But Great Britain and the United States, failing to come to any agreement as to the ownership of the seals, resolved, as they have done on other occasions, to refer the difficulty to arbitration. Each Government appointed two delegates, and they asked France, Italy, and Sweden to aid them in settling the dispute. Each of these countries sent one arbitrator.

The court met in Paris. After long and careful hearing of evidence and counsel, it decided that the United States has no control over Bering Sea outside of three miles from its coast, or right in the seals found beyond that limit, and hence that the Government of that country should reimburse Canadian sealers for the vessels and other property unlawfully seized. The tribunal also framed regulations to protect the seals from extermination. The court had no power to restrict citizens of the United States within three miles of the coast. But with this exception it prohibited the capture of seals at all seasons within sixty miles of the Pribyloff Islands, and during the months of May, June, and July in any part of Bering Sea. The use of nets, fire-arms, and explosives in seal-hunting was also forbidden.

A recent event in Manitoba which has awakened deepest interest both in the province and throughout the Dominion is the action of the Legislature and

Government in the matter of the public schools. In 1870, when the majority of the inhabitants were Roman Catholics, the Legislature established an educational system, providing two distinct classes of schools Protestant and Roman Catholic. The Board of Education was half Protestant and half Roman Catholic, forming in effect two Boards, one for each class of schools. Each had also its own superintendent. This state of affairs continued until 1890. The new settlers who had come in were chiefly Protestant, so that the census of 1890 showed only 20,571 Roman Catholics out of a total population of 152,506. In the meantime an agitation had sprung up over the educational system of the province. In 1890 the Legislature repealed the school law and established a non-sectarian school system. All denominational schools under the law were abolished. Roman Catholics were compelled to pay taxes for the support of the public schools, and if they chose to keep their own separate schools, they could draw nothing for their support from the public funds. They appealed to the Dominion Government to disallow the Act of 1890. But as there was doubt whether the Legislature had not exceeded its powers, they were advised to test the validity of this Act in the courts.

<small>The Manitoba Schools.</small>

As we have seen in a preceding chapter, the Act of Union, known as the British North America Act, passed by the British Parliament in 1867, gave to Provincial Legislatures exclusive power of making laws in regard to education. The Manitoba Act of 1870, by which Manitoba was organized, gave similar authority to the Legislature of that province. This power has, however, an important limitation as regards interference with denominational or separate schools. It is provided that the Provincial Legislatures shall not take away any right or privilege with respect to such schools which any class of persons had by law at the time of Union, or which they may have gained since the Union. It is further provided by these Acts that if a provincial authority deprives a Protestant or Roman Catholic minority of a right or privilege of separate schools established by the Legislature after the Union, the aggrieved parties may appeal for redress to the Governor-General in Council. On such appeal being made, the Governor-General in Council is authorised to ask the provincial authority to remove the grievance complained of, and if redress is not afforded, the Dominion Parliament is empowered to make such remedial laws as the case may require.

The Roman Catholics resolved to test the power of the Legislature to pass a law depriving them of their separate schools. If no such power existed, the law could not be enforced, and they had no grievance. The Manitoba Court decided that the law was valid; the Supreme Court of Ottawa reversed this decision. The case was then taken by appeal to the Judicial Committee of the Imperial Privy Council, which confirmed the judgment of the Manitoba Court. The Legislature had not exceeded its powers, and the law was valid. It was now too late for disallowance of the Act of 1890 by the Governor-General in Council; but could there not be secured through this channel some redress? This question was submitted to the courts. The Supreme Court at Ottawa decided that the Governor-General in Council had no authority to act in the matter. The Roman Catholics once more carried their case to the Judicial Committee, which decided that the Governor-General in Council had power to move for remedial action. And now, on being appealed to again by the Roman Catholics, the Dominion Government requested the Provincial Government of Manitoba to provide such redress as the case might require, and at the same time intimated that if relief should not be afforded, the Dominion Parliament would be asked to pass a remedial Act.

The Intercolonial Conference. Union of closely related countries under one general government is a characteristic feature of our times. The confederation of the provinces now forming the Dominion of Canada is an example of this tendency. With a similar idea of unification, some of our statesmen advocate closer relations between Great Britain and her colonies by a scheme which they call "Imperial Federation." By this they mean that the larger possessions, like Canada, Australia, and Cape Colony, shall no longer be dependencies of Great Britain, but shall form an integral part of the Empire and have a voice in the Imperial Government. Such a state of matters may be far off, but in the meantime there is a growing feeling in Canada and in other colonies in favour of promoting greater commercial freedom with each other and with Great Britain.

In the summer of 1894 a conference of delegates from different parts of the Empire was held at Ottawa to discuss matters of common interest. Besides the Hon. MacKenzie Bowell, who was chosen President of the Conference, and other representatives of Canada, there were delegates from New South Wales, Victoria, Queensland, South Australia, Tasmania, New Zealand, and Cape Colony. The Earl of Jersey also was present as delegate from Great Britain. Among the resolutions adopted was one in favour of a preferential tariff between Great Britain and her colonies, that is, a lower tariff on goods imported from any part of the Empire than from foreign countries. Another resolution favoured a British telegraph cable between Canada and Australia.

In the autumn of 1894 Sir John Thompson visited Europe, and, after spending some days on the Continent, he returned to England. On December 12 the startling news was received in Canada, through the Atlantic cable, that Sir John had on that day died suddenly at Windsor Castle, one of the Queen's residences in England. In consideration of his services in the Bering Sea Arbitration, as well as of his commanding ability and skill in jurisprudence, Sir John had been appointed member of the Imperial Privy Council, and he was now summoned to Windsor Castle by the Queen to be sworn into office and to dine with her Majesty. Shortly after the oath had been administered by her Majesty, Sir John was taken ill and immediately expired. Every mark of honour was shown to the dead Premier. The Queen, with her own hand, laid memorial wreaths upon his coffin, and the Imperial Government sent the warship *Blenheim* to bear his remains to Halifax. On January 1, 1895, the ship arrived at Halifax, where the interment took place with all the solemn pomp of a state funeral.

Death of Sir John Thompson.

The death of Sir John Thompson was recognised

as a national loss. The stroke was a heavy one to Canada, where his worth was best understood. His colleagues in the Ministry and his supporters felt that they had lost a leader who was worthy of their loyalty. His political opponents, too, with no grudging spirit or stinted words, recognised his merits. No finer tribute has been offered to the memory of the departed statesman than the glowing and poetic words of the Hon. Wilfrid Laurier, which form part of an address delivered in the Canadian House of Commons on April 18, 1895. In referring to Sir John Thompson's death, among other matters, the eloquent leader of the Opposition said :

"When a man is struck by the hand of death in the fulness of his years, after a long career of great usefulness to himself and his country, there remains a feeling, even above the poignancy of grief, that, after all, death has dealt kindly with him. Such was the death of Sir John Macdonald. But when a man is struck down before he has hardly reached the summit of middle life—before he has attained the full measure of his power—when his friends and his country could look to him for years of useful work, then, sir, death carries with it a sense of inexpressible bitterness. Such was the death of Sir John Thompson. In that respect it is, perhaps, one of the saddest, perhaps altogether the saddest, that our history records. In other respects I look upon it as one of the most glorious. This Canadian Minister, this colonial statesman, died under the roof of the old Norman kings, when he had just been sworn in as a member of the Privy Council of that mighty Empire, of which these old Norman kings laid the foundation, but which has reached dimensions which their wildest dreams of imagination never, I am sure, contemplated. Perhaps it is that such a death, under such circumstances, sad as it be, may be looked upon as a sacred consecration of the majestic principle of the unity of the Empire; unity not only of land and water, unity not only of islands and continents, but a unity of all the creeds and races embraced in that mighty Empire, giving to all, while preserving their individuality, a common aim and a common aspiration, and teaching all the salutary lesson of tolerance and mutual forbearance."

The Honourable MacKenzie Bowell, who had held the portfolio of Minister of Trade and Commerce under Sir John Thompson, succeeded to the Premiership. A few days later he received from the Queen the honour of knighthood. The most perplexing matter with which he had to deal was the Manitoba school question. During the session of Parliament which met in April 1895, he announced, in very decided terms, his purpose of restoring to the Catholic minority the school privileges of which they had been deprived. The usual supporters of the Government were divided in their views on this question, some favouring remedial action by the Dominion Parliament, others opposing coercive measures. A few days before the close of the session in July, the Ministry announced that Parliament would not be asked, during that session, to deal with this matter. It was also stated that Parliament would be convened again in the following January, when, if no satisfactory arrangement had been made by the local authorities of Manitoba, the

The Bowell Administration.

Dominion Government would cause such measures to be passed as would remove the grievance complained of. Some in the Government ranks, perhaps fearing that this was a quiet way of shelving the matter, were ill-satisfied with the announcement, and three French members from the Province of Quebec withdrew from the Cabinet.

The year passed away, and the Greenway Government of Manitoba still declined to restore separate schools or to make satisfactory compromise, and it now appealed to the people of the province to endorse its policy. A general election, held early in 1896, gave the Government the support of four-fifths of the Assembly. Meanwhile, as had been promised, the Dominion Parliament was convened on January 2. In the speech from the throne it was stated that a remedial Bill would be submitted during the session. Two days later, and before the reply to his Excellency's speech had been adopted, the House and the whole country were startled by the resignation of seven members of the Cabinet. The retiring members stated that their action was not due to any dissatisfaction with the policy of the Liberal-Conservative party, but to the feeling that the Premier did not command the full confidence of his supporters. In proof of their position they pointed to the fact that he had not been able to fill the vacancies in the Cabinet caused by the withdrawal of the members from the Province of Quebec. Several days passed, during which the business of the House was suspended, and the spirit of discord held sway amongst those to whom had been assigned the duty of guiding the ship of State. Sir MacKenzie Bowell waited upon the Governor-General and tendered his resignation; but his Excellency refused his assent. Finally the breach was healed, at least in so far as to enable the Government to go on with the business of the session. Six of those who had withdrawn from the Cabinet returned to their places; Sir Charles Tupper, Bart., entered the Government as Minister of State; and Senator Desjardin, from the Province of Quebec, accepted a portfolio.

A few weeks later the Government introduced the promised remedial Bill for the restoration of separate schools to the Catholics of Manitoba. Many of its supporters declared that they were opposed to the principle of separate schools, but that they voted for the measure on the ground that it restored rights held to have been guaranteed to the minority when Manitoba entered the Dominion. The Opposition, led by Mr. Laurier, claimed that careful investigation should be made by a Commission of Inquiry, and that the friendly offices of the Dominion Government, if properly exercised, would suffice to secure the removal of all grievances by the Government of Manitoba. Such coercion as the Bill provided for, they held, would be destructive to provincial rights.

While the debate was going on, the Dominion Government sent delegates to Manitoba for the purpose of trying to make an amicable setttlement of the difficulty. The Government of Manitoba, however, would not yield to the demands made, which were but little less exacting than the provisions of the remedial Bill, and the delegates refused to accept what was offered. The mission was a failure. Accordingly, the Bill was urged forward, even to the exclusion of voting supplies for the year. It passed its first and second readings with fair majorities, and entered upon the final stage of Committee. Every step was blocked by the Opposition, and progress was slow. The five years' term of Parliament was near its end, and, in order to carry the Bill through before the close, the sitting of the Commons was continued day and night without intermission for six days; but all to no purpose. The Government was finally compelled to withdraw the Bill in its unfinished state. A few days later Parliament was dissolved, and the people were called on to express their opinion at the polls.

Election of 1896. Before the election, Premier Bowell resigned, and a new Cabinet was formed, with Sir Charles Tupper, Bart., at its head. The Opposition was led by the Hon. Wilfrid Laurier. The canvass was short but energetic. Never was a political contest in the Dominion fought with keener interest. Old party lines were broken down, and electors, in readjusting their political connection to suit their opinion on the question of the hour, often found themselves in strange company. Orangemen, enlisted under the banner of the French Catholic leader, were ranged in opposition to the Protestant leader whom the Catholic hierarchy championed as the restorer of separate schools for their people in Manitoba. Both sides seemed full of hope and confident of victory. The Government, in espousing the cause of the Roman Catholics of Manitoba, had taken the risk of alienating its Protestant supporters throughout the Dominion; but might it not hope in large measure to balance this risk by the prospect of increased support from the Catholic Province of Quebec? Strange to tell, to the Province of Quebec the Government owed its defeat. Of a total membership of sixty-five for that province, about fifty of those elected were supporters of the Opposition! Another singular feature in the election was the fact that Manitoba, which only six months before had elected a local Legislature almost unanimously opposed to separate schools, now gave a majority to the Government whose policy it had been to urge the remedial Bill with all the energy it could command.

THE RIGHT HON. SIR WILFRID LAURIER.

Shortly after the election Sir Charles Tupper waited on the Earl of Aberdeen and tendered the resignation of himself and his colleagues. His Excellency at once summoned the Hon. Wilfrid Laurier, leader of the Liberal party, and committed to him the task of forming a new Government. Mr. Laurier deviated from the usual course of selecting colleagues from the members elect by calling in men from outside for some of the most important positions in his Cabinet. Sir Oliver Mowat, the Premier of the Provincial Government of Ontario, was made Minister of Justice; Hon. William S. Fielding, the Premier of Nova Scotia, was made Minister of Finance; and the Hon. A. G. Blair, Premier of New Brunswick, Minister of Railways. A few weeks later the Hon. Clifford Sifton, who had held the office of Attorney-General in the Greenway Government of Manitoba, became Minister of the Interior. Thus Mr. Laurier, himself the first French Premier of the Dominion, formed a Government of undoubted strength by calling to his aid the ablest and most experienced statesmen of his party throughout the Dominion.

The Laurier Government, June 1896

The Governor-General's late advisers were in ill-humour when they bade him good-bye. They had desired to fill vacancies in the Senate and various public offices throughout the Dominion by the appointment of their friends to these positions; but his Excellency, holding that a retiring Cabinet should exercise such functions only in so far as the public interest demanded, refused his assent.

Parliament met a few weeks after the election for the purpose of voting supplies—that is, a grant of money to meet the year's expenses of the Government. Little other business of importance was done during the short session.

Mr. Laurier had boldly asserted that he would make a peaceful settlement of the Manitoba school difficulty within six months. This he brought about by means of a compromise, which fell far short of the demands of the claimants of separate schools. According to the terms agreed on in the autumn of 1896 between the Federal Government and the Government of Manitoba, there are to be no separate schools in the province, but the pupils of all religious creeds are to receive secular education together. Provision is made, however, whereby separate religious instruction may be given during the last half-hour of the daily session to the pupils of different creeds by clergymen or others chosen for this purpose according to the wishes of the parents. It is also provided that schools attended by a certain number of Catholic children may have at least one Catholic teacher; and, similarly, schools attended by a certain number of non-Catholic children may have a non-Catholic teacher. *Settlement of Manitoba School Question.*

During the session of 1897 Parliament made important changes in the tariff. A higher duty was placed on tobacco, alcoholic liquors, and some other articles; on various commodities the duty was made less; while in many cases specific duties were changed to *ad valorem*, or the reverse. A clause in the Act was designed to give a preference to British goods over those imported from other countries. It was found, however, that this feature of the Act had wider scope than had been intended; for through Great Britain's trade treaties of many years' standing with Germany and Belgium, these countries could claim for their products the same rate of tariff as was accorded to Great Britain. *Changes in the Tariff, 1897.*

The year 1897 is memorable throughout the British Empire as the sixtieth year of Queen Victoria's reign, being popularly known as the Queen's "Diamond Jubilee."

The Queen's Diamond Jubilee

The sixtieth anniversary of her accession to the throne on June 22nd gave to Her Majesty a longer reign than had fallen to any one of her predecessors. The event was celebrated in London with a splendour which eclipsed everything of the kind that the world has ever witnessed, and with an enthusiasm worthy of the loyal subjects of a noble sovereign. At the celebration Canada was highly honoured in the person of her Premier, who was treated with the most distinguished courtesy. The Queen conferred on him the honour of knighthood, and made him a member of her Privy Council. Through his influence, also, Her Majesty's Government was led to terminate the trade treaties with Germany and Belgium in order that Canada's trade policy might take full effect.

Much interest was awakened throughout Canada, as well as in the United States, by the discovery of the rich Klondike gold fields along the Upper Yukon in the North-West.

The Klondike Gold Mines.

The precious metal is obtained from surface deposits of gravel brought down by mountain streams, and is separated from the sand by washing. The Klondike region is difficult of access, being shut in from the coast by high mountains, and, situated near the Arctic circle, it is made most inhospitable by the severe cold that prevails throughout eight or nine months in the year.

CHAPTER XXXV.

THE PROVINCES SINCE CONFEDERATION.

In Nova Scotia since the Union, with the exception of four years from 1878 to 1882, the Liberals have held the reins of power. *Nova Scotia.* In the election of 1867, shortly after confederation, throughout the province only three Union men were elected—Dr. Tupper for the House of Commons, and Hiram Blanchard and Henry Pineo for the local Assembly. During the succeeding eleven years three Liberal Premiers—William Annand, W. B. Vail, and P. C. Hill—were in succession at the head of Government. The Lieutenant-Governors during this period were General Sir Fenwick Williams, General Doyle, Joseph Howe, and Adams G. Archibald. On the death of Mr. Howe, his old political rival, Judge Johnston, was appointed Lieutenant-Governor. This venerable statesman was then residing in the south of France, whither he had gone for the benefit of his health. He at once set out for Nova Scotia, but on his arrival in England failing strength compelled him to withdraw his acceptance of the position. The Hon. A. G. Archibald (Sir Adams), who, as Governor of Manitoba, had already done good service to the Dominion in organising that new province, was then appointed to the office. Mr. Archibald's moderation and unwavering integrity throughout an active political life of twenty years had won for him the confidence and respect of all parties, and his appointment to this high office, which he held for ten years, was received with universal satisfaction.

In the Assembly elected in 1878 the Liberal-Conservatives had a large majority, and a new Government was formed, of which the Hon. S. H. Holmes was Premier, and John S. D. Thompson (Sir John) and Samuel Creelman were prominent members. The most important measure adopted during the rule of this Government was the County Incorporation Act, which was passed by the Legislature in 1878. This Act provides a Municipal Council for each county of the province for the management of local affairs, such as maintenance of roads and bridges, care of the poor, appointing of constables, road-masters, assessors, and other officers. The members of the Council are elected annually, one for each polling district of the county. The principal business now falling to the Council was formerly transacted in part by the Court of Sessions, which was made up of the magistrates of the county and the Grand Jury, and in part by the Town Meeting, which was a popular assembly of the ratepayers.

In 1882 a new Assembly brought the Liberals again into power, with the Hon. W. T. Pipes as leader of the Government. In 1884 Mr. Pipes retired, and the Hon. W. S. Fielding became Premier, Hon. J. W. Longley became Attorney-General, and Hon. Charles Church, Commissioner of Mines and Works. Twelve years later, in 1896, Mr. Fielding entered the Dominion Cabinet, and the Hon. Geo. H. Murray succeeded him as Premier of Nova Scotia.

Among the measures adopted during the Fielding administration were the establishment of a School of Agriculture in affiliation with the Normal School at Truro, the construction of iron bridges over many of the larger streams which cross the public roads, and an Act relating to coal-mining in Cape Breton. By this last-named Act extensive coal-fields are leased for ninety-nine years to a syndicate which binds itself to pay to the Government a royalty of twelve and a half cents per ton on the coal it sells from its mines.

With the exception of Quebec and Nova Scotia, the Legislatures in the various provinces consist of a single chamber, the members of which are elected by the people. Bills for the abolition of the Legislative Council have, on different occasions, been adopted by the Nova Scotia Assembly, but they have always met with defeat in the Council.

Since the Free Schools Act in 1864 the general education of the people has made steady progress in Nova Scotia. The average of pupils enrolled in the public schools in 1864, the year preceding that in which the Act was passed, was about 35,000; in 1875 it was 79,000; in 1885, 84,000; in 1895, 89,000. The money expended in support of the schools during these years was respectively $150,000, $594,000, $642,000, $841,000. While in some of the provinces educational affairs are under charge of a member of the Government, who is styled Minister of Education, in Nova Scotia these matters are placed under the control of the Council of Public Instruction, which consists of the members of the executive of the Provincial Government. The Superintendent of Education is the Secretary of the Council

Education in Nova Scotia.

and acts as its adviser in all matters pertaining to the educational affairs of the province. The first three Superintendents have already been named. Dr. Rand was succeeded in 1869 by Rev. A. S. Hunt, A.M., who, on his death in 1877, was succeeded by David Allison, LL.D. Of scholarly attainments and energetic manner, Dr. Allison gave new vigour to the academies and high schools of the province. On his resignation in 1891, he was succeeded by A. H. MacKay, LL.D., whose influence is specially felt in the increased attention given to the study of natural science.

DAVID ALLISON, LL.D.

New Brunswick. The history of New Brunswick is very similar to that of Nova Scotia. Of recent events the abolition of the Legislative Council in 1891 is the most important. On the resignation of the Hon. Andrew S. Blair, in

1896, to accept the portfolio of Minister of Railways in the Dominion Cabinet, the Hon. James Mitchell became Premier.

For several years Prince Edward Island had an elective Legislative Council. In 1892 this branch of the Legislature was conjoined in one house with the members of the Assembly. Connection with the mainland by a railway tunnel under Northumberland Strait is a question of commanding interest in the island.

Prince Edward Island.

The Province of Quebec stands second in the Dominion in regard to population. Its capital, Quebec City, is the oldest and most picturesque city in the Dominion. Montreal is the largest city, and has the most extensive commerce.

Quebec.

Ontario has rich and varied resources, and is one of the most prosperous countries in the world. It is the wealthiest province, and contains nearly half the population of the Dominion. Sir Oliver Mowat was Premier of the province from 1872 until 1896, when he resigned to become Minister of Justice in the Dominion Cabinet.

Ontario.

Since its organisation as a province of the Dominion, Manitoba has made rapid progress in population and material wealth. In 1870 its inhabitants, exclusive of Indians, numbered about 12,000, the larger proportion being French and half-breeds. In 1891 they had increased to 150,000, of whom about one-half came from the eastern provinces, chiefly from Ontario. Since the census of 1891 the number of inhabitants has been greatly augmented by immigration. The city of Winnipeg, whose population in 1870 did not exceed a few hun-

Manitoba.

dreds, at the end of twenty-five years numbered nearly 40,000. Manitoba and the North-West Territories are the great wheat-producing countries of the Dominion.

British Columbia. Since its union with the Dominion, British Columbia has had a prosperous career. Its Government has expended large amounts on public works and on railways, by which new vigour has been imparted to mining and other industries. The province is rich in gold and other minerals. In 1892 Premier Robson died suddenly in England, whither he had gone on public business. He was succeeded in the Premiership by the Hon. Theodore Davie. In 1893 the Legislature voted $600,000 for new Parliament buildings to be completed in 1895.

The North-West Territory. In 1882 the North-West Territory was divided into the four districts — Assiniboia, Alberta, Saskatchewan, and Athabasca — which form the beginning of future provinces. In the meantime, however, these districts were left under one Government. In 1883 the seat of Government was removed from Battleford to Regina, on the Canada Pacific Railway. In 1886 the Territory was given representation in the Dominion House of Commons and Senate, and two years later the Council was abolished and a representative Assembly was elected in its place. By recent changes the local government has been so modified that it now differs little from that of the provinces.

CHAPTER XXXVI.

THE GOVERNMENT OF CANADA.

CANADIANS may well be proud of their civil privileges; for in no country of the world can a people be found who can more justly claim the possession of self-government. Their government is in truth " of the people, for the people, and by the people." They have not, indeed, the choice of their Governors; but a Governor in Canada, like the Sovereign of Great Britain, has little real power. In his name are done many things for which he is only formally responsible. He is said, for example, to choose his Ministry or Executive. In reality he does nothing of the sort. This body is called into being by the people's representatives; it is completely under their control, and at their behest it suffers dissolution. The Ministry is selected from the Legislature, and it must have the confidence of the majority in the elective branch—that is, of the House of Commons or of the Assembly. If at any time the people's representatives, becoming dissatisfied with its policy, pass a vote of want of confidence, it must resign. The Governor then summons some leading member of the Legislature who belongs to the party having the majority, to form a new Ministry. The member thus called on, after conferring with his political friends, selects for his colleagues such other members of the Legislature as are thought to command the highest confidence of the party.

The Governor is not supposed to have any policy of his own. By a convenient fiction he is spoken of as appointing officers under the Government, such as sheriffs, post-masters, and customs officials; or he is said to call the Legislature together, to adjourn, or prorogue, or dissolve the House. All such matters are really the work of the Ministry. The Governor is bound to act according to the advice of his Ministry; hence he is relieved of all official responsibility. If he refuses to follow the advice of his Ministry, this body resigns. Future action then depends wholly on the way in which the people's representatives regard the conflict between the Governor and his advisers. If they approve of the Governor's action, they will support a new Ministry that is willing to take the responsibility of his action; if they do not approve of it, the Governor must recall his Ministry and follow its advice. It will thus be seen that the Ministry has in reality but one master, and that is the elective branch of the Legislature.

A change of Government, that is, of Ministry, often follows a general election. It frequently happens that the people become disaffected towards a Government on account of some feature in its policy. If a general election takes place under such conditions, a majority of the members elected will probably be adverse to the Ministry. The members of this body are then forced to retire, and a new Executive is formed in the manner before stated.

In addition to their general duties as members of

the Executive, some members hold what are called departmental offices, or have charge of certain departments of public business, such as matters connected with the Post Office, Public Works, Agriculture, Education, Militia, and Fisheries. A Minister who holds such office is said to have a portfolio, and he receives a salary from the public funds. On assuming office he is required to return to his constituents for re-election.

Although, as stated above, the Governor-General has little power, he possesses very great influence, through which he may mould public opinion, and the Dominion of Canada has been fortunate in having the highest official place in its Government occupied by men of eminent ability and character. In the friction that often arises from the conflict of political parties, provincial interests, differences of race and religion, and from other sources, there is evident advantage in having in this high position one wholly unbiased, in whose impartiality and judgment all have confidence.

In the history of the Dominion, on different occasions, agitation which threatened the peace of the country has been calmed by judicious action on the part of the Governor-General. A notable instance is shown in the good offices of Lord Dufferin in conciliating British Columbia. The British noblemen who have represented the Sovereign in Canada have, as a rule, performed the duties of their office with admirable judgment and tact, and they have done much to promote the interests of the country. Through their personal qualities, enriched by high culture and scholarship, and their broad sympathies, they have wielded an elevating influence, and given encouragement to science, literature, and art.

As was the case in the various provinces before Confederation, the Dominion is ruled by party government. The two great parties, as already stated, are known as Liberals and Liberal-Conservatives, the one party or the other holding power according as its policy secures the favour of a majority of the people. While grave evils arise out of the system, it is difficult, and perhaps impracticable, to devise anything better to take its place. It should, however, be the constant care of our statesmen, as it should be the endeavour of all true patriots, to guard against these evils, and resist them with unyielding purpose. Perhaps the vicious outcome hardest to repress, and of most baneful tendency, is that expressed by the false maxim, "To the victors belong the spoils." Through selfish interest electors are induced to support their party, not because of the soundness of its principles and the purity of its administration, but because of the hope that in its exaltation to power some private benefit may accrue to themselves.

It will be readily understood that the form of government here described would not be suited to certain conditions of society. No greater evil could befall an ignorant, unpatriotic, or immoral people, than to be thus endowed with the power of self-government. If a people lack intelligence, they easily become the dupes of designing demagogues, and if they lack principle and patriotism, they are ever ready to barter their country for gold. No position in our country demands more wisdom and integrity than that of the legislator and the statesman. The privilege of choosing such men should be regarded as a most sacred trust, to be used under a deep sense of responsibility. The man who sells his vote should be deprived of the privilege which he so criminally abuses.

We have briefly traced the history of our country through a period of nearly four hundred years—a long time, even in the life of a nation. The progress made seems scarcely commensurate with this long period of growth. Different causes have tended to hinder more rapid development. For over a hundred years at the beginning, as we have seen, systematic colonisation was wholly neglected, while explorers and adventurers came and went, leaving the country as they found it. For another hundred and fifty years the struggle for supremacy between France and England kept matters in a state of unrest and uncertainty, so that little over a century has elapsed since the ownership of this country was finally settled. Then, during the greater portion of English rule, or until 1867, the several provinces remained isolated from each other, with comparatively little influence, national sentiment, or community of interest. Meanwhile, a neighbouring country, consolidated as one people, with strong national vitality and absorbing power, drew away from the provinces many of their natural elements of growth.

Conclusion.

In the meantime, however, the provinces were gathering strength, though slowly and obscurely. They were striking root downward and accumulating energy, which, under the present more favourable conditions, is developing an abundant fruitage. By toil and self-sacrifice our fathers have left us a noble inheritance to cultivate and adorn. The Dominion of Canada is called upon to compete, in industrial, intellectual, and moral progress, with the nations of the world. The resources and possibilities of our country should stimulate us to cultivate those habits of industry, intelligence, and virtue, without which neither individual nor national greatness is possible.

APPENDIX.

THE value of goods exported from the Dominion of Canada in 1896 was $121,013,852; the value of goods imported was $118,011,508.

The trade of the Dominion is chiefly with Great Britain, the United States, the West Indies, Germany, Newfoundland, France, Belgium, Holland, Italy, China, Japan, and the various countries of South America.

The revenue of the Dominion is about $36,000,000.

The public debt is about $258,000,000, the greater part of which has been incurred in the construction of railways and canals. The expenditure on railways in construction by the Government, and in subsidies to companies, before and since Confederation, amounts to $233,542,000. The total number of miles of railway in the Dominion in 1896 was 16,270, of which the Government owned 1397 miles. The amount expended on canals to June 1894 was $62,237,000.

The principal canals are those of the St. Lawrence, above Montreal; the Welland Canal, between Lakes Ontario and Erie; the St. Mary's Canal (completed in 1895), between Lakes Huron and Superior; the Rideau Canal, between Ottawa and Kingston; the canals of the Ottawa, Richelieu, and Trent rivers; and the St.

Peter's Canal, in Cape Breton. The canals are owned by the Government. The St. Lawrence River and the Great Lakes, with their connecting rivers and canals, form a water route to Port Arthur, on Lake Superior, 2260 miles from the Gulf of St. Lawrence.

CENSUS OF THE DOMINION IN 1891.

	Area in Square Miles.	Population.
Nova Scotia	20,550	450,396
New Brunswick	28,100	321,263
Prince Edward Island	2,000	109,078
Quebec	227,500	1,488,535
Ontario	219,650	2,114,321
Manitoba	64,066	152,506
British Columbia	382,300	98,173
Territories	2,371,481	66,799
Total of Dominion	3,315,647	4,833,239

POPULATION OF CITIES AND TOWNS HAVING OVER 5000 INHABITANTS.

Halifax, N. S.	38,556		Kingston	19,264
St. John, N. B.	39,179		Guelph	10,539
Fredericton	6,502		St. Catherines	9,170
Moncton	8,765		Brantford	12,753
Charlottetown, P. E. I.	11,374		Belleville	9,914
Montreal, Que.	216,650		St. Thomas	10,370
Quebec	63,090		Stratford	9,501
Trois Rivières (Three Rivers)	8,334		Chatham	9,052
Levis	7,301		Brockville	8,793
Sherbrooke	10,110		Peterborough	9,717
Hull	11,265		Windsor	10,322
St. Henric	13,415		Port Hope	5,042
Sorel	6,669		Woodstock	8,612
St. Hyacinthe	7,016		Galt	7,535
Toronto, Ont.	181,220		Lindsay	6,081
Hamilton	48,980		Winnipeg, Man.	25,642
Ottawa	44,154		Victoria, Brit. Col.	16,841
London	31,977		Vancouver	13,685
			New Westminster	6,641

RELIGIOUS DENOMINATIONS IN CANADA.

NOVA SCOTIA.

Baptists	72,731	Disciples		1,728
Free-Will Baptists	10,377	Methodists		54,195
Roman Catholics	122,452	Presbyterians		108,952
Church of England	64,410	Salvation Army		1,377
Congregationalists	3,112	Others		5,181
Lutherans	5,882			

NEW BRUNSWICK.

Baptists	54,960	Disciples		1,003
Free-Will Baptists	24,674	Methodists		35,504
Roman Catholics	115,961	Presbyterians		40,639
Church of England	43,095	Salvation Army		993
Congregationalists	1,036	Others		3,021
Lutherans	377			

QUEBEC.

Adventists	3,364	Jews		2,703
Baptists	6,854	Lutherans		1,385
Free-Will Baptists	1,127	Methodists		39,544
Roman Catholics	1,291,709	Presbyterians		52,673
Church of England	75,472	Salvation Army		297
Congregationalists	4,296	Others		9,061
Disciples	20			

ONTARIO.

Adventists	447	Jews		2,501
Baptists	96,969	Lutherans		45,029
Free-Will Baptists	7,869	Methodists		654,033
Brethren	9,343	Presbyterians		453,147
Roman Catholics	358,300	Quakers		4,350
Church of England	385,999	Salvation Army		10,320
Congregationalists	16,879	Others		60,129
Disciples	9,106			

APPENDIX. 441

PRINCE EDWARD ISLAND.

Baptists	5,749		Disciples	531
Free-Will Baptists	512		Methodists	13,596
Roman Catholics	47,837		Presbyterians	33,072
Church of England	6,646		Salvation Army	180
Congregationalists	11		Others	944

MANITOBA.

Baptists	15,829		Methodists	28,437
Roman Catholics	20,571		Presbyterians	39,001
Church of England	30,852		Salvation Army	399
Congregationalists	1,815		Jews	743
Lutherans	6,545		Others	8,036

BRITISH COLUMBIA.

Baptists	2,960		Presbyterians	15,284
Roman Catholics	20,843		Congregationalists	775
Church of England	23,619		Salvation Army	298
Lutherans	2,083		Jews	277
Methodists	14,297		Others	17,736

TERRITORIES.

Baptists	1,397		Methodists	7,980
Roman Catholics	13,008		Presbyterians	12,507
Church of England	14,166		Salvation Army	85
Lutherans	2,676		Others	15,065

DOMINION OF CANADA.

Adventists	6,345		Methodists	847,765
Baptists	257,449		Presbyterians	755,326
Free-Will Baptists	45,116		Protestants	12,253
Brethren	11,637		Quakers	4,650
Congregationalists	28,157		Salvation Army	13,949
Roman Catholics	1,992,017		Tunkers	1,274
Church of England	646,059		Universalists	3,186
Disciples	12,763		Unitarians	1,777
Jews	6,414		Others	123,111
Lutherans	63,982			

INDEX.

ABBOT, Sir John, 407, 408
Abercrombie, General, 150
Acadians, 106, 112, 114, 124, 128, 138, 181
Acadie, 68, 95, 102
Accommodation, the, 209
Aix-la-Chapelle, Treaty of, 120
Alabama Claims, 361, 379
Alexander, Sir William, 38
Algonquins, 40
Allison, David M., 428
America, 3, 14, 18
American Revolution, 182
Americus Vespucius, 18
Amherst, General, 153
Archibald, Sir Adams G., 339, 375, 376, 425
Archibald, S. G. W., 282
Argall, Captain, 36
Arnold, Benedict, 186, 190
Ashburton Treaty, 313
Astoria, 263

BAGOT, Sir Charles, 302
Baldwin, Robert, 267, 268, 269, 294, 302
Baldwin-Lafontaine Government, 302, 305, 322
Ballot, voting by, 390
Baptiste, 95
Barclay, Captain, 232
Barry Riot, the, 279
Batoche, 401
Beauharnois, Governor, 109
Beauséjour, Fort, 129, 137
Beaver Dams, 230
—— skins, 75
Bering Sea Arbitration, 410, 411
Berlin Decree, 217

Biard, 36
Bidwell, Marshall, 267, 294
Biencourt, 35, 36
Big Bear, 402
Bigot, Intendant, 130, 152
Blake, Edward, 384
Blanshard, Richard, 347
Bolton, Major, 374
Boston Tea Party, 184
Boucherville, 408
Bougainville, 156
Boundary disputes, 346, 347, 349, 380
Bowell, Sir MacKenzie, 417, 418, 420
Braddock, General, 133
"Brandy Dispute," 280
Brant, Molly, 136
Brébeuf, 49
Breda, Treaty of, 69
British Columbia, 345, 347, 348, 349, 377, 378, 389, 430, 438, 440
British North America Act, 357–360
Brock, Sir Isaac, 221, 222, 226
Brown, George, 323, 326, 329, 330, 366

CABOT, John and Sebastian, 16, 17
Camosin, Fort, 347
Campbell, Sir Archibald, 278
—— Sir Colin, 280, 307
Canada, 188; debt of, 437; government of, 431–434; railways of, 437; religions of, 439, 440; revenue of, 437; trade of, 437
Canada, Land Company, 244
—— Temperance Act, 390

Canadian Pacific Railway, 378, 389, 396
Canals, 248
Canso, 114
Cape Breton, 196, 249
Carleton, Sir Guy (Lord Dorchester), 187, 196
Carleton, Thomas, 195
Cartier, Jacques, 21
—— Sir George E., 328, 331, 372, 383
Cataraqui, Fort, 81 (*see* Frontenac)
Catholic Emancipation, 253
Cavalier, Robert, 81
Champlain, 28, 32, 34, 39–52
Charlottetown Convention, 353
Chateaugay, battle of, 233
Chauncey, Commodore, 228
Chauvin, 27
Chesapeake, the, 231
Cholera in Canada, 244
Chrystler's Farm, battle of, 235
Church, Benjamin, 97, 102
—— Charles, 426
Clergy Reserves, 252, 270, 321
Colborne, Sir John, 270, 291
Colebrooke, Sir William, 312
Coles, George, 317, 336
Collins, Frank, 270
Colonists, English, 91
Columbian Exhibition, 408
Columbus, Christopher, 10
Company of New France, 49, 51
Confederation, 341, 352, 353, 354, 356
Constitutional Act, 197
Continental Congress, 185
Courcelle, Daniel, 71
Court of Appeal, 390
Craig, Sir James, 208, 219
Creelman, Samuel, 426
Crowne, William, 69
Crown Point, 137, 186
Customs and social condition, 212

DALHOUSIE, Earl of, 273, 275
Daniel, Père, 58
D'Anville, 116
Daulac or Dollard, 64
D'Aulnay, 66, 67

Dawson, Sir William, 340, 342
Dearborne, General, 226
De Callières, 98
De Chaste, Aymar, 27
Deerfield, 101
De la Roche, 26
De la Tour, Charles, 66
—— Claude, 66
De Léry, 21
De Mézy, Saffray, 71
De Monts, 29, 39
Denonville, 84, 86, 87
D'Estournelle, 117
De Tracy, 71
Dieskau, 132
Disputed territory, 284, 313
Dominion of Canada, 357–368
Dongan, 83
Donnacona, 23
Dorchester, Lord, 187, 188, 196, 208
"Double Shuffle," 331
Douglas, Sir James, 348–351
Doyle, General, 425
Draper Ministry, 303, 304
Drucour, 138, 148
Dufferin, Earl of, 385, 395
Duquesne, Fort, 151
—— Governor, 131
Duquesnel, 114
Durham, Earl of, 292, 293, 299
Dustan, Hannah, 96
Duvivier, 114

EARTHQUAKES in Canada, 65
Education, 245, 319, 341–343, 380, 427, 428
Edward, Duke of Kent, 204
Election, first Dominion, 368
—— Law, 390
Elgin, Lord, 304, 318, 326

FALKLAND, Lord, 308
Family Compact, 251, 266
Fenians, 363, 364, 377
Feudal system in Canada, 76, 322, 327
Fielding, William S., 422, 426
"Fifty-four-Forty or Fight," 346
Fisher, Charles, 312, 313, 335
Fisheries, 380, 390, 391

INDEX. 445

Fitzgibbon, Lieutenant, 230
Five Nations, the, 41
Fleche, 35
Forrester, Rev. Alexander, 341
Fort Camosin, 346
—— Frontenac, 81, 150
—— la Tour, 67
—— Lawrence, 129
—— le Joye, 149
—— Louis, 37
—— Pitt, 151
—— Victoria, 346
—— William Henry, 95, 145

GALISSONIÈRE, 130
Germain-en-Laye, Treaty of, 51
Ghent, Treaty of, 241
Gordon, Governor, 355
Gosford, Lord, 276, 291
Gourlay, Robert, 267
Government, early, in the provinces, 199
Government of Great Britain, 285
Governor-General, his power and influence, 431-433
Grand Pré, 119, 139

HALIBURTON, Thomas C., 253
Halifax, settlement of, 122
Harvey, Colonel (Sir John), 229, 279, 310
Head, Sir Edmund W., 326
—— Sir Francis Bond, 271, 294
Henry the Navigator, 9
Hill, P. C., 425
Hincks, Sir Francis, 302, 323, 324
Hochelaga, 23
Holbourne, Admiral, 144
Holmes, Admiral, 159
—— Simon II., 426
Howe, Captain, 129
—— Joseph, 281-283, 307, 335, 337, 356, 357, 370, 383, 425
Hudson's Bay Company, 85, 86, 257, 371
Hull, General, 222
Hunt, Rev. A. S., 428
Huntington, 385
Hurons, the, 40, 42, 47, 57, 58

IBERVILLE, 96
Indians of Nova Scotia, 125, 126
Indian tribes, 40
Intercolonial Conference, 414
Invasion of Canada, 186
Iroquois, the, 40, 56

JAMESTOWN, 36
Jesuits, the, 36, 54, 62, 76
—— Estates Act, 403
Johnson, Sir William, 135, 136, 154
Johnstone, James W. (Judge), 308, 335, 337, 339, 425
Jolliet, 79
Jonquière, 118, 130
Jumonville, 132

KEMPT, Sir James, 273
Kennedy, Arthur, 351
King's College, 204
Kirk, David, 50
Kondiaronk, 88, 99

LA BARRE, 83
La Chine, 89
Lacolle, 238
La Corne, 128
Lafontaine, 302
La Jonquière, 117, 118
Lake Champlain District, map of, 136
Lake Country, map of, 227
Lalemant, 59
La Salle, 81, 82
La Tour, Charles de, 37, 66-69
—— Claude de, 37, 66
—— Fort, 67
Laurier, Sir Wilfrid, 416, 420-424
Laval, Bishop, 62, 63, 70
Lawrence, Fort, 129
—— Major, 129, 138
Le Borgne, 68
Le Loutre, 126, 129, 138
Leopard, the, 218
Lescarbot, 33, 34
Lévis, 143, 156
Lincoln, President, 363
Liquor traffic, 63, 75
Long house, Indian, 43
Longley, J. W., 426
Long Sault, 64

446 INDEX.

Lorne, Marquis of, 395, 397
London, 141
Louis XIV., 74
Louisburg, 111, 115, 146
Lower Canada, 197, 198, 207, 253, 272-274, 290-294
Loyalists, 192
Lundy's Lane, battle of, 238

MacCulloch, Thomas, D.D., 246
Macdonald, John Sandfield, 333, 383, 384
Macdonald, Sir John A., 325, 327, 333, 366, 387, 392, 395, 405
McDougall, William, 371-373
Machillimackinac (Mackinaw or Mackinac), 222
MacKay, A. H., 428
MacKenzie, Hon. Alexander, 367, 384, 386, 388, 392, 394, 405, 406
MacKenzie, Sir Alexander, 260, 261
MacKenzie, William Lyon, 267-270, 272, 294-298
McNab, Colonel (Sir Allan), 295, 326
McGee, Thomas d'Arcy, 333, 368, 369
Magellan, 19
Maisonneuve, 55
Manitoba, 375, 411-413, 418-421, 429, 438, 440
March, Colonel, 103
Maroons, the, 205
Marquette, 79
Marys, the three, 55
Mascarene, Paul, 113, 114, 118
Massacre at Grand Pré, 119
Mason and Slidell, 360
Masse, 26
Memberton, 34, 35
Mercier, 407, 408
Metcalfe, Sir Charles, 303
Mines and minerals of N. S., 337
Miramichi fire, 250
Mississippi, the, discovery of, 79
Mohawks, the, 72, 73
Molson, John, 209
Monck, Lord, 333
Monckton, Colonel, 137, 149, 153

Montcalm, Marquis of, 143, 145, 157
Montgomery, 186, 187, 188, 189
Montmagny, 53
Montreal, 46, 55, 75, 325
Moravian Town, battle of, 232
Mowat, Sir Oliver, 329, 334, 368, 384
Munroe, Colonel, 145
Murray, General, 153
—— George, 426

Nanaimo, 348
National policy, 392, 395
Nelson, Dr. Wolfred, 290, 291
New Brunswick, 195, 205, 277, 311-314, 353, 356, 380, 381, 438-440
New Caledonia, 345
New England, 60, 61
New Orleans, 241
New York, 72
Niagara, 210, 236
Nicholson, 104, 113
Noble, Colonel, 119
Northmen, the, 7
North-West, the, 370, 372, 375, 393, 438, 440
North-West Fur Company, 257, 265
Nova Scotia, 37, 113, 307, 308, 335, 337-342, 353, 369, 370, 377, 383, 425-428, 438, 439

Odell, William, 312
Ohio Valley, 131
One Hundred Associates, 49, 53, 65
Ontario, 383, 384, 396, 429, 438, 439
Order of the Good Time, 34
Orders in Council, the, 217
Oregon, 345
Oswego, 143, 238
Ottawa, 329
Otter, Colonel, 401

Pacific Ocean, 19
    Railway scandal, 385, 386
Palmer, Edward, 316, 336
Paris, Peace of, 172
Parliamentary customs, 201
Parliament House in Montreal burned, 306

INDEX. 447

Papineau, Louis J., 209, 274, 290, 291, 298
Party government, 434
Pepperell, William, 110, 116
Phips, Sir William, 92, 93, 94
Pictou, 178
Pipes, W. T., 426
Pitt, William, 146
Pocahontas, 36
Political agitation, 250
Pontgravé, 27, 29
Pontiac's Conspiracy, 170
Pope, Joseph, 315
Port Dover, 238
Port Royal, 31, 50, 69, 104
Postage stamps, 320
Poundmaker, 401, 402
Poutrincourt, 32, 33
Prevost, Sir George, 203, 210, 220, 231, 240
Prideaux, General, 153, 154
Prince Edward Island, 149, 254, 314–317, 343, 354, 382, 429, 438, 440
Prince of Wales, 331
Privateers, 102, 103, 191

QUEBEC, 55, 104, 404
—— Act, the, 176, 196
—— Convention, 354
—— efforts to recapture, 166
—— *Gazette*, 173
—— occupied by British, 166
—— Province of, 391, 429, 438, 439
—— scheme, 354
—— surrender of, 168
Queen Anne's War, 100
Queenston, battle of, 225
Queen Victoria, 287–289, 403, 424
Quit-rents, 254, 255, 314–317

RAILWAYS, 320, 336, 385, 436
Ramesay, 118
Rand, Theodore h., 342, 381
Razilly, Isaac de Launay, 66
Ready, Colonel, 256
Rebellion in Canada, 290
—— in the North-West, 373, 398–403
Rebellion losses, 304

Reciprocity Treaty, 325, 363, 390
Red River Settlement, 263
Remedial Bill, 419
Representation by population, 329
Responsible government, 310, 314, 316
Riel, Louis, 373–377, 387, 399, 403
Roberval, 24
Robinson, John Beverly, 270
Rolph, Dr., 267, 294, 295
Royal government, 70
Royal William, the, 249
Ryerson, Dr. Egerton, 253, 319 384
Ryswick, Treaty of, 97

SACKETT'S HARBOUR, 230
St. Castine, Baron, 75
St. John's Island, 205, 206
St. Lusson, 76
Salaberry, 220, 234
Salle, Sieur de la, 81
San Juan, 350, 380
Schultz, 374
Scott, Thomas, 374
Scott Act, the, 390
Seigniorial tenure, 322
Seven Years' War, 142
Seymour, Governor, 351, 378
Sherbrooke, Sir John C., 203, 238
Shirley, 120, 133, 137
Simcoe, 210
Simpson, Sir George, 265
Smith, John, 36
Stadacona, 23
Stamp Act, 184
Stanley of Preston, Lord, 403
Strachan, Bishop, 245, 252, 270
Strange, 402
Subercase, 103, 105
Sulpicians, the, 62
Sunbury, 179

TACHÉ, Sir E. P., 333
Talon, 71, 73
Tecumseh, 233
Telegraph cable, 339
Temple, Sir Thomas, 69
Thompson, Charles Poulett (Baron Sydenham), 300, 307
Thompson, David, 261

INDEX.

Thompson, Sir John, 408, 415–417, 426
Three Rivers, 109
Ticonderoga, 110, 150. 186
Tilley, Sir Leonard, 355, 356, 395
Townshend, General. 153
Tracy, Marquis de, 71, 73
Treaty of Ghent, 241
—— of Ryswick, 97
—— of St. Germain, 51
—— of Utrecht, 108
Tupper, Sir Charles, 337, 395, 420, 421

UNIACKE, James B., 335
United Empire Loyalists, 192
United States, 192, 332, 360–363
Upper Canada, 196–198, 210–212, 266–272, 294
Utrecht, Treaty of, 108

VAIL, William B., 425
Vancouver, Captain, 262
—— Island, 347, 348, 351
Vaudreuil, 104, 109, 132, 156
Vergor, 138

Verrazano, 21
Vetch, 113
Victoria, Queen, 287, 403, 424
Victoria City, 347
Vignau, 46
Villebon, 95
Vimont, 56

WALKER, Sir Hovenden, 107
War of 1812, 225–242
Washington, 240
—— George, 133, 135
—— Treaty, 379
Webb, 145
Wentworth, Sir John, 202
Winthrop, 94
Wolfe, General, 153
Wolseley, Sir Garnet, 375

YORK (Toronto), 211
Young, Charles, 317, 336
—— John (Agricola), 245
—— Sir Aretas, 314
—— Sir John (Lord Lisgar),
—— Sir William, 335, 340

THE END.

www.ingramcontent.com/pod-product-compliance
Lightning Source LLC
Chambersburg PA
CBHW051738300426
44115CB00007B/613